DOT CHESS
The Cricket in Between

Saumil Bhukhanwala

www.saumilzx.com

Mumbai, India

January 2007

This book is dedicated to

every sports-enthusiast who made an effort

to compete

at various levels in their sport,

and pushed

the best to where they are.

Why would a book by just another 'fan',

—with little competitive experience—

be credible to even consider reading?

Half the answer lies on the top half of this page,

and the remaining half on the next…

With the help of

spontaneous observations

and

systematic abstractions—

one can 'arrive' at facts

which are remarkably significant and

often alarmingly obvious!

The important point, however,

is not *who*

arrived at it—but rather,

what was arrived at

and *when* it could be relevant.

So be ready to find out what you already know!

Dot Chess– The Cricket in Between
Written & Published by Saumil Bhukhanwala
1st Edition, January 2007
ISBN 978-81-7525-824-2

more information & distribution queries:
www.saumilzx.com

for purchase online
amazon.com

Cover Design: Saumil Bhukhanwala
Photo of chess king, licensed from SurroundStock™ image
library, Thats Our World Creative Solutions Pvt. Ltd.
Mumbai, India.

CONTENTS

Acknowledgments   12
Preface   14
Purpose of writing a sports book   17
Introduction to some assessment methods   25

PART I: FORMAT OF CRICKET

1. Dot Nature of Cricket

1.1 Why are there dot balls in cricket?   32
1.2 Evaluating a dot ball   33

2. Intention & Execution

2.1 Intention & Execution gap in various sports   35
2.2 Implication of margin of victory   37
2.3 Implication of multiple attempts to prove a theory   38
2.4 Light Gray Shots!   40

3. Who Initiates Play?

3.1 Initiate and Control Disciplines   41
3.2 Inititate-React Combinations   42
3.3 Inititate-React-Terminate in Cricket   43
3.4 Implications of runs/wicket not being absolute   44
3.5 Implication of weak or strong connectivity of steps   44

4. ZX Fomats

4.1 Zero Error and eXtra Effort Demands of sports   47
4.2 Implications of Z-demand on Batting   49
4.3 Implications for X-demand of Bowling   54
4.4 ZX of Cricket as compared to other sports   57

5. Sparse or Dense Scoring?

5.1 Cumulative Scoring in various sports   59
5.2 Bowling is sparse, Batting is dense   60
5.3 Scoring pattern reflects shot quality?   60

6. Classifying bowling by intent

6.1 Three ways of bowler overcoming shot execution 64
6.2 Some combinations and mixing types 68

7. Sequenced or Simultaneous Participation?

7.1 Cricket in context of other sports 71
7.2 Implications of bowling & batting order flexibility 72

8. Symmetric or Asymmetric Skills?

8.1 Cricket is different, again 78
8.2 Implications to bowling & batting skills 79

PART II: CHESS OF CRICKET

9. Applying Chess to Cricket

9.1 Chess as a way to explain & solve problems 86
9.2 When can chess be applied to cricket? 87

10. Strategy and Tactics

10.1 Strategy and Tactics are not the same! 97
10.2 Strategy as an underlying plan or policies 98
10.3 Tactics as forced activity and calculated ploys 99
10.4 Putting them together. 99
10.5 Features of Strategy and Tactics 102
10.6 Applying both to Cricket 104

11. Development, Open or Closed Plays

11.1 The Concept of Development in Chess 110
11.2 Control of Key Squares 111
11.3 Activation of Resources 111
11.4 Altering Balance 113

12. Tempo, measuring beyond time

12.1 Tempo in Chess 115
12.2 Applications in Cricket 118

13. Chess Summation

13.1 Keeping options open and mixing approaches   121
13.2 Recognizing when the 'chess advantage' is yours   124
13.3 How much chess is good in human sports?   127

14. Deriving Ideas from Tennis as well

14.1 Tennis analogy to sessions/matches of cricket   129
14.2 Execution Precedence over Match State   132

PART III: APPLICATIONS & CASE STUDY

15. Test Matches are limited over games!

15.1 110-170 Overs per innings!   138
15.2 50 overs, for 2 wickets   140
15.3 Balls played by batsmen   142
15.4 Assessing the effort as runs and wickets   144

16. The Great Dot Dilemma

16.1 The Dot State   145
16.2 Dot Undefined   146

17. One Shot Bowling

17.1 It is not so special   152
17.2 but yet batsmen cannot just score   152
17.3 even if it is predictable   153
17.4 The chances for the bowler during one shot   154
17.5 Light Gray Options for Batsman   156

18. Draws in ODIs & Twenty20s?

18.1 Solving the dot exploitation   157
18.2 Wickets in ODI and Twenty20   158

19. Chess in Shot Production

19.1 Tempo within the context of execution/reaction   160
19.2 Sachin Tendulkar & Brian Lara   163

19.3 Releasing Tempo: Ponting and Hayden   169

20. Chess in Team Roles

20.1 Bradman sacrifices the tail after counter gambits   172
20.2 Jacques Kallis, the Defensive Queen   173
20.3 Shahid Afridi, the Crazy Knight   175
20.4 Andrew Flintoff, Queen of the Ashes   177
20.5 Shane Warne, as a Chess Shot   179
20.6 Jason Gillespie, as Pawn Outpost   180

21. Tendulkar Dot Chess

21.1 Nasser Hussain in India, 2001-02   185
21.2 Tendulkar Deflected at Natwest 2002   187
21.3 Pakistan loses on type 1, World Cup 2003   188
21.4 Offside Defensive Tactics, Melbourne 2003-04   189
21.5 Tendulkar 'Karpovs' the Aussies, Sydney 2003-04   191
21.6 Aussies take revenge, ODI Final 1, 2003-04   194
21.7 Deflection Continues, Srilanka Asia Cup Finals'04   196
21.8 Tendulkar Walls, but Afridi gets him, Pak 2005   197
21.9 Tendulkar vs Inzamam, Recognizing the chess   200
21.10 Undriving Vass- winning a wait 2005   202
21.11 Murali Exploited on a Skewed Attack, 2005   203
21.12 Exhanging Queens, vs Pollock in India, 2005   205
21.13 Shoiab Deflected on Skewed Condition, 2006   207
21.14 Accepting the singles gambit! Pak ODIs 2006   209
21.15 Overcoming inswinging one shot Pak 2006   210
21.16 Waiting on Nimzo-Pollock, 3rd Test 2006   211
21.17 Adelaide Boomerangs in Cape Town   214
21.18 Out-dotting West Indies in ODIs 2007, India   216

PART IV: ASSESSMENT & STATS

22. Team vs Individuals

22.1 Cricket as a Team Game and Role of Players   222
22.2 Then assess the roles, with different stats!   223

23. Match Winner vs Fighter

23.1 Match Winner- as keeping uncertainty away 226
23.2 Fighter- up-front and fight-back 232
23.3 Why it is natural to be a fighter in sport 234
23.4 Evaluating Match Winning Performances 237

24. Playing when it matters

24.1 How often can it work out? 241
24.2 Understanding the Natural Pattern of Success 241
24.3 Comparing Performances to the Natural Pattern 244
24.4 When does it matter, and filtering it right. 246

25. Match Winner vs Tournament Performer

25.1 Learning from Tennis 254
25.2 When can match winners win tournaments? 254
25.3 Consistent above-par outcomes in a tournament. 255
25.4 Winning Single-Handedly? Handle with care... 256

26. Presenting known stats in a better way

26.1 Sunday Stats 257
26.2 Short term indicators- based on Dot aspects! 260
26.3 'Breaking' Averages 262

27. New types of stats from agreeable concepts

27.1 Normalized Scores 266
27.2 Runs or Runs( )? 268
27.3 Comparative Analysis 270

PART V: APPENDIX

Towards a formal assessment system 274
Axiomatic approach for rule changes & variants 277
My Background & Personal Acknowledgments 286
Jan-Ove Waldner & Tendulkar; and the rest... 288

Acknowledgments

My work revolves around software development, photography, publishing and travel product development. So not many are aware that I am involved in such a book or working on theories pertaining to sports as such. To begin with, I owe my parents for their tolerance on every activity, and colleagues who have supported my other projects– Komal Kataria and Pravin Rai who have worked on other web & travel publishing projects (and have no choice but to listen to my cricket analysis), Ashit Sheth at Earthlinks for co-working on travel projects. Since this is my first attempt at a sports book I have a list of personal acknowledgements about friends when I played many a sport (see Appendix). My school friend Shahid Pabaney, for proofing and offering suggestions on most of my content driven projects.

I must thank all cricket channels and the panel of past legends for bringing cricket to us from around the globe. Needless to say, Richie Benaud, who is one of the great contributors to cricket off the field (besides his contribution to Australian cricket on the field), is perhaps one of the few who can make statements on the history of the game, as he has seen it evolve right into the twenty20 era. If there was only one person I could afford to give a free copy of my book, it would be him. Hopefully, I will be able to spare more.

Online resources such as **cricinfo.com** are a boon, especially when we have to track scores and commentary during work or from abroad. Apart from cricket, important online resources I have come across are the chess databases and websites by chess experts explaining the basics of chess and also the nuances, for enthusiasts like me. **Chessbase.com** is popular, and so is **chessgames.com** (my personal favorite, since their Java interface works well). Besides, there are thousands of PGN (Portable Game Notation), for playback on desktop and PDAs. I also admire search tools like Google for making the internet more click-worthy, and **wikipedia.org** for information of all kinds. In fact, they also have a explanation on chess theories, chess openings and profiles of Grandmasters. **Amazon.com** does feature a great variety of chess books, though not many on cricket (this one will add one for sure).

Preface

So Cricket is about runs, wickets and strike rates? It sure is, but there are many ways to get there and significant ways to make an impact by which these are controlled. Needless to say, cricket situations and conditions such as newness of the ball, nature of the pitch, weather, etc. are crucial factors which we are indeed aware of but can often ignore in our evaluation. But there are other basic aspects, which are being exploited and these are now changing the way cricket is being played. Fitness and training methods, new ways to analyze a game (with computers and videos), modern equipment, and the impact of ODIs have altered the game, for better or worse (depending on which era you were born).

Game play is substantially intricate, nowadays- although most of us would like to just see it as a skill of bat and ball. But unfortunately, it is not just about see it and hit it, although that is one of the ways of approaching it! There is lots of 'chess' between players, between a player and the match situation (role needed), and in regard to strategy and tactics. Like chess pieces, players get in and out- thereby altering the balance of resources by which these runs or wickets are achieved in the first place. So let's see what exists in-between the runs and wickets equations. Let's explore the chess in cricket!

I am working on creating an assessment system for cricket which will put stats and numbers in a better perspective. Also, we will have a wider vocabulary to explain certain situations, when stats cannot do due justice. Why bother? Because stats do get flashed around (in this age of instant-access to technology) well before a player can even make his way back to the pavilion. So if numbers do get posted, they should be fair and just to the players, taking in the effort and not just the result (yes, the result is what matters in the end, but players play well before it ends and the impact of their effort is often lost due to improper assessment).

> **As fans and spectators, it is wrong to watch a sport**
>
> **for its entertainment value and then pass comments**
>
> **on the competitive aspect.**

This book is a preview for such an assessment system. I have solved a lot, but need to address many more issues. Till then enjoy the prelude, which I hope offers relevant observations and lots of interesting ideas, and a few answers. In my view, an assessment system which does a definitive job than the *ad hoc* statistical methods used today, is much needed and I have a working model already. However, I hope to refine it, and would in the meantime, like to present this book - as a diary of ideas - and in turn study the relevance of the entire exercise, once feedback and ideas get triggered around.

And even before working on cricket theory, I have been working on a universal system of expression for all sports– an abstract and formal way to describe a situation in any sport using a limited but well defined vocabulary of special terms (some of which are seen in the first part- Format of Cricket. Again, the framework is in place, but this is much broader in scope, as it is supposed to address every sport with one theory. It will take a bit more time to formalize..

Note: In certain discussions, where we compare and contrast aspects of various sports, it may appear that a particular sport or discipline is 'easier' than the other. That is not quite so, because the rules are same for all players in every sport (even if some aspect is easy, it is the same for the opponent) and any competition is always demanding, it is just that the nature of skills and format varies.

Also, many examples in the discussions are around Indian cricket, because of the amount of Indian Cricket I follow, being an Indian. So when I acknowledge the effort of certain Indian players, it perhaps could be that many others were more apt in that case study, but have gone unnoticed as it was not possible for me to watch every game.

Purpose of writing a sports book

Books are usually written by experts and players of vast experience– so as a mere follower of many a sport, why get into the process at all? Here are but a few reasons, why ardent fans should be looking to get involved in the process:

1. Our free time is endangered!

If you ask what most of us do in our free-time, beyond work and sleep- the answer will usually relate to some form of relaxation and entertainment. A huge number of people, will eventually say that they spend a lot of time playing or watching sports, besides other creative processes such as music, movies, art etc. If we do the maths, then perhaps 30% or more, of our quality free time can get connected with such creative activities. We therefore need to have better systems and institutions in place, so that we maintain the traditions and evolve our art as well, in an apt manner. It is about time that many of the steps, should be driven by fans and that we put forth our commitment to what we love and often live for, even though we are just 'fans'. We live in a era where technology and media can contribute just as much as it can erode the traditions. We surely do not want to end up with 3,000 TV channels and find ourselves searching for more.

2. Sports is more academic than most of think it is.

Talent is of primary importance in just about every field, but most of us think that academics is more or only about science, literature and all those subjects taught in school. I used to think that way too, and that is why my table tennis remained stagnated at a certain level (I played at a junior level in Mumbai). Here is an event that changed my views within a span of a few moments, which nonetheless had a lasting impact.

During my school days, I used to practice table tennis with my friend Sanjay Kava (in the same club; he was from another school- Jamnabai Narsee). He had tremendous 'natural talent' and had scant respect for any opponent on the table. He would watch a player ranked in the mens' draw and say he was going to smack that guy. And he usually did, if in his uncanny assessment he could do so. He also won his first inter-school title, by beating a brilliant opponent to whom he had, in fact, lost to, a few months back. He told me he wanted to beat him under 10 (21 point games in those days) and he actually smashed it 3-0, and by huge margins.

Then one day he was pitched against the Parthiv Vyas (an Asian junior sensation, who unfortunately for India, passed away in his teens). He told me, he had no chance, as Parthiv was a player on another plane. But that evening, after the match he returned with a smile on this face. He would never carry a smile if he lost, so I thought he had done the impossible. Not quite, but he was proud he did win a game in the five set match, and he knew that it was more demanding than his other tournament titles. He kind of felt a strange sense of satisfaction, at finding out really where he stood, in context of an international player. He was not like the other schoolboys who would revel in displaying his medals to his uncles and aunts. So all in all, I thought of Sanjay as a super talented player. However, he had actually failed a grade or two in school, so I never really saw him as a 'good student'. But that was about to change.

As most gifted sports enthusiasts, Sanjay was a natural at soccer, basketball, volleyball and cricket as well. One day at our club, many friends praised his cricket in an 'intra' school match (against regular players of his school team). They told me, that his cricket was even better than his table tennis! So that evening I asked him if that was so, why was he not playing for his school (their coach Mr. Solomon, was a sincere man and had invited him to the nets). He grinned and said he preferred to focus on table tennis. Then I asked him if batting was indeed easier to him than table tennis, as our friends were suggesting, to which he replied bluntly "are you crazy? in batting, I get out on my first mistake, but here (in table tennis) if I hit 10 right and 7 wrong, I am winning". It was just another casual statement from him, as when I recently bumped into him, he did not even recollect it. But that had a big impact on me.

What he had said, well, we all know it (and as we shall see later, this statement is only half the truth). But he actually took advantage of the format and honed his attacking skills accordingly, tried shots from the weirdest angles, all with an understanding that the percentages will dictate the outcome. Such insight was way beyond his age and also indicative that it was actually his sharp mind which nurtured his 'natural ability' and his confidence came from his ability to understand the nature of the game, and not his 'killer instinct' or magical skills, which most of us saw with great awe.

On the other side, I used to believe I was academically good, since I could handle maths and science with ease in school. Nonetheless, my science aptitude, howsoever practical, was yet derived from books and theorems created by others. Here was my friend, who was regarded as a 'failure' in school, but could time and again come up with assessments and statements which were not only potent, but were actually his own. He was not better than most of us at table tennis simply because of his natural abilities– but was actually ahead, because of superior mental application.

That evening was a humbling experience for me. I had just realized that the guy whom I believed was merely a natural talent, was in fact academically superior to most of us- just that his terrain did not fit the gamut of our school 'syllabus'. It explains why I failed to improve beyond a point (after all, I thought academics was for school exams and sports was about skill alone), whereas he made strides, year after year, because he was academic about what he was skilled at. And, if at all he only went so far ahead, it was because he practiced with many of us, who never gave him enough 'mental competition' beyond basic skills.

In school, we were being imparted 'knowledge', whereas he was already into the fine art of 'knowing'- based on instinct and first hand experience. Folks, Sanjay Kava did not fail at school– let's just say that our school system was a failure instead. He was ahead academically, by miles- it is just that our scope of what constitutes 'studies' was not good enough to encompass many great disciplines- such as sport- at which he excelled. I am sure that many Sanjay Kavas have been lost into oblivion, on account of our narrow vision of what constitutes 'studies'. They always told us in school that studies come first. But they rarely stressed that you should, therefore, study your sport or art just as well!

There are essentially two points that come out of this:

1. Whenever we see talent, at the top level, even at national or state level, be assured that they would have made strides academically, at

least in regard to fine tuning their skills, to get to where they are, irrespective of whether they were naturally gifted or just trained hard.

2. However, it may not mean that the best players, who are academic in their style of play, may have great overall knowledge or have academic inclinations relating to the scope of possibilities in their sport, beyond their specialization. This is true in most fields, where specialization takes up a lot of mental effort, often at the cost of the larger picture–like say science and technology, where engineers may have perfected certain production skills, but may not necessarily know the scope and possible uses of the very technology they create and how it affects the way people eventually adapt to it in the real world.

So we need to respect the fact that every sports-person has been academic in their department and skills, else they would never be near the top, but also accept that in the larger context of their sport, even when the best performers of the game are put together, views will differ and may often fall short, when new theories and broader issues are involved.

3. Appreciation of effort & crediting players at various levels

Another aspect which is being lost in the entertainment is the ability to acknowledge quality of effort. We might be tempted to say that the result is what matters in the end, but as mentioned, we forget that players play before it ends and the effort often goes unnoticed. As humans, we do not have total control over results, and in a team game this is even more so. Besides, in sport, even when you do things right, the result is often not as expected, due to the nature of the format and conditions, and most importantly, the fact that your opponent will offer stiff competition. So eventually, any good assessment system should be indicative of the effort and credit the result, in the proper perspective.

For instance, in cricket, we will be well served if they show highlights which retain the ratio of scoring shots and dot balls during the entire match to emphasize the variety of effort. This way, crucial dot balls will make their way into key moments shown each evening. Superb defence, well-lefts, near misses, great fielding, should get priority over inside edges, and shots played with 'enough bat' and land somewhere for runs.

Regarding effort, there is another aspect which needs inspection, not just in cricket but in every sport. **We need a better way to credit top international efforts, apart from just the winners.** Take the example of Anju Bobby George, India's foremost athlete and world-class long jumper. She often ranks in the top five, in major world competitions. Each time she 'ends up 5th' the media reminds us that she has disappointed once again and has come back with her hands empty. Sure, India would like her to be a medalist at an Olympic event, but just lets put it in perspective a bit.

For instance, in my field, I have met many great programmers and tech-whiz kids, many have worked at Apple, Microsoft, Intel, Sun, Texas Instruments and other great companies. Sure, we cannot compare an industry to say long jump, which is a specific discipline within the world of sport. But even if we take their specific field of specialization- which demands life-long dedication, just as long jump is in sports– I can say that many outstanding engineers would often not be in the top 5 of their own company!

If the guys I knew are just about the best I was fortunate to meet, it is beyond my brains, to figure out the effort Anju might have put in, to be in the top 5 of the world and if we cannot figure that out, it is perhaps just right for us to shut up, as we would be clueless in helping her go from 5th to 3rd or better. Just stand up and salute her. We do not need TV announcers, who perhaps may just be the 5th best in their own newsroom to comment on her performance.

Or take the case of Indian tennis sensation, Sania Mirza. She broke into the top 30 of the world in women's tennis and then went back in the rankings a bit. So we have ever so eager, wayside pundits complaining about her advertising contracts and glamor gal image being her 'downfall' (they surely do not give tennis rankings based on glamor). To be the best in a country of millions of teenagers, by a mile, is not considered an achievement? She deserves her dollars just for that. Surely, to be in the top 30s of the world, even if you are yet in your teens, is obviously not the end of the world, but it is no mean accomplishment, nonetheless. As I said, just try to assess how the best professionals around you, for whom you have high regard, would be rated in the country. After that, you need to see where their contributions would perhaps fit in the world, if at all. Apply the 'tigers in their own backyard' yardstick, to other fields, and find out which species they end up as. In fact, being a tiger in your own backyard is not bad, if the backyard implies the entire country, but we often see that sports persons are ridiculed for not measuring up to world standards, even if we cannot question their standing at a national level.

Sure, the ultimate in sport is to be on top. But the way to get there has more to do with competition back home at the grass roots. In cricket, Australia, is a great example of how the local standards are so good that a player such as Mike Hussey, makes his international debut and tops the world rankings within a year or so. Next time you see an Olympic athlete end up last in the finals, it needs to be looked into as who let the country down- the local sports situation as such or the athlete who finished 8th in the world.

Perhaps, the Olympics and other sports bodies should create a formal system of points, for top 75% of the positions achieved in major events, apart from just the medal winners. This should then go into the 'country' points tally, across all sports– making it possible or even mandatory for certain sponsors, TV rights dollars, and sports institutions to split a tiny fraction of the budget or ticket revenues from a sports event to achievers in their own sport and to other sports as well, in proportion to points earned. Some sort of a shareholding in a collective sports pool. Youngsters will then be encouraged to continue a sport, or choose a lesser popular sport but where they can provide competition, earn 'minor-points' at state level, and yet get a piece of the pie. As fans, we will be served better, as the 30% or so, of our free time is in the good hands of good competitors, at each and every level.

Introduction to some assessment methods

How should we assess a sporting moment?

If you ask ten different experts to just explain a sports situation in a clear manner, let alone assess it, you will come up with different answers. So it is no surprise that most of them will end up with different assessments as to what went wrong, what was the strong point, and what is required next. Besides it is hard to ever agree on what would have happened or could have been, if something was done or was not (you can often do such analysis in chess, since chess pieces always behave the same and from a given board position, you can often refute or confirm a winning line).

Here are few ways to arrive at what I believe can help us assess and appreciate situations better.

1. Watch & Play TV! Acknowledging Effort and Skill.

When you watch a player execute a shot, be it cricket or any other sport, try to play it as if you are that person—just as it unfolds—as if you are playing that shot along with the player (if you do this on the replay, it will still have some value but when you do it 'live' you will really 'get the shot' in context of the reaction time). You will at once feel the effort that goes in, and often the technical nuances, even in simple defensive shots. When you play along with a player—as if you are the player—for a session or a phase of play, it will be like a first hand experience of what happened– how many times a player was beaten or managed to squeeze in some good shots, because it is like you are playing and sweating it yourself. Then describing the performance in context of the moment will be as if you are explaining what you went through.

2. Plan & Watch TV! Understanding Strategies and Approaches.

Watch the best players play a game– this time before the shot or ball, just try to think what you would have done, at that instance. Surely, your idea may not match, but that is when you ask, why that player attempted a shot of that type or bowler bowled it that way. Again, you can do this with other sports and you will be surprised where your questioning can lead you. Just keep in mind, that often the player perhaps executed the shot poorly but the idea may yet be apt. So do not discard that option. Sports can be as academic as science or maths, and often more challenging since there are no common methods for all players and there are many (correct) ways to approach a problem.

3. Assess based on what you would take as an outcome.

Let's say you are at position A and after a certain phase of play, you can get to position B. Would you take that position B? If yes, and you have a workable method to get from A to B, then that method could be an option, because you can say– I can accept this match position (B). You also have to consider the consequences in case of not reaching there. Remember that a position is more than runs, wicket, and overs left– as player involvement, conditions and tons of other factors that can play a part. Also, since there may be many methods—seemingly absurd as well as directly relevant—keep them in your memory bank (more important than the computer memory), just as chess players do, you will never know when it gets used. There will be many bizarre counterplays involved, because unlike an exhibition type of art, sports is a competitive art form. You will find an opponent who matches your intentions, even if they cannot match your skills, forcing you to consider possibilities which go quite a bit off your 'natural' game.

Here is how I got into 'playing a player' while watching TV:

When I was a grad student in the US, I had a freelance job as a photographer at the campus newspaper. Although, into Computer Engineering, I took photography very seriously, as my research was in digital imaging. So once I was assigned to shoot a basketball game, I was a bit circumspect as this was not a game I was too familiar with, and getting the timing on the shots would be tricky, as players move around quite quickly. Around that time I saw a training video by renowned Austrian photographer Ernst Hass, about how he applied eastern philosophical concepts of 'becoming the mountain' while shooting a mountain or any other event. This gave him a real good feel of what the subject/moment was all about. He sure did, as his photography was very spontaneous and captured the feel of the moment.

So I began recording basketball games on TV, and tried to play along with players and use my TV remote to 'freeze' the frame, as a practice of clicking a shot. This did help, as I did manage to get a bunch of decent shots in a few games I covered (I usually did not shoot sports, as many other colleagues would usually line up for such events to get free passes as well). Anyway, thereafter, I have been watching every sport in a different way- as I often try to 'play the player' rather than just watch. It is quite a bit of fun but requires a lot of focus, for sure. Try it out, you will be amazed at what you can experience, right in your living room.

Tips from a rickshaw driver

During the World Cup in South Africa (2003), a day after India defeated England, I was heading out to office in a rickshaw. I love talking to these rickshaw guys, as you do get to know a lot of stuff about what is happening around town. Apparently, the rickshaw-wala (driver), loved to talk as well. He said he was also on his way towards my office and then he was going to buy some fire-crackers for the India-Pakistan match. He was hoping that Sachin Tendulkar would play some of the shots like he did against England. I quickly reminded him about the pace attack of Waqar, Wasim, Akhtar etc. It did not bother him a bit. Then I asked him if he was referring to the six he hit off Andrew Caddick, (pulled from not too short a ball from outside off). Well, that was not what thrilled him, he was referring to a shot, where the ball climbed up and into Sachin—a bit more than expected—but he adjusted and hooked it finer than the fine leg fielder. It landed safely, but this in his opinion was an indication of the form he was in, to adjust his shot this way! I connected with him immediately, since I was 'playing Sachin' and remembered that shot very vividly. However, that was no reason to believe that Sachin would play one of his best knocks against the great Pakistan bowling attack. Maybe, the rickshaw-wala knew better than us. By the way, I did not have the time to ask him if he watched TV and 'plays the player' as I often do. But the fact is that if you observe with some degree of focus, you will get closer to the crucial moments, even though they were not featured in the highlights of the day. In fact, in that World Cup, Tendulkar hardly gave a chance on a defensive shot and also had a great strike rate. If he was really truly beaten in defense during the World Cup, it was by Wasim Akram who cut him in half, but the ball went over the stumps. Funny game this, his weakest defensive effort was also in his best innings.

To create a system of assessment, we need consistency in our expressions– for which we need a specific set of terms and apt nomenclature. Then we can try to construct phrases using only such agreed terms, to achieve consistency.

Studying the format of cricket and other sports is therefore the first step, in identifying possible abstractions, which can have a broad usage across sports.

PART I: FORMAT OF CRICKET

1. Dot Nature of Cricket

1.1 Why are there dot balls in cricket?

In other 'point based' games such as tennis, table tennis etc., every instance of play results in a scoring effect. Then there are sports such as soccer, snooker etc., where every instance or attempt will not score. The reasons are obviously related to skills and the rules which were invented or designed to test certain skills in that sport. The rules and format for a given sport, usually will undergo refinements during its early development phase, and then change only when deemed necessary (as after the Bodyline series, England in Australia, 1932-33). However, certain rules or concepts may perhaps never change—even though a sport is a man-made activity and we can define things the way we like—because it would make little sense to alter rules to an extent that there is no latitude for skills to be unleashed.

For instance, in my view **the dot ball in cricket is a necessary concept due to the disparate skills of batting and bowling** (a 'dot' ball is a ball where no runs are scored, but in general, however, we will apply this term to those balls, where no scoring took place–either runs or a wicket). Since bowlers initiate play and provide momentum with their own 'inner' abilities and batsmen do have a tool—the bat—to make use of this momentum, it is just fair to say that bowlers will need some margin to bowl around a larger area than the stumps (wider/higher). Likewise, since cricket is played on a natural surface with a ball which can behave or misbehave, a bit more than what a bowler often intended, it is meaningful to give the batsmen some breathing time to 'select' the shots.

> Welcome to the world of dot balls! You can invent any variant you wish, be it Twenty20 or a one over game, the day dot balls disappear from cricket, you can assume that cricket is finished as well. Dot balls are the underlying basis of cricket– in skill as well as planning.

1.2 Evaluating a dot ball

Since there is no change of score on a dot ball (no runs or wickets), it appears that nothing is happening. That is not quite so, either from the entertainment angle or from the competitive perspective. There will be dot balls, where the bowler had to earn it, or those which 'square' the batsman completely or some which were extremely 'well left' by the batsman. These are special to watch (used to be?). Sure, there are dot balls which just went wide or were easy to defend. But even those dots, have a value in the match context. **Some dot balls are 'positive' for batsmen, some are 'positive' for bowlers, and some are neutral for both.**

For instance, in a test innings, during the first new ball phase– when bowlers are expected to take a couple of wickets, dot balls are in many ways 'positive' for batsmen. Every dot ball implies fewer balls left from the 6 or 7 overs that most fast bowlers are likely to bowl up front.

Likewise, from overs 50-80, dot balls are 'positive' for bowlers, as that is the phase, bowlers may be in their third spell and the ball is old. It is mechanically demanding for bowlers to prevent batsmen from scoring. Likewise, in the middle overs—from 25th to 50th over—dot balls are perhaps 'par' for both. Bowlers need wickets and batsmen need runs to make sure the runs to wicket equation is tilted accordingly. Obviously, these are general rules and each match will be different. Nonetheless, this is the case in general.

So what about ODIs? Dot balls are in general very, very, very, positive for bowlers in 50 over One Day Internationals (ODIs), since they do not have to take 10 wickets to win the match (it is nice to take wickets, and put pressure on the new batsman, but a dot ball is always a plus for the bowler, even in the first 5-10 overs of an innings. As we will see, Australia have exploited this concept of focusing on the dot balls in ODIs, superbly in the last few years.

Who says one day cricket is a batsman's game? Skill-wise it is still diffi-cult for bowlers, as their wide ball margins are reduced. But format -wise they can turn things upside down, by not trying to take wickets, or rather getting wickets without bowling wicket-taking balls. Low scoring ODI games may be common in future, even on good pitches!?

We will see the significance of the dot ball in cricket as we proceed. Just about everything revolves around these dots, as we explore both cricket and 'chess' as applied to cricket.

2. Intention & Execution

2.1 Intention & Execution gap in various sports

There is a gap between intention and execution, in everything we do. So what so new about it. Do we all not know that? What we may have planned may not work out, because we are human. Sure, but there are shades to it. Whenever we assess a performance in cricket or another sport, we should keep in mind the nature of the sport and competitive framework. This gap is a lot trickier than it seems, and needs to be put in perspective for fans and spectators– who often expect magic and miracles from their heroes. Further, even the analysts and experts often ignore the fact that a plan did not work out due to certain degrees of execution failure. Sometimes the failures may be just errors, sometimes blunders, and in some cases, failures can be a lack of doing better.

For instance, the trickiest assessment happens in a game such as **soccer** (with my limited following). The toughest aspect of appreciating soccer is that even after good planning and superb execution, the goals may not come through, as that is the nature of the game. Maybe a defender just managed to get his foot in time or a great shot at the goal was tipped by an acrobatic goalkeeper. It can be harsh, since execution by the strikers was excellent—but no goals—as there is no exact science for conversion. Commenting on a soccer game based on the goals scored, can be the most misleading. You perhaps have to see what happened and then pronounce whether the plan was poor or the execution; or perhaps both were good yet.... was it just the nature of the game.

Then there are **cue-sports such as pool and snooker**, where intention and execution, can at least be analyzed theoretically. Sure, even the best players miss seemingly easy or regulation shots, but we can at least agree, about the if-then scenarios, since the balls and table are consistent enough to behave in accordance to the laws of physics. Further, in cue sports, you execute shots by yourself and not as a reaction to an opponent (see initiate and control *Ch 3.1, p41*). So if your are at peace with yourself, you can say that 'my execution will at least be as good as the chances of accomplishing that shot'.

The other extreme is a game like **chess**, where if your plan is apt, the execution can be (or can expected to be) in synch, based on your expertise. This is surely true at the level of each move (if you know 'the' correct move at a given position, playing it is no problem- chess being a 100% mind game and the board being 100% consistent and pieces always behaving as they always do). At a deeper level (over many moves), obviously the plan and execution may not be in synch, since your opponent could have worked out variations, to keep you considering deviations as well. But if in chess, you can prove logically that a certain line of play wins or equalizes, from a given board position, you can always repeat that, the next time you encounter the same position (unlike other sports, where execution of a shot is reaction-based and the same situation may lead to different possibilities). This notion of exactness leads to a fact that a win in chess against a top player can rarely be a fluke (if he is better and experienced, he can repeat what he knows, and work out what he does not—and then since the pieces behave exactly—he should win against lower ranked players, and sometimes playing 25 of them at a time!). A loss in chess often leads to the weirdest of ego clashes. Aaron Nimzowitsch, noted chess theoretician and amongst the best players of his time, once lost a game which he reckoned he should not have. After the match he stood on the table and expressed his feelings– "why must I lose to this idiot?". You are not supposed to lose in chess, if your knowledge is better, because execution is expected to be flawless on a flawless board. This means that losing implies a shortcoming within the player, which even the best may not accept.

In other games, it may not be easy to analyze the impact of certain moments. In **cricket**, if a catch was taken, then what would have been the match like? (Ashley Giles dropping Ricky Ponting in the second test of the 2006 Ashes, when Australia were chasing 500+ and had lost quick wickets inside 100 runs). Obviously, it was very very costly, but we cannot prove for sure, what the batsmen who came in next would have achieved if the catch was taken. Perhaps they would then play differently and adjust their game or have another story in the second innings. Assessing such if-then scenarios is indeed difficult in cricket.

All in all, this aspect of **intention and execution gap being different in each sport, needs to be kept in the forefront of our assessment, and we always have to hold back on the comments, considering that this gap can be filled in various ways.**

2.2 Implication of margin of victory

The implications of any sport where the gap between intention and execution can be uncertain (both in terms of bad luck and good), a team has to ensure that it must try to win with some margin, because it is the nature of the game that so many wickets will not just fall in the last session nor can one rely on the lower order to sneak in runs with unreasonable time or target chases. Sure it is memorable and nice to win 'down the wire', but better is to do things right and to keep a clear margin. Great teams such as the West Indies (70s-80s) and Australia (today), are great because they could win with a innings or at least with clear margins. The best guys take unpredictability out of the equation.

Note: in a game such as chess, a pawn advantage can be held and converted to a win in the 'end' game, simply because of the exact nature of piece and board behavior. However, to achieve a one pawn margin is not easy against top players. In cricket, if you can be 100% sure that certain advantages will come your way later in the game, such as a weak fifth bowler in ODIs (has to bowl, since 10 overs per bowler) then that can be exploited in the later stages for sure.

2.3 Implication of multiple attempts to prove a theory

Since cricket is a game in which execution can fail and some failures can have catastrophic effects, such as dropping a catch of a major batsman or getting the openers out early within the new ball spell, plans can go awry very easily. Apart from failures, something that was planned, perhaps did not work because the opposition did very well or the conditions were way too tilted in favor of batsmen or bowlers, to get the theory tested, under reasonable conditions. So for any theory to be proven, you have to give it multiple tries. Likewise, the fact that a plan worked once, does not indicate that the theory behind it is sound, for the same reasons! However, it is frequently seen, that we make our conclusions on the basis of a game or two, especially when the results were not what we expected.

Recently, in the last and **third Test against England (Mumbai, 2006)**, Rahul Dravid opted to field first, when just about everyone would have expected to bat (England were 0-1 down in the series). Perhaps the logic was that the pitch was so good that only 3 innings might be completed. In which case, the team batting second would win or draw (that is how I saw it anyway, there might be other reasons). But India batted not quite as expected, and failed to draw the game on the last day. However, India dropped almost a dozen catches or near about. So can we pass our conclusion about a theory based on the result of indifferent batting? Below par batting can happen and a theory perhaps needs to address that, but dropping so many catches can never help the cause of any theory.

However, such a notion that the first failure implies that a theory lacks substance, existed earlier as well. During the infamous **bodyline series (England in Australia, 1932-33)**, England, under Douglas Jardine, had implemented a bowling theory with fielders packed on the on-side and fast bowling into the batsmen and often into the ribs. This meant that batsmen could not play any meaningful shots, as horizontal bat shots to the leg side would result in getting out or no runs due to most fielders on that side. Sir Don Bradman missed the first match, which Australia lost. In the second match, he was out for a duck in the first innings but scored a ton in the next, by playing unorthodox shots on the vacant off-side (by backing away outside leg stump, making room for shots on the off, risky but thats all that was possible). Australia won a low scoring encounter with 10 wickets from legendary leg spinner, Bill O'Reilly. However, England persisted with the same tactics and won the series 4-1. Later, O'Reilly went on to say that had Bradman (*ref: Art of Bradman*) played the first match and Australia had won that match, this theory would perhaps have been refuted and abandoned after the first match itself. Perhaps only Jardine can answer that, but the fact remains that when you try something 'out of the box', and then lose the match, 'let's put it aside' would be the reaction, more on account of external pressures and not on account of adequate testing.

2.4 Light Gray Shots!

Scoring of lucky edges has always been a part of cricket. However, I remember the time in the 1970s when as kids we watched cricket at the Wankhede Stadium in Mumbai. If a batsman, especially if it was of the class of Gavaskar, got runs to third man, off an outside edge or through the slips, there would be a pin-drop silence in the stadium. Today, we have fans celebrating the boundary! Times change and so do the celebrations. However, in a modern context to be able to play an attacking game, means that you have to explore 'light-gray-shots', as the modern bats offer you that advantage. Even if you do not hit it from the middle of the bat, there is every chance of the ball going over the in-field or often for a six. We are not discussing stray instances of chinese cuts or unintended edges. **We are talking of taking intended-risks with the knowledge that slightly 'light gray' shots, as long as they have 'enough bat' are good enough to fetch you runs, perhaps more than a regulation** drive or a leg-glance. Another case to explore on the intention to execution aspect. The sad part is that even when orthodox shots are available, batsmen opt for wilder options, and per-haps with even fewer risks than shots intended along the ground (as mistiming such shots to be played along the ground, can scoop up to a close in fielder, but giving it a whack, ensures you find fewer fielders, if any).

The whole point is that intention and execution issues need to be treated with sensitivity, as the 'normal pattern of outcomes' for a bats-man or bowler is derived from this aspect (*Ch 24.2, p241*). Unfortu-nately, our mental energy, before and after a game– takes off in the wrong direction, because too much is often read into each game, espe-cially if there was failure.

3. Who Initiates Play?

Who initiates every instance of on field action (be it a delivery, a shot, a move or a point) and how does the execution proceed? This is the most significant factor, in determining strategy and dictating the nature of play.

3.1 Initiate and Control Disciplines

For instance, in most classic **Olympic events** such as track and field, gymnastics, swimming etc., you initiate action and control what you do without your opponent interfering (at least not directly in an execution sense). Likewise in **golf** for instance, you are almost completely responsible for your performance. These are all initiate-and-control disciplines. The advantage is that you can play your game the way you want but the downside is that you can perhaps only play as well as your game is worth– there are not many options to just outplay an opponent tactically, when it is not your day. Your preparation therefore counts a lot. **Cue sports** are to a great extent similar but you still can compel your opponent to play from positions you leave for them. However, when you are cueing and playing your shots, you initiate and control the proceedings.

The common characteristic of initiate-and-control disciplines, is that in such sports, you can play or **practice all by yourself** to quite a large extent, as no one else is needed during shot execution. The second aspect is that **scoring in such games can be treated as 'absolute', within a given course or conditions**. A break of 120+ in snooker is superb, no matter who your opponent was. If you scaled a golf course in just so few shots, your score is an indicator of performance for that course, even if you played alongside your grandkids. Likewise, if you could jump or throw so far, or break the record in swimming or sprinting, it sure was a great performance, even if the others in the field were not of great stature. No one ever asked who the competitors were, when Sergei Bubka bettered the pole vault world records about a few dozen times in his life.

3.2 Inititate-React Combinations

Absolute scoring or playing all by yourself, is not the case with say tennis, table tennis or other team games such as soccer, basketball etc. The player or team is essentially reacting to 'a play' initiated by the other. In **tennis and table tennis**, a player serves and then there can be a series of reactions (a rally). In **soccer and basketball**, possession is key and the other team defends. But you can seize initiative by stealing possession (a bit different from tennis or table tennis where so many serves are guaranteed). Then there is **boxing or wrestling**, where any of the players can initiate some activity or react to what your opponent did. (again different from the others mentioned). **Nonetheless, your are always initiating and reacting based on your opponent's style, skill or strategy.** These games are not about playing with yourself. Likewise, such sports are not absolute in the way scoring happens (if you win 11-3 in table tennis or 95-65 in basketball, or you knock your opponent in boxing, the first question someone would ask is against whom?). Another question is what kind of advantages did you have or the opponent have in terms of conditions, playing surface, team strength, state of competition (league stage or knockout) etc.

3.3 Inititate-React-Terminate in Cricket

Cricket and baseball are in the second category (initiate-react rather than initiate-control), but a bit different. Bowlers initiate action, batsmen react to the delivery and fielders terminate (if the ball went to them). Now since the bowler and fielders are on the same side, it looks like the batsman is up against 11 players! Fortunately, the reality is not quite that drastic as usually only one of the fielders may come into play during a given shot.

But bowlers will always hold the key to strategy, and have actually unconsciously or have been forced to use this fact from time to time to keep batsmen at bay, whenever the game got stacked in the favor off the batting guys, over the history of the sport.

Again it is important to remember that runs are not absolute, neither are wickets. They are always in relation to who was bowling or who was batting and the advantages of the conditions. Unfortunately, statistics get flashed all over, as if they are self-garnered scores as in snooker or billiards.

Note: just because you play and make breaks without your opponent's involvement in cue-sports, it is not easier by any means, because the skills being tested have their own intricacies. And when something is not working while everything from cueing to execution is apparently right, it is often not easy to figure what is going wrong- since in such self-controlled skills, there will usually be many hard to define 'inner gauges' and ways to 'feel' the shot to get it just right).

3.4 Implications of runs/wicket not being absolute

There are many ways to get a better indicator to better reflect the runs in testing conditions, runs scored against good bowling, and runs scored in different phases of an innings. The sooner we adopt a better way to display that, we would be doing justice to both batsmen and bowlers. However, in many ways it is not possible to measure certain contributions from players as statistics, although a lot of it can be done.

For instance, Shane Warne has not been greatly regarded for his performances in India. However, in the 2004 Test Series in India, when Australia won for the first time in so many decades, he did something in the first test at Bangalore, which had a massive impact on the series. Although, he had poor figures of 4 wickets for 193 runs in the match, he knocked over VVS Laxman twice (bowled him pitching leg and knocking off, and then got him lbw in the second innings when Laxman was perhaps trying to cover the line). So statistically, he was say two-three wickets short of having 'par' bowling figures, but to keep Laxman off the reckoning in an Australian context, was a series defining moment for sure. Forget the stats, Australia will take the Laxman dismissals anytime. How does someone measure a process of de-nemesification?

3.5 Implication of weak or strong connectivity of steps

There are certain games such as **chess and cue-sports, which are very well connected from the first move to the next series of moves,** which may naturally follow. In fact, in chess, the first two or three moves define the nature of the contest—open or closed, draw-like or dynamic, clear or complex—as certain lines of play logically follow the first few moves. Contrary to this in a sport such as **tennis, table tennis, soccer** etc., after every run of play initiated by one party, and well replied by the opponent- the connections are 'reset'. This means in the **next instance the initiator can try something totally different and unconnected to the prior activity or repeat the same stuff, if it is still deemed fruitful**. Connectivity of executing the next steps in such games is only indirect, based on match state and possible ploys that may work (and may be unrelated to past ploys). But the fact remains, that there is no rule as such, which imposes that the next run of play must be in some way a progression of the line or approach that just was. The next steps can be totally different or they can also be exactly same, and it depends on the initiator!

Cricket too, is only indirectly connected in execution steps, at best, and depends on the initiator of action (the bowler). The notion about—why does this batsman not just smack the ball over square leg or play it inside-out over the in-field to extra cover—sounds possible, but one thing is certain, the bowler will not bowl the next ball from square leg or extra cover, he will come back and initiate the same ball, if he still deems it to be risky for the batsmen or he may try something totally different, as a surprise. The point here is that, **bowlers initiate play and bowlers to a large extent can dictate the style of activity, since they are not forced by law, to change their next delivery or next over,** even if the batsman had a 'moral victory' in the past over(s). So in every sport, who initiates action, matters a lot and the style of play is dictated based on context of move or step connectivity of that sport.

The best example of this again would be the **bodyline series**. Although, Sir Don Bradman did score a century in that series, the manner of shot production was unorthodox and risky as well (as mentioned earlier, shots had to be scooped from leg to off). The reason the laws of field placing had to undergo changes after this series, was due to the weak connectivity from ball to ball in cricket.

To digress a bit, let's see what happens **in chess, when someone does something obtuse** and off the norm (as was Jardine's bowling plan). Say a player complicates the board by playing a closed game (pawns inter-locked and most pieces are stuck behind), and then gradually shuffles the pieces in strange ways or unleashes some streaky tactical play. If the opponent encounters such line of play the first time, there will be headaches for sure to find a solution. But if the opponent is equal or better, he will reply and it will usually be just as obtuse and weird, to achieve counter play (as Bradman had to). **But having given a fitting reply, albeit obtuse, the next move or line of play in chess, will proceed from that new board position.** If the reply was indeed compelling, the initiator of this obtuseness will have to alter his play and the onus to reply will now be on himself, as he has to reply from the new position, and look for other options or revert back to something 'normal'.

Now compare this with cricket– after the batsman gives a fitting reply, countering an obtuse delivery with an unorthodox or risky shot, the bowler can get back and repeat the idea, with or without variations, which forced the batsmen to take risks. The batsman will have to pass the test again, since risky shots can get him out (although his knowledge is better with each instance due to predictability, the intention to execution gap is relevant in a reaction skill such a batting). Of course there is a limit to which a bowler can repeat this, as giving away runs is not very exciting either (yet much less costly than a wicket). And in the case of Sir Don Bradman, giving away an average of 56 runs/innings in the series, was a worthwhile bargain!

4. ZX Formats

4.1 Zero error and eXtra effort demands, of various sports

If we study the reward and penalty system of various sports, for bad/poor outcomes and for good/better outcomes, we can get a broad way to classify the basic 'demand' of a sport or a sporting situation.

If the poor or bad outcomes in a given discipline can result in a catastrophic loss or has a strong adverse impact on the state of play, such disciplines will have a demand (or priority) to reduce or eliminate errors. We can classify such disciplines as **Z**-demand (**Z**ero-error demand).

Likewise, if the good or better or special outcomes have a strong impact on the state of play, such disciplines will have a demand/priority for extra effort or special activity. Such disciplines will be classified as **X**-demand or X-based, since the e**X**tra effort (special effort) will be demanded.

Z-based disciplines require that even the simple or basic attempts must be at least 'sufficiently proper' as mistakes are costly.

X-based disciplines will require that your strong and good attempts are much better than the competition.

In short, in **Z**-demand disciplines, even your worst outcomes must be good, and in **X**-demand disciplines, your
best outcomes have to be better.

Batting is a **Z**-demand skill (first mistake and you could be gone) and
Bowling is an **X**-demand skill (how much better were the good balls—
good enough to get wickets?). This does not mean that **X** (special big
shots) does not matter in batting, or **Z** (avoiding loose balls) does not
matter in bowling. It is just that the demand or priority has to be met
that way, and then you look at the other aspect.

**This Z-X can be illustrated up by recent comments by West Indian
legends (as heard on TV).**

When Sir Vivian Richards was asked about the batting of some batsmen of today's era, he mentioned that they are good but they often try
to run before they can walk (a **Z**-sided view, and that too from one of
the most explosive batsman! Essentially because mistakes are costly,
even if it be just one. The basics come first in batting).

Likewise, when Michael Holding was asked to comment on bowlers
taught to focus on line & length basics, often at the cost of sacrificing
speed—he was very clear—if you have the pace, a bowler must not be
asked to let it go, but make him work on the basics, keeping the gift of
speed intact (an **X** -sided view, since you need the pace to get the better
of batsmen, and it has to be substantially better to get them out, so
pace can make the difference, between being beaten or getting out. You
can then bowl slower if needed in certain conditions). Both views are
spot-on for the disciplines they represented.

4.2 Implications of Z-demand on Batting (non-commutativity!)

For Batting: not only are the errors costly in batting (they are costly in soccer or snooker as well, for instance), they are **non-commutative** with the good that can happen by a batsman. This means that a sequence of (9 good + 1 bad + 2 excellent + 1 poor shot) is not the same as (1 poor shot + 2 excellent + 1 bad + 9 good), as it might be in conventional mathematical addition where $(A-B+C-D=C-D+A-B)$. This is so because the first mistake prevents any good that might follow. This has major implications to all batsmen either at school level or test level, as nobody on the planet can ever tell when your first mistake is going to happen (let alone predict when the next unplayable delivery might come your way). Moreover, even if a batsman does not make any mistake, if bowlers force the batsmen to play unorthodox or risky shots at the beginning of an innings, there is again a type of pressure, exploited by this non-commutative aspect (even if such a batsman can play those unorthodox shots, it is difficult to do so early in the innings, on account of the non-commutativity of the good and bad).

For instance, Sir Don Bradman once sent the no.9, 10, 11 to open the innings in wet conditions, **3rd Test against England, 1936-37** hoping that the sun would shine the next day. Does that sound like the greatest batsman of all time feared the conditions (perhaps having to bat 1-down)? Instead, we can all see that he understood the real nature of batting– it is not about how many good or exciting things you can do, but understanding that it just takes one sneaky ball to make you walk back, even if you are all set to play a big knock (and in this case, you may not even make a mistake, it is the pitch that will do you in). He batted lower down, in this pressure Ashes match, and made a double century to win the game for Australia. His greatness was in the fact that he was aware that he was the best batsman in the game, yet was humble enough to realize that nobody is perhaps ahead of the game itself.

Some implications of Z-demand & non-commutative aspect–

1. Just play you natural game! Sure, but putting into practice- ball for ball, is no easy task. A shot which works 9 out of 10 times would work in other sports (or even in bowling for example), and might work for a batsman as well. But does that 1 out of 10 chance of failure happen on the 3rd shot or 9th shot– or even the first shot? Nobody knows, but it will always be criticized.

2. Talent can be double edged– it often happens that too much flair can lead to downfall, due to the non-commutative nature of batting. This is why often, lesser batsmen top up in a test series, because they cannot do certain creative things which others might, which in some cases is a blessing, as they only focus on the merit of a ball and mistakes are less likely. This is not the case with bowling– talent is needed by truck loads (although you may at times have a restricted plan), as you need to better a batsman by some degree, often at the cost of a few runs.

3. This batsman should have at least made 30-40 runs, if he could not make a big score. This is again a meaningful ask from a batsman, as after all they are not hired to make mistakes. But it is not about mistakes, its about *one* mistake. If you expected a batsman to make 40 runs at least, then when he gets out to a ball immediately after 40, it could be that he receives the same ball, when batting at 5, 11 or even 0 runs on the board.

4. This batsman is in such great form, then what happened? Again, great form implies that most of the balls you face, you will defend well and score promptly as well. But it is about that *one ball* which might get you. Sure, being in form is simply great, as you will at least score runs in a positive manner, when you do get yourself in. There is a **very thin line between confidence and over-confidence in batting**—which perhaps no one can define—since a mistake can be due to getting 'carried away' or it can occur, due to a slight shortcoming in execution.

So terms such as 'confidence', 'form' etc., can all be better treated if we keep the non-commutative nature of batting in view, before we jump to conclusions. We will **try to assess form, based on studying the frequency of balls a batsman is beaten** *(Ch 26.2, p260)*. Again, the answer lies amidst the dot balls!

5. Shot selection, anybody? Now this non-commutativity helps us explain one of the most undefinable aspects of batting– shot selection. Which ball to defend, which to leave, which to play constructive shots and when do you go for some big shots. No matter how high the percentages are for pulling off certain shots (including tricky 'well-lefts' over the stumps), it is difficult to explain what to do when. Because **percentages only indicate the ratio of good to bad, but does not guarantee the order of acceptable and failed outcomes**. If such an order cannot be predicted, then in a non-commutative format, you will need some luck (or call it bravery), so that the failed outcomes happen only after a string of successful ones.

The same cannot be said for bowling, because **bowling is fairly commutative**— 1 good ball, 1 excellent ball, 2 bad balls, followed by 2 decent ones can be same as 2 bad, 1 good, 2 decent and 1 excellent ball. This means bowlers can bowl according to percentages- and try to probe around with risky variations or surprise balls (this does not make bowling easier, as there are other aspects which can frustrate bowlers, which keep the game in fair balance).

Primary fact of batting:

> No batsman can even claim to 'play well' in a particular
> innings even against a very very weak bowling attack, no
> matter what form he is in, since nobody knows when his
> next mistake will be (or may receive a superb delivery).

Does all this sound as if batting is the scariest discipline around? Sure this non-commutative aspect leads to pressure, which cannot be eliminated or even defined. However, there is another way to look at things-since you do not know when your next mistake is about to happen, maybe it might not happen immediately, but later on. So if you 'apply' yourself and do hang in—and definitely not try to fabricate shots, but play on the 'merit' of each ball—it seems like "not knowing when my mistake might happen" can work the other way as well!

For a moment, let's see just how bizarre this pressure of 'first-error and you are out' is. If it was so horrendous, it looks like no batsman should ever last more than a few overs (20-30 balls?). **Do not the best tennis players, make a mistake every 5-7 points?** What the heck, in tennis, you can double fault twice in a game and might still have a decent chance to win it, as you can cover four points before giving two, on your serve. Are these 'point' based games, therefore easier than batting? (*p18-20*, refer to my friend's comparison). Not quite. Surely, in such games a player who is much better will usually win, but there is more to it. In tennis or table tennis, every point is scored. So at every instance of play, you will have to try to seize the initiative to win the point (else lose it). So to win the point, you need to try to better or outplay your opponent on every point. The meaning of a mistake must be seen in this context, as you have to produce a compelling (if not overpowering) reply on each instance. A batsman does not have to do that in cricket. He need not counter the bowler with an equally dominating reply on each instance. He can drop the bat dead to the best of deliveries (not easy, but yet no need to get the better of the bowler). Welcome again, to the world of dot balls! Batsman, can hang in there (with some grit and technique), even if they cannot start off with a bang. No such breathing space in tennis. If you are not on the button even for a short phase, points will flow away and you will not be able to dot yourself back in contention.

So now we have the secondary fact of batting.

> Since we do not know when a batsman will make his next mistake, and the format does not demand that every ball be met with equal dominance, it might well be that a mistake might be avoided to a large extent! Therefore, we cannot even say that out-of-form batsmen or tail-enders may not contribute meaningfully!

Sachin Tendulkar had to struggle for runs in Australia 2003-04. However, he took comfort in the fact that holding on is just as much an advantage in batting, as is the 'first mistake and you are out' disadvantage. He scored nearly 500 runs without getting out from two tests– Sydney and Multan (Pakistan 2004). I am not sure what a record for test runs scored without being dismissed is, but this was as some effort for sure. He did offer two chances during the last phase of the innings, to push scoring rate, once in Sydney and in Multan. But a good example of why you can hold on, in spite of Z-demand.

In modern times, Jason Gillespie has been a great tail-ender (see pawn outpost, *Ch 20.6, p180*), and he sure understands this advantage of 'holding on', as it is not imperative to even have a backlift– all you need is to align the middle of the bat to the line of the ball, with more of a 'pendulum' swing.

So in batting, just as a mistake can do you in, on the first ball (**Z**-demand & non-commutative), not making a mistake can hold you in for just as long. This is the hold aspect (**Z**ero error-demand still persists, but you can hold on, as dot balls offer a margin). Two seemingly contradictory truths, but true because of the dot nature of cricket.

Both facts are best explained by Sunny Gavaskar's approach to batting– give the bowlers the first hour of the day (as **Z**-demand can be exploited by bowlers with the new ball) and the rest of the day belongs to you (hold on— now it is up to you not to make a mistake and score on merit, as bowlers tire).

4.3 Implications for X-demand on Bowling

So all this zero-error demand on batting seems like bowlers should have a good time? Unlike batsmen they do not get heavily penalized for their mistakes, let alone their very first mistake (the worst ball might yield a four or six, but nothing like being 'out'). And unlike say tennis, where a tennis player will lose points in a batch, if say few serves do not fire right (and thereby lose the service game, since each game is just 4-5 points). Bowlers will have the luxury of bowling a dot ball here and there, and may get around bowling a couple of 'safe balls or an over or two', before getting warmed up.

Sure, these can be some advantages of bowling, but there is a serious aspect which makes the demand on bowling very **X**-tilted. They will have to put in such an e**X**tra effort that they produce adequate balls to beat or rather overcome the defence of batsmen. Moreover, they may yet go wicketless! The fact that batsmen can dot the best yorker or flipper, even if he is tested to the core, it remains a dot. Bowlers may not face the pressure of uncertainty of the 'one' mistake as batsmen have to, but for sure they have to bear the frustration of bowling well for many a spell and go wicket-less, as wickets (at least in Tests) may not come due to batsmen mistakes, but may have to be earned in a manner where there is often no correlation to the quality of the ball. Surely, the gap between beating a batsman comprehensively, and actually getting the wicket is undefinable and far from an exact science. Whereas, in batting if you do last for a session or two, you can hope to have some valuable runs on the board, as runs can be scored in many mini-constructive ways (just getting the better of a bowler by a bit, might fetch you a single or two). As we shall see next up, about sparse and cumulative scoring formats.

Primary fact for Bowlers:

> A good bowler, when playing weak batting sides, can say that he will produce many compelling deliveries, but cannot say that he will at least take so many wickets in a given innings– since no bowler can say which ball will beat a batsman and get him out as well.

Now you can see why Wasim Akram, Waqar Younis, Alan Donald, Shane Warne, or Muralitharan were reckoned as the most demanding to face (in this era). Their special stuff is usually good enough to get the better of the defence of most batsmen, and with sufficient frequency, that even though the conversion ratio of beating a batsman and getting him out is not an exact science- they would perhaps be better so many times, that the probability for such a conversion would be high indeed. Need to fulfill the **X**-demand for bowling? All of these can be great bets.

However, just as in batting there was both a disadvantage (due to the demand) and an advantage (due to some leeway as dot balls), there is such a duality in bowling as well. Again, it has to to do with the dot buffer– which gives both batsman and bowlers some margin and not be forced to fulfill the demands of their disciplines.

So for bowlers, there is an **X**-demand, which implies that the best attempts of a bowler must better the batsman by a substantial degree (and then hope that it is good enough to get a wicket). However, since dot balls are possible and a mistake is not catastrophic for a bowler, there is no need to try to better the batsman on every other instance (delivery). He does not have to fear failure in either trying to bowl a series of dot balls and then try something fancy ever so often.

Secondary fact about bowling.

> Surely we do not know how often a bowler will better a batsman and yet not get a wicket, but the format does not demand that every ball be compelling— the bowler therefore need not try to push too hard on each attempt, but can try to hang-in and mix in probing deliveries. Therefore, we cannot even say that out-of-form, tired or part-time bowlers, may not contribute meaningfully!

Modern day bowlers like Courtney Walsh, Glenn McGrath, Shaun Pollock, and Anil Kumble seem to be tireless marvels? Every bowler gets tired, and these are no robots. They understood that there is no need to give too many knock out punches (as the **X**-demand would usually push most bowlers to do so), just the right mix of dots and probing deliveries will give you the results.

The **X**-demand, and the leeway of dots and even some errors leads to many bowling ideas. Bowlers can be flexible or strict, can try variations or surprise balls/gambles. Since a few errors are permitted (not too many), the scope of experimentation is usually wider in bowling, than in batting (unless the situation allows).

Bowling is commutative on good and bad attempts– to some extent bowlers can ignore failure, if chance of success is fair. You can see that this is the commutative aspect of bowling. The good and bad can even out, unlike batting, which we saw is non-commutative. Just that in bowling, the 'good' may not result in a wicket. So it is commutative but tricky.

As Wasim Akram has mentioned, Imran Khan asked him to ignore his problems with no-balls during the World Cup 1991/92. Wasim was a top notch bowler, and there was no point spoiling the rhythm for a few no-balls or extras. Sure, bowlers need to keep sight of extras, but fix their problems in the nets, rather than upset their rhythm in a match. Few 'extras' are not as significant as say, losing a wicket or the chance of getting one (What if you get a wicket off a no-ball! tricky one).

To sum up, the **Z** and **X** demands to impose certain requirements on batting and bowling– and lead to primary facts. However, the buffer of dots balls, allows a margin to both batsmen and bowlers— the secondary fact— so that they can meet demand without being forced into it directly.

4.4 ZX of Cricket as compared to other sports

If batting has a **Z**-demand and bowling has an **X**-demand, how **Z** or **X** are they? How do they compare with other sports?

This is what my first book was supposed to be about, but if you go deep into this stuff, you will be amazed at how you will begin to correlate across sports. We perhaps do not have much space to get into this, but if you assess the penalty for bad/worst outcomes and reward for good/best outcomes for every sport, you will get an outline. For instance, **snooker, soccer, 9-ball pool, chess** are tilted towards **Z**-demand since failures are catastrophic. Whereas many Olympic throw/

jump/lift events are on the **X** side– since your best attempts have to be better; whereas gymnastics, diving, shooting, are **Z** tilted– as one or few indifferent outcomes will pull your total well below the pack. Then there are 'point' based games such as **tennis, table tennis, volleyball** are balanced in Z-X, where your slightly better outcome and the best shots will fetch you one point—no more—and the poor or wild misses can lose you no more than a point. However, how each point is earned has many other nuances, which make the **Z-X** balance tilt (based mainly on serve). **Basketball**, is also centered as the scoring is dense, but with a tilt on the X-side since not attempting to score does not lose points and your scoring attempts have to better the defenders and also land inside the basket (and within the shot clock). Finally, take **golf**– it is very 'fair in commutativity' for both **Z** and **X**, as good and bad outcomes have proportionately as good or as bad an impact. Your worst outcome will be penalized by as bad as it is (further away from the hole). Likewise, a better shot will get as closer to the hole, by as much better it is (unlike point based games, where the scope of penalty/reward on each instance, is maximum within a point). However, with bunkers and hazards, the **Z**-aspect will be a bit more prominent in golf.

The most important thing to remember is that the **Z-X** balance, is the basis or a pre-requisite for each format. Even in **Z**-demand formats the **X** aspect will come in, and vice-versa. For instance, batting is **Z**-demand so you have to do everything in a zero-error framework, but you have to better the bowler in various degrees singles, twos, orthodox fours etc. Likewise, for bowling, the **X**-demand implies that bowlers have to better the batsmen, but errors cannot be out of control, as you cannot give many fours or even regulation singles/twos, or at times waste dot balls in favorable times.

In every sport, you need an eye on errors as well as pushing the limits, but it just happens that every sport has its own priority due to format.

5. Sparse or Dense Scoring?

5.1 Cumulative Scoring in various sports

Cricket uses the simple process of addition to score. Runs and wickets are 'added' to see how much of the game remains or if the target is achieved. Sounds silly to look at it this way, but that is not always the case, that we 'total' the scored moments.

In many **Olympic events**, only the best attempt counts (jump/throw events, whereas in **gymnastics/diving** attempts are averaged (cumulative). In **9-ball pool**, there is no concept of a score within a rack— whoever sinks the 9-ball wins, even if the other eight balls were sunk by the opponent (but you have to follow an order of potting from smallest ball to higher, to get into position to sink the 9-ball). Likewise, **chess** is a good combination of cumulative and non-cumulative format, since material gain is about accumulating piece value (although no points are scored as such) and getting to strong positions from which you can gain advantage eventually leading to a checkmate, is a positional aspect.

It may surprise you that the scoring formats in various sports differ so much, that the game strategy and tactics are naturally chosen or altered to fit the format. A good example would be to compare **soccer and**

basketball. In soccer, there might be a goal or two scored, whereas in basketball perhaps 70-90 points may be normal, in similar time frames. This means that in basketball, playing aggressive even in defence is normal, and in soccer you need to be circumspect in pushing too many players forward. **Chess and 9-ball pool** being very positional, and all the material is just to get to the objective (the king or the 9-ball)– chasing material at the cost of the position is therefore not prudent. **Tennis and table tennis, and point games** score every point, although tennis is not about simple addition (you may win 6 service games easily, but the opponent may win his 6 service games narrowly, but the set goes into tie-breaker even though you won more points as such. The cumulative process is sort of multi-tiered).

5.2 Bowling is sparse, Batting is dense

Now cricket is different again for batting and bowling. Scoring for batsmen is usually progressive and there are many options– singles, twos, fours, sixes etc. Whereas scoring for bowlers is sparse– a wicket every 50-70 balls is usually very good. So there is a **fair imbalance about the rate at which batsmen get some reward as compared to bowlers,** although the reward of getting a wicket is worth a lot more, perhaps about 20-30 runs (roughly, based on bowling averages).

Nonetheless, this run and wicket disparity in frequency has been addressed very well in modern times, as we will see in later sections. This cumulativeness is a simple fact, but crucial nonetheless, and we will revert to it in analyzing run, wicket equations and many other situations.

5.3 Scoring pattern reflects shot quality?

One of the burning questions of modern times is the manner in which the game has 'moved on' or 'evolved', wherein runs can be scored in a manner which make a mockery of the past. Firstly, it is not apt to talk of 'evolution', as is done in natural sciences, since games are invented by humans and can be controlled. There is scope for new formats and inventions, but we need not digress from tradition, just because of technology (lighter bats, protective gear, covered pitches, etc.). Chess is a great example of how the moves have remained the same through the ages, and yet there are tons of newer variants, and also inclusion of computer aided analysis, and matches against computers etc.

However, in cricket, like tennis or table tennis, the bat has essentially changed (got better), with pitches getting flatter and boundaries shrinking in. Whether this is good for the game or not, is beyond the scope of our discussion, but one thing is sure the **scoring pattern is falling out of tune with the quality of shot making**.

When cricket scoring was being formulated, numbers were perhaps attached to the 'deemed' quality of effort for various degrees of shot making— a single if you just pushed the ball in the gap, a two if it passed a gap, a four if it was timed well enough to beat the inside gap and boundary fielder, and with some power *and* timing you could earn a six.

The degree of difficulty of shot making has shifted, not yet completely, but has shuffled for sure, as hitting a six is not as different from a four as it used to be, and perhaps getting a four often is easier than a two or a three on smaller grounds. If the bats and conditions are not kept in check, we are dangerously approaching a situation where the pattern is nearly reversed! Then hitting a six would be perhaps easier than a four, since finding the gaps would be unnecessary, scooping a one-bounce four safer than orthodox drives, and so on..., till getting singles would be seen like a leg-bye, incidental and might as well run for it.

So the next time we witness games such as the remarkable game of **South Africa vs Australia (5th ODI, Johannesburg 2006)**, where

South Africa chased 434, we have to go back and see if the pattern has shifted— are the numbers (runs) associated with shots, in-tune with the degree of difficulty. This game was still a great game, as it was played in an era where 300 is considered a match winning score. But it may not be so in the near future.

But as Barry Richards pointed out that if such games are the norm, nobody would ever like to be a bowler!

Eventually, there would then be a need for a new pattern, to re-map 'numbers' to shot type as if we are just inventing the sport in the technological era (as this is a man-made game and it can be done if needed, especially to prevent making a mockery of past eras, where the skills were just as good, if not more diverse). Hitting sixes should then perhaps fetch you a 'three', or even be given out (tennis players still need to control the ball within the court, even with modern gear) and one bounce fours as twos, and perhaps threes should be declared a six? It may sound like a joke, but we have to remember that **numbers attached to a shot must be in tune with degree of difficulty and they were man made to begin with**. Hitting the ball out of the boundary gets you 6, because the game was invented that way, and tomorrow, if it is not six times as tough as a single, humans should have every right to change it. (like basketball is kind of fair to all skills with 2 and 3 point shots, and free throws earning a point each; likewise billiards also has a two/three point approach to all shots, and perhaps there is a case to score certain interesting shots, such as multi-cushion cannons differently. But by and large billiards allows everyone to play various shots, especially before getting to the top of the table).

Sir Don Bradman hit about 46 sixes in his entire cricketing career, including first class matches (The Art of Bradman, *Sundries, p234*). He obviously choose not to score that way, as playing along the ground would ensure longer innings. You do not want to be watching a brand of cricket, where it would be hard to correlate how Bradman's scoring pattern would fit into the format— and yet call it cricket.

6. Classifying bowling by intent

There are different types of bowlers and different bowling conditions–so classification of proper line, length, speed and degree of spin will vary. You can describe bowling as attacking, defensive, negative, etc., or by the nature of line and length. However, when we want to study the pattern of mind-games and competitive tussles between bat and ball, I have found that **classifying each ball based on the intent of the bowler-** as to what level of shot execution (by the batsman) he intends to overcome, works superbly from the standpoint of scope and possible line of play that can follow, since intent and shot type cover mind as well as matter (physical possibilities). Here is how I classify such bowling intent.

6.1 Three broad ways of bowler overcoming shot execution

Here is a helpful way to classify based on level of shot execution a bowler wishes to control:

Type 1: Bowling, wherein the bowler tries to take a wicket by actually overcoming the batsman's defence.

This type may be knock-out bowling by producing deliveries which are just too good for the batsman to offer a defensive reply (Shane Warne,

Wasim Akram, Muralitharan?). You may even beat a batsman's defence by bowling many deliveries and 'setting him up mentally or technically' to bowl a particular ball which beats his defence, due to dubious execution (Bedi, McGrath?). Likewise, you can try to bowl tight spells, where each ball is tough to defend as such and one of the balls may get you (Kumble?). Obviously the patterns will be endless and each great bowler would have mastery over some trademarked combination. But great bowlers will produce enough balls which beat the defensive abilities of good batsmen.

Whatever the method, the bowling in this type is about ball(s) which actually gets the better of a batsman's defence- how one goes about it will vary from bowler to bowler.

Advantages of type 1: if you have the skills and variations to beat the batsman in defence, then you better get him out.

Downside of type 1: this often gives away runs, as you bowl near the batsman or the stumps— within reach of the batsman. So if the ball does not achieve 'enough', you may go for runs, Also, errors can happen when you try to do the special stuff, which results in runs as well, eg. a yorker going down the legside, or flipper landing short.

Type 2: Bowling which betters the batsman in terms of overcoming shot production, not necessarily beating the defence.

This can refer to bowling where you bowl wide/high enough, to prevent a batsman from playing proper shots. Or bowling line-lengths which squeeze the batsman for space (no room to free swing the bat) and/or for time as well (length is such that footwork cannot get you to the pitch nor can you buy time off the back-foot). Another way, is to just be so quick that, it is demanding for the batsman to react and play a shot. Not to forget the modern development of slower balls, in many different ways (watch out for the W'indies). Again there will be many ways to prevent the batsman from effective shot production, ranging from quality bowlers to even Jayasuria, Chris Gayle or Tendulkar.

Obviously, lot of test bowling and classical ODI bowling is about this kind. Ambrose and Shaun Pollock can probably achieve this kind of activity, while having breakfast.

Advantages of type 2: your ticket to a dot ball, by cramming the batsman or bowling just out of reach. You can focus on basics, with a bit of speed change and wobble, rather than try something fancy. You can always surprise the batsman and keep the chance of a wicket alive.

Disadvantages of type 2: reduce the chance of getting a batsman out, since the balls are not perhaps into the stumps (eg. shoulder height), or does not have 'enough' to beat his defence. Further, error in the basics, will allow the batsman to free his arms. You may give runs anyway.

Type 3: Bowling which actually allows shot production!

Sounds silly? One can understand the other two types, where the bowler tries to get the better of the batsman in some way at least- if not beating the defence (type 1), then by preventing shot production (type 2). Why would a bowler allow shot production, unless we are referring to some sort of occasional deliveries (as a gamble) encouraging a lofted shot, inviting a drive with slips waiting for an edge or a square cut off a straighter 'arm' ball...). Such gambles or invitations may be used for tactical purposes and have always been used by spinners and pace bowlers.

However, today this type of bowling has been developed as a type of stock bowling, not just for surprises or gambles. We will soon see when and why it works. Aussies are masters at it, followed by South Africa. Amongst batsmen, those who assess it the best, includes Sachin Tendulkar, Brian Lara and Inzamam-ul-haq (I am not sure about elsewhere, though).

Advantages of type 3: You can hope to be consistent, since the balls bowled are expected to be just 'good enough', not special. Further, you can prepare to cover the batsman's 'natural' replies– to bowl dot balls or give singles and keep it quiet. Another aspect is that on certain type 3 balls, there can be some margin of error, since you were never trying to be too accurate in the first place– as in full-wide or short wide balls.

Disadvantages of type 3: only certain types of balls will be available to a bowler, from which a batsman's reply can be within an anticipated framework. You also relinquish or reduce your chances to take wickets, unless the batsman tries to fabricate a shot. Being predictable, will allow batsmen some time to prepare and wait for the right time as well.

Summary of the intent types

To summarize, these 'types' are broad categories to explain or analyze bowling intentions in regard to what level of shot execution (by the batsman) the bowler intends to overcome. Moreover, **in a spell or even one over, the bowler obviously can mix any of the types,** depending on bowling style, pitch conditions or to target specific batsman.

Further, and most importantly, as with most classifications in any art, these categories are not quite discreet in a mechanical sense- **a particular ball may fall into both categories or almost in one category, with a little bit of the other,** since there are so many in-between possibilities between different types of balls. There are no discreet areas on the pitch or the trajectory, which make a ball fall into this type or another. In fact, this is the fine art of bowling, where the intention is subtly disguised, and the ball just falls out of the criteria of an intended type (a short ball inviting a square cut (seems like type 3) but it gets closer to the body and crams the batsman for space (ends up as McGrathian type 2). The tough thing for a batsman is that a ball does not carry a tag indicating bowler intent—which type it is or if it is a blend of the types.

6.2 Some combinations and mixing types

The examples are just to illustrate how recognizing intent type helps in explaining or dealing with specific bowling approaches. These instances are based on my limited observations of what I have seen or enjoyed. They may be off the mark, as judging intent, is best left to those in the middle. But I hope the examples do help in clarifying the matter.

Type 3 surprises: Bishen Bedi was an absolute master at slipping in innocuous balls with lethal consequences. He would allow a batsman to cut or drive (type 3), but with variation in flight to induce a mistake. His stock bowling was type 1-2 stuff, which would beat you test you in defence and not give you much to score either.

Type 3 stock: A different exponent was E.A.S Prasanna- he could bowl—many balls at a stretch—wherein the batsman actually plays good shots, but they just seem to go to one of the fielders. This can frustrate a batsman more than perhaps getting beaten, since you are achieving dots by playing good shots. This is not something invented by spinners in India, though during Bedi and Prasanna era, the spinners over bowled themselves by a few dozen overs and had to explore the spectrum of possibilities just that much more (in addition to the type 1, 2 which all good test bowlers will need).

Type 1-3, one shot? It is well known that Sir Alec Bedser did have some success against Sir Donald Bradman, by bowling in-swinging balls, for which the natural replies were covered by fielders behind square and just in front on the leg side. We need clarification if the balls were just type 3 (allow the shot on the leg side), or compelling enough to defend as well, targeting the stumps (type 1). It could be that the a ball could be of mixed type 1 & 3. Allow shot production but also can get out if batsman misses.

Type 1 Variations: Warne on Tendulkar, trying a dozen plans– when Shane Warne first came to India (Test Series 1998), he had a tough time stopping Tendulkar. He has explained on TV, that he used to have many plans, and after each failed, he went on to the next, and then would repeat plans with little success. This is an example of a great bowler, trying to find ways of getting a batsman out by perhaps having many 'type 1' plans. As mentioned, in a type 1 scenario, the batsman also has scope to score, as balls which are to be well defended, can provide orthodox scoring options for the batsman. Perhaps, he could have done some type 3 stuff- allow him to play, but say only certain shots– pitching full outside off stump and turning further, again and again? He could perhaps do many such things 'just to keep things inactive'. But knowing Warne, this would be too dilute, an approach. He has the best type 1 repertoire, after all, and he would accept it if a batsman got the better of him on his best variety. Let's hope such 'your skills vs my skills', rivalry stays on in cricket. It is looking less likely, I'm afraid.

Type 3, example from tennis: Leander Paes & Mahesh Bhupati (Athens Olympics 2004). This is India's famous doubles pair, which has won many grand slams and although their individual rankings may not be high, as a doubles pair they are in the top echelon of doubles seedings. Many in India, and around the world believe that they are this good simply because most top players do not focus on the doubles. Somewhat true, but yet this pair would be compelling on account of many different skills required in doubles (Indians are better off in reflex-play and touch shots, but perhaps not as athletic to match-up in singles). They were pitched against Roger Federer (already world rank 1) and Yves Allegro in the second round. Federer perhaps participated in the doubles event to win an Olympic medal for Switzerland. Sounds like the Indian pair would struggle? It turned out quite the contrary. Federer could not reply to Bhupati's serve effectively, and Bhupati was not serving aces at sharp angles, just solid serves near the body! Actually, Federer replied quite well, but those replies were good for a singles format, where returning the ball in the other half of the court (not the half from which the serve was sent in) would be considered compelling, as the server would have to cover ground to stay in the point. In this case, Leander Paes, waiting at the net, used to accept it gleefully and win the point. This is similar to the type 3 bowling, wherein you allow shot production, but so long as the result of a 'proper' reply can be taken care of (in the case of cricket, it is hoped that the good shot will go to the fielder; in tennis doubles- the good service return ends up to your partner).

After the bodyline series (1930s), perhaps nothing has been as drastic in cricket, on account of fielding restrictions on the on-side, and maximum of two behind sqaure-leg. However, ideas will always be explored whereby the bowlers repeat only one type of ball, with field placing to force unorthodox shots (perhaps without the ungainliness for which the bodyline series is remembered). The degree of repetition by bowlers will depend on the target batsmen and situations.

You can bowl type 3, to the best player in a team but it is difficult to apply it to all the others. You can target a player, and actually allow him to play specific shots. As a bowler, you will restrict the batsman to singles and dots, but reduce your chances of getting him out. You cannot do the same type 3 stuff to every other player in the team, as you cannot give singles to everyone, and will need better chance of wicket taking, as most batsmen do get out early on or even mid-way.

7. Sequenced or Simultaneous Participation?

7.1 Cricket in context of other sports

Sequential or Simultaneous Participation? This is another aspect of the format in which cricket is played. Do all players (actively) participate-simultaneously or sequentially? This aspect has a huge impact on the strategy and tactics of a match. **Batting is very sequential and irreversible** (since batsmen usually get back to the dressing room when out, and in rare instances if injured). So the batting order is always a matter of debate, just as pawn structures in chess (since a pawn cannot be moved backwards again, in case required). At a time, only two batsman are active, and the others follow sequentially, upon a negative event (a wicket). Compare this with most other sports- **soccer, basketball, volleyball** etc., players will be playing on the pitch simultaneously- or may alternate in brief periods, as in cue sports (In fact, in **9-ball pool** and **English Billiards**, players can garner racks or breaks, and make the opponent sit for a long time, never allowing the rhythm to develop). **Chess** is a great hybrid– pieces have to be moved one at a time, but at given moment, many pieces can be a likely option for that move. Further, every piece already influences certain squares, by the fact that it is on the board . Such influence and interaction between each other pieces, is simultaneous. Further, whenever a piece moves, it is not the only piece to be focused on, as it perhaps opens the path (a file, a diagonal, or a rank) for another piece, which then has a different influence without moving.

In cricket, **bowlers also are active two at a time, but the process is not exactly a sequence, but rather a flexible combination or a cycle**. Although bowling is not simultaneous (within a given period only two bowlers bowl), but still reversible (since bowlers can come back to bowl again) and can be activated in various combinations. Within a session or phase, bowling can be seen as quasi-simultaneous as compared to batting, where even if many wickets fell, it was always a strict sequence (albeit the order is flexible).

Also, it must be noted, that fielding is almost simultaneous (since field placing happens collectively and all at once, although usually only one fielder may be involved in receiving the ball or chasing it). This is a key factor, that the collectivity of field placing can be used a lot more effectively than just considering them as 9 discreet fielders. Like soccer or chess, fielding can achieve 'a whole is greater than the parts' like effect more directly than you can say so for batting or bowling.

7.2 Implications of bowling & batting order flexibility

So what are the implications of this sequential and simultaneous aspect? To begin with, you can think of a bowling attack as an arsenal, from which you can pull up the right weapon as needed, to a great extent, whereas in batting, the sequenced nature, makes thinking about your batting resources a lot differently. Thinking about the strength of batting resources, and putting it into action is tricky indeed— even assuming it will work.

Take for instance why partnerships are considered important in any form of cricket. Well, since batting is sequential, we do not know how the batsmen yet to bat, will perform. And since batting failures can happen due to the first error– which are often beyond prediction– it is just right to make sure that partnerships consolidate whatever was needed in that context and also tire the bowlers. Predictions are always difficult, but when it comes to batting, it is not even easy to talk in the continuous present tense, as the sequenced nature makes it it difficult to connect what might happen based on what is happening, as most batsmen are not yet activated (this may not be the case with say bowling, where in a shorter period you may see all the bowlers or in simultaneous games such as soccer or basketball, where you can at least say the team is playing well).

This sequential aspect is taken for granted (by viewers) that we often fail to forget that when the conditions are favorable for bowling it is imperative on the part of the batsmen at the crease to shut the prospects for bowlers. Bowlers can run through with a batch of wickets only when they can get one wicket, in the first place. So batting order is not about the weakest link in the chain, as the tail and other batsmen can be shielded by the seasoned ones ahead.

Further, when we talk of batting as sequential, the basic exception is about opening batsmen, since they always go out as a pair- together. So any opening batting analysis should be done as in simultaneous disciplines. And when there is simultaneous participation, the·weakest link matters. Therefore openers have to both be seasoned specialists, if they are to shut the bowlers in anyway from attacking the sequence to follow. As far as India is concerned, we have struggled even during the Sunny days. One Gavaskar cannot do it, even though he was perhaps as good as they get. India did have a few other sincere openers then, but somehow as an 'opening pair', the Indian story, has been largely unfulfilled and the results show overseas, till today.

In batting, running between the wicket, is again an aspect which falls under simultaneous analysis, since it happens by both batsmen running together (and in cases of runners, it gets simultaneous and confusing). The important thing is that the weaker link must be taken into account, as this is not like each one batting at his own pace.

Another aspect of imbalance of batting and bowling sequence/ simultaneous issues, is that there are lots of tactical possibilities which often do not get exploited as much.

Imran Khan had a great knack of sending in lower batters to alter the pressure when bowlers are on top, in low scoring games. Batsmen have to play themselves in from scratch due to this 'one at a time' sequential nature. It is easier for lower order batsmen to play a valuable cameo- as they do not play constructively anyway, and can alter the run-wicket balance. Recently, South Africa did well to send in Shaun Pollock in the last innings (3rd Test South Africa vs India, Cape Town, 2006). He played a bit more freely and could come down the track to throw the Indian bowlers from getting into good rhythm. Incidentally, when Kallis and Prince came in shortly thereafter, they struggled to get the scoreboard ticking, as the Indians did put pressure by forcing a defensive line, with some options for wickets. If such a sequenced imposition was not the way cricket is played, they could have got someone else to pinch a few temporarily- as you might in chess, by looking for gambits or weird movement of a knight jumping about in a zig-zag manner. South Africa eventually won, but low scoring tests and ODIs in general, can benefit largely if you recognize bottlenecks due to sequenced format.

On a side note, this also means partnerships can shut any other good or possible experimentation that other batsmen stuck in queue, have to offer- like undeveloped pieces in chess. This also means that having 'wickets in hand' in an ODI, must be handled with care, if say 8 wickets are left with 10 overs to go. Unfortunately, the other remaining batsmen will not all be able to come in and bat simultaneously! Lack of 'breathing' overs for each new batsman, often leads to more dot balls, as batsmen cannot 'get going' immediately. This nullifies the 'wickets in hand' aspect.

From the bowling angle, captains have usually exploited the fact that bowlers can be mixed around (as in the last few overs at end of a day). But even then there is perhaps more scope to shuffle bowlers, in my view, especially in certain batting friendly conditions and in ODIs.

Sri Lanka have been superb in this regard under Arjuna Ranatunga and later, by quickly bowling the slow bowlers, in bits and pieces, with batsmen finding it hard to adjust. It must however be understood that this was done with Sri Lankan batsmen who bowled the fifth bowler quota, who perhaps are not expected to take wickets anyway.

Recently, in the Ashes 2006 in Australia, Ian Chappell made a point as a commentator, to start the day with McGrath and Warne (the innings was already underway the previous day), to test the footwork using both pace and spin, even if it be for an over or two of spin. If it did not work, then pace at both ends could be used to exploit any morning dew. Although Australia did well, this is a case, where bowling can be seen in a 'more simultaneous' context of options available, even when only two bowlers, usually string in overs to make an effective spell.

Time of Soccer vs Cricket: here is an interesting way to look at the duration of a soccer match as compared to a test match. Since soccer is completely simultaneous, and all players are active together. Further, at a given time, almost half the team will not only be active but involved in moving about briskly. So in soccer for almost about 2 hours, considering stoppage and/or extra time, all 22 players are active, and perhaps about of 12-14 are directly involved around the area of focus (6-7 from each side). Soccer is easily about 28-30 'man-hours' of high activity, in a 2 hour format.

Now compare test cricket, in context of batting and bowling. At a given moment only 1 bowler and 1 batsman (with perhaps a fielder) are directly involved. So in a five day test match, with 6 hours per day, you have 5x6x3= 90 man hours cricket.

A five day cricket match is not that much longer than a soccer match, if we consider batting and bowling as the key focus then from execution as well as spectator interest, a test match is 60 batting-bowling hours, whereas soccer is about 30 man hours (we cannot ignore fielding and the fact it is tiring, but the idea is to compare the primary focus). A test match therefore from player time and spectator interest, is only about twice or thrice the duration of soccer! And if you take just about an innings each, then test cricket and soccer are almost equal in man hours.

This means that any shorter variants of test cricket– say a one inning first-class match or an ODI are involving players actively for the duration which is similar to that of soccer. Although, such a time comparison is perhaps not exactly measurable, as the games do demand different degrees of athleticism and reflexes, we can get some idea of any shorter version from say 50 overs ODI, is then cutting the breathing time for player execution too fine.

In my view, twenty20 may perhaps need to look at how many players might bowl or bat. It is never easy to say that a 20 over game must have only two bowlers of 10 overs each to give bowlers a fair chance (as the balance is then tilted to 9 batsmen a team). But they can say that two twenty20 matches can retain the same sides, and over the two games, 8-10 overs per bowler should be fine. Likewise, batting teams will get 10 wickets over both games. These are to be played as two different games, with a result each (which is what the spectators want), but it would be an historic move to connect player involvement across two games. The unfinished bowling quotas would transfer over to the next game, and so would wickets remaining– just that the next match starts at 0 runs each. This would make things more interesting as in every game the team will have to optimize resources for the next match and still try to win the present one. This obviously is a suggestion, arrived at by comparing duration of sports and execution scope, and the fact that the sequenced nature of the cricket is squeezing away, the room to breathe in twenty overs.

In test cricket bowlers may in favorable conditions take a wicket every 40-60 balls. In twenty20, with flat pitches, it is unfair to even expect a bowler take a wicket (by beating the defence) in 24 balls. Bowlers will get wickets, but on account of bad shots. Rather use bowling machines in twenty20!?!

8. Symmetric or Asymmetric Skills?

8.1 Cricket is different, again

How symmetric is the format in terms of player skills, during a particular phase in play?

When we talk about symmetric nature of skills— we are comparing the kind of skills one side is involved in as compared to the skills the other(s) is involved in, at a given moment or phase in a match. **Cricket (and say, baseball) is extremely asymmetric.** When one side is bowling the other is batting (both arts are radically different). Batting and bowling are so different, that except for a few great all-rounders, most great batsmen can barely bowl and many great bowlers could hardly ever bat (although they were expected to!).

Compare this to most other sports, like **cue sports, soccer, basketball, volleyball** etc. Both teams are employing similar skills, at a given phase, and their objectives are similar- to score goals or points in a given phase of play. It must be noted that in subtle ways, in every sport, at a given moment there will be some asymmetry. In **soccer and basketball,** one side might be trying to covert their ball possession into a goal, whereas another is trying to defend (slightly different skill). In **tennis and other court games**, someone has initiative of a serve, and may at least for the first few shots in a rally, employ different skills than the receiver of the serve. In **chess,** the board and pieces are symmetric. However, in chess, the tempo advantage is with White and creating imbalance by developing pieces out of symmetry is the prime objective. But this imbalance is part of the skill and has to be achieved. So chess skills can broadly be applied to both sides, although the approach is quite different for Black as compared to White. But the whole point is that, in most sports, both sides usually work around similar skills (in a broad sense) in a phase of play, but in cricket this is radically different–since a team could be batting or bowling for sessions or even a day, which means sides are using dissimilar skills, for sessions and often perhaps a day or two.

8.2 Implications of difference in bowling & batting skills

So why are we getting so caught up in this symmetric or asymmetric aspect of skills?

Well it has implications- such as the toss (did anyone complain of the toss on a soccer field? In cricket, batting and bowling are rarely ever equally favorable on a pitch). Or take the idea about follow-ons (the Laxman effect on Aussie loss in Kolkata 2001? Teams have been avoiding follow-ons, on account of fatigue due to asymmetric skills).

Moreover, it also means that it is difficult in cricket to assess a game, at a stage where only one side has batted or in the third innings- since the others were more involved in bowling (asymmetric!). We had seen earlier that it was difficult to talk in the 'continuous present tense' for batting, on account of sequenced nature making it hard to tell how the others will play. In this case, it is difficult to make a comment on match state, as to who is winning because of the asymmetric aspect being prolonged over various sessions. This why explaining 'who is winning' to a stranger to cricket, is a bit more difficult than many other sports, since the skills are asymmetric—one team is trying to score runs, whereas the other is trying to take wickets— and we only know the value of a wicket in terms of runs after the match or couple of innings.

During the 70s and early 80s, there were many formats in India, where the first innings score determines the outcome, if the match was drawn, This often meant that teams would try to bat out the other, and rarely ever declare. However, there were instances, when the team batting second would declare before the opposing team total was reached, if an outright win was possible or desired. Ashok Mankad, captain of Mumbai, often made such premature declarations, to use his spin bowlers (Shivalkar, rated highly by Gavaskar, was amongst one of them) to bowl over the opposition quickly and then chase a new (4th inning) target. Such interesting declarations, surely happen where 3 or 4 day matches are played. The abstract explanation is that declaration in such cases is a tool, to alter the skills you want to be involved in, at a given time, which are favorable to your strength or the pitch conditions. Declaration is not therefore not just about runs piled, but a tool to spend more time doing the skill you prefer or is favored– tilting the impact of asymmetry on your side.

On the note of asymmetric nature of the skills, there is an important implication in ODIs, where conditions are radically different in morning & afternoon or between day & night as the case may be. Different conditions is nothing new in cricket, as in test cricket this has always been the case, that sudden showers or pitch deterioration was never equal to both sides. But in test cricket, a batting side has the scope to defend in such adverse conditions and a draw is an option as well. You have enough time in test cricket to surpass your opponent and avert the conditions. However, in ODIs where strike rates are key, any variation in conditions is quite unfair, considering that most games are fought on margins of a few overs.

There is a way to kind of address this issue by splitting the 'toss' alternately, during a series. But here is a possible ramification to the game itself. After 25 overs, we can perhaps 'pause' an innings, let the second team bat another 25 overs; then continue the first 'paused' innings for the remaining 25 overs, starting at same runs, wickets, overs per bowler etc. Then finally chase the target by the chasing team. This will be fair in context of condition variations, and also be interesting in tactics, avoid one sided games to an extent, and also avoid complexities such as the Duckworth-Lewis (D/L) method for assessing of incomplete games, as both sides have batted 25 overs ('the pause' can be at 20th over?). Also, some notion of follow-on can be brought in. It is still an ODI with one 50 over innings per side, but each inning played over two phases. Just a possibility, and perhaps fairer than many day-night games and much better than D/L outcomes.

Symmetry of chess pieces: since this book has a lot to do with recognizing and exploiting imbalance of resources in various contexts, from the point of symmetry, here is what chess has to offer. As noted, chess players have a common set of skills, in achieving a checkmate but with different plans for Black or White. As far as symmetry on board is concerned chess pieces are always arranged in the exact same fashion, and equal & opposite for both sides. However, this results to known and memorized openings to such an extent that only certain lines are favored and the process has lost a lot of spontaneity, due to sameness of starting line ups.

Chess legend Bobby Fischer, has formalized a new variant to overcome the problem– by shuffling the pieces randomly. But what about the symmetry?

Symmetry in Fischer Random Chess (Chess 960): in this variant of chess, the back rank has pieces shuffled in random order at start of play to eliminate the advantage of those who memorize openings in standard chess (where the pieces always start the same way each time). In this format, except for pawns, every other piece can start at a square which was conventionally for another piece, with certain restrictions (one bishop must be on a light square and the other on a dark square, rooks must be on either side of the king). So for instance, the queen can be where a knight or bishop might normally be, and the knight may be at the corner, where the rook usually stands. So the starting lineup for rank 1 (a1-h1) will be shuffled by randomization (and since 960 unique combinations are possible, it is now called Chess 960). However the most important aspect, Black pieces are not randomized, but are mirrored exact and opposite to White, (after the White line up was shuffled and ready). This maintains the fairness of equal and opposite piece value & position in chess. Symmetry is maintained, albeit randomly.

Maintaining symmetry at start up is a key concept, since one of the most essential test of skills in chess, is how players introduce imbalance by arrangement of pieces or exchanging material in different combinations. Chess is a subtle art of recognizing, creating and exploiting imbalance. The mirror-symmetry of starting line-ups retains this art in both formats of chess– the conventional as well as Fischer Random.

Chess possesses all possible competitive motifs, and hence can be 'applied' to most sporting situations or problems where the parameters are defined. The beauty is in trying to identify how to 'map' a sporting situation to a given position or aspect of chess.

Since cricket is a game where resources come and go, as in chess, there are bound to be even more correlations. Eventually any assessment system for cricket, must account for the 'positional aspects' as well, as they do in chess.

PART II: CHESS OF CRICKET

9. Applying Chess to Cricket

9.1 Chess as a way to explain & solve problems elsewhere

Chess is a game which has all possible competitive motifs. Since various chess pieces have a different value, on account of mobility and style of movement, it is possible to use (and has been) **chess as a way to solve many real world problems, where the parameters and exploring of options are actually expressed as a particular position in a game of chess** (like popular chess puzzles). Then one can solve the chess puzzle—which computers can do very well, complicated or otherwise—and translate back to the domain of the real world problem. The tricky part, however, is to be able to successfully represent a problem as a chess position (may not need to use all pieces; and often different piece combinations can be used which differ from the normal set of pieces in standard chess, such as three rooks or two queens).

So it is no wonder that we should be able to apply chess theories, with appropriate considerations to most other sports. Obviously, the key factor is to determine which aspect of chess corresponds to which feature of the sport, where an analogy is intended. Chess can be applied in various ways, such as, a combination of pieces to analyze teamwork, studying the nature of action & replies on the chess board to analyze psychological interactions and possible approaches, general principles of strategies and tactics (most of us think both are the same things, but not quite) and ideas of development of pieces (in chess, pieces have to be brought out from their bank rank, to get them 'in-play', but in a manner that gives you an advantage and makes competitive sense).

Chess can also be used to study execution of shots since certain parameters, such as footwork, swing, grip, balance, power, rhythm etc., work in different combinations for different players. We can draw great inspiration from chess and find the right situation or theory from chess to describe how those parameters should 'come together', just as pieces in chess combine to meet a target (which in cricket might be to 'middle the ball' or 'aim for the off stump').

So let's just say that chess can be applied in analysis of teamwork as well as individual skills; you can use chess principles in context of a competition (a match) or in meeting a target in context of execution criteria. **The greatest advantage of using chess as an analytical tool, is that a game of chess puts things in visual and logical perspective.** It just helps you see options, which can be missed out and also help you overcome empty threats, which have no basis.

Since this is not a chess book, we will consider chess ideas in the broadest and most relevant manner to understand the application to cricket (I am just an admirer of chess, not a player, but the internet has made it possible for every enthusiast to follow chess to the level you want to, without being born in Russia).

9.2 When can chess be 'applied' to cricket and when not.

How would chess relate to cricket? Before we start making transformations between chess theories and cricket, we have to understand that broad concepts or match sessions, should be the reference to move between the domains of each sport. If you take chess, move by move, in a literal sense, you will not be able to find parallels in cricket or any other sport directly, as equivalent concepts or player types may not exist in the other game. For instance, chess has a concept of 'checkmate', where you can win by attacking the king and trapping it, even if you have less material on the board. Now such a concept does not exist in cricket, as you win by scoring more runs, rather than a possible knock out (if by hitting some type of shots or say by achieving a hat-trick, a team could win, then that would be similar). Whereas, in a game such as boxing, even if you have fewer points, you can knock out your opponent and win as in chess.

However, within a narrower context, such a 'knockout of a king' does exist in cricket. For instance, if you study 'the chess behind an instance of purposeful bowling and various shots played in reply, then the stumps are the 'king'. No matter what replies you give as a batsman, attacking or defensive, you have to protect the stumps (On India's tour of Australia in 2003-04, Greg Chappell demonstrated why bowlers have to be accurate in Australia— if you pitch it up, most good batsman will drive or work the ball around, whereas if you drop it even a fraction short, the ball usually sails over the stumps, on account of bounce. No threat to the king, then no problem).

So let us explore the similarities and differences between chess and cricket.

1. Team Composition: To begin with, both chess teams (of pieces, not players) are perfectly equal- since the mix of pieces are the same and arranged as a mirror image as well. Both sides have one queen, two rooks, two bishops, two knights, and eight pawns (and the king!). In chess, although there are not 'points scored' for material gain, pieces have been assumed to have certain value (based on experience of

Grandmasters, or GMs). A knight or bishop, although very different in movement, are rated approximately the same and about the value of 3 pawns. A rook, which is perhaps as mobile orthogonally as a bishop is diagonally is worth 5 pawns (a bishop's drawback is that it covers either only light squares or only dark squares, whereas a rook can cover both). A queen is worth 9 pawns, and is the most valued piece on a chessboard.

Now, talking about cricket, if you compare players to the pieces, it is clear that most sides are not equal. For instance, a team such as Australia, today has a stronger team than most other world teams. if we assume that a knight or bishop 'has average value', then a lot of Australians would be like a rook on the chess board, very efficient and above international standards. Amongst batters, Ponting would be like a queen today, as Hayden was a couple of years ago. But remember that a queen in chess is at best worth two rooks. So when other teams with their share of Tendulkar, Lara, Inzamam etc., who are queens of their own teams (in a batting context), compete with Australia, those teams cannot still match the batting line up, since there will be many others in their team who will be much less than a rook or even a bishop in value. And we have not yet begun to compare the bowlers yet!

So the next time you hear on TV, as to why teams struggle to beat Australia, what went wrong? "how was the captaincy?", "is it killer instinct?".... well, do not look that far, they are that much better to begin with, it is natural that they will end up winners more often than not. Ask a chess GM to play a game with normal pieces, but against another astute player who has both bishops and both knights replaced by four rooks instead. The GM may not take this on, even if the opponent further replaced his queen with a rook. Australia are ahead in Test cricket, because of what they do to build the team in the first place. I am sure they have some more 'Husseys' in the waiting.

Compare this to an Indian context, where we do not know who will even open the innings, in test cricket. Before a psychologist, we need orthodox openers. Ask a chess player to open with other pieces prior to the **d or e pawns**? And as mentioned earlier, this is not a modern day problem, even during Gavaskar's time, India never consistently managed to produce a combination which was nearly as potent as Greenidge-Haynes or Hayden-Langer (as a pair, refer sequenced-simultaneous discussion, when the weakest link counts; *Ch 7.2; p72*). We need openers to open the innings. We also need Virender Sehwag, not to build pawn formations, but perhaps to blast around later.

The whole point is that the first notion of imbalance is in the team composition itself (diversity of player types within each team, and then one-to-one comparison to the other team). Strategies will be designed around this, to exploit the imbalance and make sure resources remain matched (or mismatched) as deemed best for a competitive advantage.

The team composition therefore has implications. **Players have a pre-match value,** just as a chess piece has a value before play begins. The basic difference is that a chess piece behaves the same each day, and is 100% predictable, whereas a human player will be moody and may do better or worse. Yet, it is important to assess players and estimate them, otherwise, how would we ever select or leave out players when making the 11 or 16 member team. (see the Gilchrist effect in the opposing team's declaration, *Ch 21.13, p207*, even before he plays an innings).

Then there is a **pre-development effect,** usually a deflective one. If you are the strong batsman or bowler, you will attract the best bowlers or batsman, from the other side towards your moments of activity, thereby deflecting them away from other activity, as is common in chess (see Tendulkar Dot Chess, *Ch 21.13, p208*).

Team compositions differ, and even a few 'stars' who may be the 'queens' of international cricket, cannot alter much as we saw that a team with many rooks instead of other pieces will be more effective. Apart from that there are small but crucial pieces, such as the major front line pawns, who do not move much—but occupy and prevent—and therefore impact the dynamics of play, as to which piece must be active at the right time and situation. Only perhaps the captain of a team knows by instinct what is really missing and where they stand. No matter how good a captain you are, a team can only compete to the best of its capacity, which often may not be good enough.

2. Resource Activation: another aspect of chess and cricket, is that resources (piece, players) are active at different times, and they also go off the board (like batsmen), and may be skewed off or deflected (like bowlers) in different ways. Based on identifying imbalances from the team composition (as in point 1), the next step is to see how the participation and activation occurs. **The fact that participation happens in a 'development manner' and player involvement can be terminated or sidetracked, as in chess, this aspect of cricket is most akin to chess.** And the fact that runs and wickets, are not absolute, but always in context of quality of bowlers, batsmen, and positions of advantage, it is very important to value runs accordingly.

3. Small piece can knock big piece? if so, then relevant 'roles' can be assigned to lesser players as well.

In chess, a pawn or minor piece can strike the queen or stronger piece, and capture it. This is unlike a board game like *Stratego* (a combat game where army, protects a flag, which is like the king in chess), where piece value is hidden from the opponent. In this game, an inferior piece cannot capture a superior piece, even if it strikes first. Most real world sports are in between these two approaches, since humans can at times lose to competitors who are inferior, at least for a few 'points'. Since the **Z**-demand of batting implies that such things will often happen, there will always be crucial roles played by lesser players and even the best may need support to ensure that they are not exposed to such wobbly or unpredictable bowlers or tricky conditions. In chess, pawns and minor pieces are usually developed first. This is because pawns can do the job of preventing strong pieces from getting into key areas, and minor pieces can begin to initiate advantages, or get exchanged with other minor pieces to develop a favorable position. In chess, except for the rapid formats, you will rarely see queen activity very early on. The essential point is that, in cricket as in chess, certain roles have to be played by different levels of players (and vary as per current match context), in order for proper execution of any strategy or plan.

It must be noted that, since chess is an 'exact' game, where piece behavior is defined and always the same (a knight or bishop cannot work differently, unlike say in a human team sports, where runs or goals may be scored by players beyond their role or capacity). This means that if a position is proven to be lost or won, then on another day when the same position occurs again, even the greatest GM cannot alter that, since the move sequence can always be repeated with certainty.

So when we derive analogies from chess to most other sports such as cricket, certain aspects have to be kept in mind.

1. Chess is played under exact conditions, so theories can work repeatedly in chess. This is why certain openings and defences, once refuted or shown to be weak, will be so that way. Whereas in cricket or other team sports, when a logical theory is applied, you need to consider factors such as mood or fitness of players, nature of pitch and ambient conditions etc. There is a lot of theory in every sport but some ideas may be applicable even if they failed earlier, or often may not be usable just because they succeeded elsewhere (see intention-execution gap, *Ch2.3, p38*). When we compare player roles to chess pieces, there is scope in human sport for passion and impromptu skill, to override theory (there is a little Afridi in all of us).

This means that what works in chess, can be applied to other situations in other sports, but with anticipating a success ratio in a statistical sense.

For similar reasons, there is another interesting note here– **many theories of chess which are 'obsolete'– such as certain openings or other thumb-rules, can in fact be apt in other sports.** In chess, a theory which may be compelling or meaningful, in a broad sense, may lose favor, simply because after certain depth of move combinations, it has been refuted or leads into weakness– by *just* a move or by *just* that extra pawn or weak square. 'Just' weak in chess can be totally weak, on account of the exactness —that move sequence is always repeatable—which leads to logical refutation of that theory. But that theory may still have strong implications—as a potent concept—to be used in other sports, since players play with variance each day, unlike chess pieces, as mentioned earlier.

2. Further, in cricket, player involvement is different for batsman and bowler as we have seen earlier– very sequenced for batsmen but more flexible for bowlers- who can be shuffled and brought back again. This makes certain concepts of development and combination-play of chess a lot more apt for bowling, but may not be applicable, or rather, needs different application for batting (where the batsmen are waiting, often too long before someone gets out).

3. In terms of format (initiate, ZX aspects)– the biggest difference between bowlers and batsmen, when there is a game of chess going on between them, there can be clear advantages to a bowler, since he initiates play, every ball. This means a bowler can play according to a plan or suddenly deviate from it, even for just one ball. Batsmen on the other hand have to wait for the ball to be bowled, and play accordingly. So why can they not change the plan and also do something predetermined to counter a bowler who follows some weird pattern of play? Well, batsmen can get out on the first failed attempt to do something different (**Z**-demand), whereas bowlers can get back to the bowling mark and revert to the same stuff, even if hit for a four or six. **Think of bowlers playing a game of chess, wherein they get to take back a move—a few times not more—but batsmen cannot take back moves,** unless they like to play chess in the pavilion. Further, batsmen even after having replied to a weird ploy in an equally weird manner, may have to repeat the same, as there is no rule as such on bowlers to change the fielding or their line of attack (see phase connectivity, *Ch 3.5, p45*).

However, the truth is not all that bad for batsmen, as bowling to very 'set plans' repeatedly, is far from easy and batsmen may not get out due to predictability (although they may not be able to score easily, due to well covered fields for specifically that kind of bowling). **The Bodyline series was an extreme example where the 'chess prevailed' for bowlers,** on account of being able to repeat with risks (vacant off-side) but batsmen finding it difficult to repeat unorthodox shots (since they get out). Had Australia replied with the same tactics in bowling, the outcome surely would have been closer.

4. There is no 'knock-out to win' concept in cricket, as explained earlier, since there is no equivalent of a 'king' being 'checkmate'. However, you can conceptually treat the most important thing (and yet not directly a scoring feature) such as the defending the wicket, or forcing a bowler to alter line/length, as a chess knockout at least for a temporary phase.

5. Differentiating when the human players, compete on skills and compete on chess, especially in team games, this is indeed the trickiest aspects of 'applying' chess to other sports. Very often the competition remains one of skill, as in trying to bowl out a batsman with a very good ball.

Then at times instead of skill,

> **you 'apply chess' in a sport, when you just choose certain options—for which there are only few known 'natural' responses— and therefore, you can prepare for the known, or force 'unnatural' replies.**

For instance, giving a single to a strong batsman by bowling full and wide, with sweepers on the fence, is more of chess than skill, as the natural reply, although proper, is known and can be kept in control.

When to compete on skill, and when to get into chess, is perhaps the most difficult to debate. How much of a chess piece a player should be (as life is not about being so mechanical) and how much should be left to passion and flair to 'go for it'. Both aspects are relevant as human beings play it because they love it (like an art or form of expression), and yet your opponent will not be so nice to be an audience or admirer to let you prevail (because it is a competition).

Note on chess in real world problems: can we apply chess outside the realm of sports, in real life and business situations? Sure, theories of chess can be applied in different aspects of our day to day living, so long as the terms and possible options are within defined scope and limits, and unpredictable events are assumed not to affect the plans.

> However, often chess theories will not work very well in real life, as parameters are vague and their scope may keep changing as the relationships or industry changes– it's like playing chess with changing rules or invalid pieces.

For instance, politicians can make moves not agreed upon, business and branding may demand dollars which are never at a level playing field. Besides, life can have many different situations where emotion and mood take over. Would you try your bargaining skills with a cab driver to save a few dollars, and afford to miss a spectacular sunset on the few precious days of a vacation? (especially when you are with someone special or as the personal preference goes, all alone with a camera,).

Nonetheless, within a range of meaningful assumptions, and some crazy events do not disrupt your plans, chess is 'on' for sure. Anyway, with or without chess, you would have to make certain assumptions. So if indeed your assumptions do hold, during your project– the 'chess' that you apply will indeed help you see options, which you would otherwise miss out, either long term or temporary.

10. Strategy and Tactics

10.1 Strategy and Tactics are not the same!

In real life projects and most sports, usually the terms "strategy" and "tactics" are used interchangeably. However, chess players will never do so, as these two terms differentiate the nature of chess games and players as well.

Even if you never explore chess theories, just knowing what strategy and tactics refer to, will help you make inroads into your own way of working and thinking. You can apply it to other business projects or any other aspect of life or work where problems need to be solved or analyzed. Such a pair of terms will exist in every field—such as in software development, you have stable modular design vs implementation issues/hacks. In business, there may be a marketing plan and also promotional ploys. Or for that matter, investing in shares of established companies vs cashing in on fresh opportunities. Sounds like a long term plan vs short term gimmicks, kind of thing.

And if you do explore and learn from chess—you will get one thing very clear—both strategy and tactics are important in their own sense, and there is no universal approach to situations. I guess most of us are aware of that, because every problem has its own peculiar issues, which may seem like something else before, but are often totally new and demand investigation right from scratch or the basics. **However, what chess teaches us is the need to explore various options, however ridiculous or unlikely they may seem, and often choose those which may even contradict the crux of your objective,** as you need to get to some other point from which you can try to get to the objective. If it was always a straight line to get to your goal, it is perhaps no goal worth seeking. Often temporary solutions may help you keep going in a crucial phase; likewise long & winding paths may need to be followed to ensure you avoid or overcome 'competitive traffic'. Chess has all competitive motifs– from well established principles to bizarre deviations from what is deemed 'normal'.

From the perspective of spectators, fans and analysts of any sport, it is therefore incorrect to look at a given approach of a player or team, and pass conclusions, just because it looks weird or contradictory to the need of the hour. Players often have to go through phases which do not look exciting, but are required, to get to some other known position from which your style is better suited— as it never comes to you on a platter.

10.2 Strategy as plan to arrange resources at certain time & place

On a chess board, strategy refers to a plan which tries to get pieces in 'good' or 'effective' positions, to ensure things are under control and allowing you to conduct your game in a manner appropriate to your style or competitive need. **Strategy is also therefore almost interchangeably used with the term 'positional play'** (although tacticians also seek to achieve positions, but in a different way).

When you make sure you have a sound overall position, you will be ready to explore any advantages in mobility, time, opponent's weakness, imbalances of resource distribution (piece strengths may be equal, but imbalance in formations, implies certain possibilities for both sides), key or weak squares, and support to pieces and the king.

10.3 Tactics as forced activity and calculated ploys

If strategy defines what kind of positions are strong or solid in giving an overall strength to a side, tactics involve looking at sections or specific pieces which can be engaged into some forced activity for a short period of time- to actually get to desirable positions. Tactics in chess usually involve direct threats to major pieces, pins or a check to the king, exchange of pieces or even sacrifices to actually alter the balance by 'making something happen'. However, tactics can be fruitful, usually when the new position achieved is sound as such and makes sense positionally or can allow you to further push on with an initiative gained to make in-roads. Tactics are often risky or need quick calculative abilities, since you are trying to force some activity, and often with sudden impact. Tactics can be short-sighted, as they may work only within limited scope (few pieces or certain area) and for short time. But within the short span, if they can impact the overall balance, they may be worth the risk.

10.4 Putting them together

It is obvious that both strategy and tactics are important, and have to be used to achieve your target—to win (checkmate in chess) or to get to positions of advantage from where you can build from. However, you can usually reach a position in many different ways, or reach different positions which are good as well. Therefore, it is no surprise that players prefer to employ a varying mix of strategies and tactics, and sharp or solid stuff in between. But in any case, all top chess players will be well versed in both, as you need to be able to read what your opponent is working out, even if you prefer not to be too tactical or too strategic a player (positional players).

For instance, GMs—Vishwanthan Anand, Bobby Fischer, Mikhail Tal are great tacticians—since that is what they are always looking out for. But they obviously have great positional assessment as they are not employing tactics for the heck of it. They just have an uncanny knack to throw in a bunch of moves which can make the chess board look like it is falling apart into unsound positions. However, once the storm is over, these guys very often end up with a resultant position which actually falls 'in place' in *their* scheme of things. It is no surprise that Anand is even better at rapid chess formats since it tends to favour tactical players.

Likewise, strong positional players like to attain solid overall positions and then explore ways to get slightly ahead or use sharper moves to gradually achieve better positions (accumulate mini advantages or squeeze out their opponents on some aspects). These include GMs—Anatoly Karpov and Michael Adams, for instance—who can often take long & winding routes, if needed- as long as it it is error free. It's like finding the right stepping stones in uncertain waters. Nonetheless, these positional masters, have to be wary of tactics by opponents who can throw their 'error free plans' off by a mile, and all gradually accrued advantages will then be rendered meaningless, if the opponent's tactics ushers into a 'new' position or alters the tempo towards his side. Tacticians would look to create waves in the water, to throw you off the stepping stones or they might alter the course of the waters, in such a way, that your stepping stones lag behind or are directionless.

In modern times, such demarcations in style are perhaps not too visible, since theory has evolved so much, that it makes sense to memorize certain lines of play, that positional play can be extended to great depths. Likewise tactical play, which may demand a quick and complex calculation of moves, has been given a boost by computers. So certain lines of play are totally out of reckoning, as they are logically 'explored out'. Draws are perhaps more common, although it is a natural outcome in chess, being a game of exact moves. Also, a chess draw should not be mixed up with a draw in cricket, wherein all innings have not ended because of time constraints. When chess games end in draws, they are like tied games of cricket— the game has ended and both sides are equal (even if the draw was agreed upon earlier, both players estimate that it will be equal at the end). **Since cricket has uncertainties of intention & execution, tied games are rare, but not so in chess.**

Further, games of chess are more complex than just saying some were positionally intriguing or tactically exciting. There are so many combined approaches and just on or two moves in between as a surprise can have an impact (called 'shots' in chess). GM Gary Kasparov has been regarded as a complete player, on account of being able to play dynamic chess as well as battle out complex 'locked-up' positions. Moreover, when he faces tactics or sharp play, he easily works out replies to defend, which be dynamic or complex as need be.

When Jose Capablanca, the legendary Cuban Grandmaster, and World Champion of the early 1900's was asked how many moves does he think ahead, he said 'one move—the best one'. It may be that simple for Capablanca, who could look at the board and find out which move looked right, but it does convey that chess can be played move by move, and without classifying things as tactical or strategic. Sort of like playing cricket– ball for ball, as it comes. However, in chess as well as cricket, there will be phases which demand anything but simplicity. Players usually prepare for so many lines of play, that the only options left are the ones which never seemed sound, and perhaps might often be the right answers.

When to use which? Although this will depend on what you need to achieve and what skills you possess, going with a positional (strategic) approach when you need to consolidate and ensure resources are in a relevant place, is prudent. Such strategic aspects generally refer to fewer risks, on account of using more of regulation type of skills, often time-tested theories. Tactics, are often seen as a means to get to your positional plans, when good opponents will not let you get where you want. Tactics include surprises and forcing methods– often tricks or gimmicks, and other calculated combinations to make something happen within a short span of time or directed towards certain resources (players or conditions). Tactics can misfire and all the explosive effort can have limited or worse outcome, and hence are seen as risky. However, it depends on skills and match context as well, as not doing certain things can be just as risky and often being more active, can seize initiative and reduce risk, as you dictate what goes on, and you are more at home with whatever the ploy is. As mentioned, just like most chess players are proficient in both, and there are approaches which fall in between– **sharp positional play** (concerned with getting resources to desired places, which may not exactly be conventional– but precarious or skewed), and **controlled tactics** which do refer to direct threats but in a less vicious manner, so that there are retreating options as well.

10.5 Features of Strategy and Tactics

Positional play is often described as 'defensive' and tactics as 'attacking'. This has a lot of truth in it, but the purpose they are employed for will be a better indicator to how attacking or defensive an approach is. You can often attack by just making potent and sharp maneuvers. and you can defend possible threats by using tactical activity such as quick exchanges or forced deflections, to gain momentum and defend 'just in time'. Tactics can buy you *tempo* due to forced activity– the tempo gained may be for an incisive attack or to consolidate defence.

But there is merit in well known chess concepts–

1. Tactics flow from good positions (if your overall resource allocation is sound, then you are better placed to use some of them in specific targeted activity). This is an explanation by Bobby Fisher, on tactical play.

2. Positions matter, but you need tactics to get you there (based on an Vishy Anand interview online, when being questioned why he does not opt for sharp positional play. He prefers using forcing tactics to get to the desired positions).

An example from recent cricket is how Brian Lara and Sachin Tendulkar have played Danish Kaneria. Lara coming down the order after Gayle and Sarwan have given a decent platform (the position), launches into an attack to force Kaneria out of the bowling spell. His ability to hit sixes against spinners, is perhaps as flawless as it can perhaps get. This is an **example of tactics flowing from sound positions.** (Lara is one of the players who has used modern bats to improve upon what he used to do well, unlike many younger cricketers who are using modern approaches to make up for their technique in hitting sixes, such as driving short balls or slogging fuller ones).

Now when Tendulkar faces Kaneria, it has usually been after Sehwag has tactically smacked the attack apart, piling runs unlike any conventional test opener. Tendulkar has therefore often come in when both runs and strike rates are strong (else he is in, inside 5 overs). Now, not giving a wicket, is what you need on the scoreboard, **as consolidating a position which was arrived by tactics, is prudent.** The risk has paid off (Sehwag's style), now make sure you are not pick-pocketed. The scoring options will open up as the bowlers are forced to take risks to get back in the game (being behind on the runs/wicket equation). The 1st Test, Pakistan in India, 2005, was a such as case, and Ganguly's 21 of 74 balls was not as useless as most thought it was (India did not win, even after getting 200 ahead, and going into the last day with Pakistan being just about 50 ahead and 4 wickets left. India or anyone would take that, as even 100 more runs from the tail, would leave India half a day to get them. Credit goes to Kamran Akmal and Abdul Razzaq for earning the draw.

10.6 Applying both to Cricket

Now lets see what can constitutes *strategy* and *tactics* in cricket.

Batting tends to be positional, again due to the non-commutativity of good and bad, due to the first error being fatal. So you have to be constructive and judicious in shot selection. However, there are obviously batsmen who have flair in scoring and holding their wickets as well. On the other side– **bowling naturally lends itself to tactics,** even earlier on in an innings, perhaps, as miscalculations can be permitted to some extent. Nonetheless, since wickets are sparse (on account of no certainty between being beaten and getting out), bowlers who just rely on tricks and ploys, cannot sustain long enough without having consistent stock bowling, based on specific line length issues.

Here are some examples (as I see it, based on my limited knowledge, but hope it explains the ideas. Also, if some player was missed, it is not due to their not following any strategy or tactic! it is because what follows is not an exhaustive list).

For instance, classic opening batting such as Sunil Gavaskar or Geoff Boycott would be examples of **sound positional play**– as they ensure that batting resources are well placed for the middle overs and beyond. Modern day players who would also qualify as strong positional players would be Rahul Dravid and Jacques Kallis (last of their kind?). All of these positional players, use their technique to defend and to score runs as well.

Likewise, **in bowling, strategy will basically involve the basic length to bowl on a pitch** and what general approach to adopt in field placing- to set up the game plan. The manner in which bowlers might surprise batsmen, like short pitched stuff or **bowl to fields which are unusual but with an intent to make things happen- are tactical**. For instance, when Shane Warne bowls round the legs into the rough, it is with strong intent to knock the batsman over, since he can sneak in variations on or outside leg stump line even if a batsman pads. The same situation, when Ashley Giles or Paul Harris (recently against India in South Africa, 2006), bowl outside leg stump, it is a **strategic approach, of waiting** and gradually getting the batsman to play within a restricted plan). So the intent and bowling variety with what kind of field placing is being used will dictate if something is strategic or tactical– is that your theme (as part of the nature of bowling) or a quick combination of unusual ideas, to make something happen.

However, players such as Sanath Jayasuria, Adam Gilchrist or Virender Sehwag, can dent orthodox bowling attacks by playing shots (although with different styles), which throw equations off track. These are examples of **extreme tactical play**. Sehwag has demonstrated that by some smashing shots and deft ones which may nonetheless just go over the in-field, he can erode the attack and score big hundreds. Gilchrist, may not score as big centuries as Sehwag, but for a wicket-keeper, he has plenty of big scores and his smacking fifties in both tests and ODIs is sufficiently dangerous that he can make bowlers bowl wides before the bat talks (World Cup Finals, Asutralia vs India, 2003). He has been the best example of tactical play, and with brisk footwork and bat speed ('tactics flow from good positions', as applied in an execution context).

Then there are **sharp positional plays– wherein you try to dictate merit, by playing shots which score in a different pattern from**

what the bowler expects– such as working the ball off the legs, or using quick footwork or deft touch, to get the ball where it was perhaps not intended for. This has lesser risks than calculated tactics of 'going over the top', but is tricky nonetheless. Tendulkar in ODIs (and earlier in tests) and Ponting in tests & ODIs, fit this mould amongst players today. Viv Richards was ahead of his era, in this regard, and his ODI strike rate is great even today.

Brian Lara tends to **alternate between rapid tactics and smooth positional play,** but tends not to favor in-between stuff. Hayden is another in this approach, exemplary in defense and drives, and slog anything short over mid-wicket. They both score big hundreds this way, by being firm in one or the other aspect. You would normally expect that those who have big strike rates in test hundreds, should in fact have a very high strike rates in ODIs. This is not quite the case here for Lara and Hayden. The reason is that this split approach– fully positional or fully tactical works great in alternating phases (tests), rather than ball to ball activity, which ODIs are all about. Of course, it is foolish to ignore Lara or Hayden in ODIs, once they get in, they know when to switch gear. But if you ever wondered why there is disparity, it is about how they plunder between phases or overs. Sehwag is another apparently inexplicable case, where the volume of runs in ODIs is not quite like his monumental test innings. He also alternates tactics and positional play, between short phases or overs, but since he begins with a tactical approach, no matter what the format, he has a huge strike rate in ODIs, nonetheless.

The above mentioned variations in style, are just that. Tendulkar, Lara, Inzamam, Ponting, being the best around, have the all the competitive motifs, and will play as required– in both tests and ODI.

Likewise in bowling, McGrath, Pollock and Kumble can be considered as **positional, in the sense, that they keep working on the batsman's defence** and have subtle variations, to actually squeeze in a ball, which follows up on the advantages (effects) of past deliveries. There can be other set-ups which are tactical, when the bowler does force activity to happen and then get through. However, these great bowlers do not necessarily need to force a batsman into anything unconventional, rather they want batsmen to react to what they are planning. Sooner or later, their little efforts will pay big dividends. Then there are other **tactical bowlers- who rely on knocking over the batsmen with some special or compelling stuff-** such as Waqar Younis, Shoaib Akhtar, Bret Lee, Harmison. The likes of Shane Warne, Wasim Akram or Muralitharan have the complete gamut between positional play (lots of potent stock bowling) and tactical punches (special balls to knock over, even if there is error free batting). Andrew Flintoff, used to relish mixing short stuff with yorkers- but has developed into a stock bowler for England as they rely more on his bowling. Likewise, his batting has now become a lot more constructive, apart from the mighty shots he is known for.

Sri-Lanka showed in the 90s that **tactical play early up, by letting go a few wickets** (like a sacrifice in chess), can put you in strong positions later- for the likes Arvinda De Silva. Aggressive hitting up front was always done in ODIs, but Sri Lanka took it further and redefined it by having about 3 batsmen going for it, thereby increasing the chance of success– as the gamble needed the luck, and trying it with one batsmen going for it, would be neither here nor there. For instance, if Jayasuria alone were to go for the hyper-smacking, he could be out and then to normalize play would be more of a gambit than a sacrifice. This Sri-Lankan ODI approach was similar to rapid chess games being tactical, since rapid chess players have to make moves within time constraints, in such a manner that there may be no time to explore positional depth. Likewise, in an ODI if you assume that all batsmen anyway will not be used up, as Sri Lanka did, those loss of wickets will not be caught up by bowling sides, due to 50 overs for each side anyway.

Examples of strategy and tactics related to field placement.

Fielders placed at positions where the ball never went to. You might often see a fielder say at fine leg to a fast bowler or long-on to a spinner, even if the ball never went there all day. This is a **strategic aspect,** to ensure that the batsman perhaps does not play a shot of a particular kind or if he does it is covered or he can get out, if he lofts it. This fielder is achieving a purpose—to impact the nature of a batsman's approach, and thereby giving a bowler a way to work with options he actually is trying to explore.

Likewise, **not having a fielder at an expected position can also be part of a long term strategy,** as that fielder can be used up in sweeping some other area, where the correct shots would go to. Since you may say, that incorrect shots may anyway not be in control of any fielders, especially in a third man type of region as the ball flies away, quickly. This could be a gambit type of approach, as give a little bit away, but open your plans elsewhere. The idea of a strategy is usually of long term effect, and helps to make the batsman participate in your plan— whether it may be by conventional approach or a more open 'give & take' approach.

On the other hand **forcing a batsman to give a specific reply to a quick set of compelling deliveries** which attack say the body or the stumps in direct fashion and with a testing combination– bouncers and yorkers, aided by fielders which can catch a failed defensive shot, and perhaps inviting him to hit over an in-fielder is a typical **tactical**

ploy. This is to test out weakness directly and in a threatening manner. Bowlers, can surprise with balls not meant for the field either.

For instance, having a 7-2 field, with many fielders at 'good' and some at unorthodox positions on the offside, and two fielders to take care of straighter balls on the on side, would be a **sharp positional play**. It is still strategic, since you are ensuring that you cover what is possible but are still indirectly telling a batsman to alter his shots, as some fielders are not in normal positions (perhaps due to a pitch condition or the way a bowler chooses to bowl). Here are two quotations from great chess players, which I find apt—

"Strategy requires thought, tactics requires observation." *—Max Euwe, former World Chess Champion*

(my comments: this now relates to the fact that tactics are direct forcing means, but to threaten a weakness, you need subtle observation. To observe, is a direct way to sense a condition and to be spontaneous as well; whereas strategy being indirect and with knowledge of what is as such good, stems from thinking. It is the kind of difference you attach to being wise and being smart. The best always have both, and more importantly know when to exercise which, as the next saying goes).

"Tactics is knowing what to do when there is something to do; strategy is knowing what to do when there is nothing to do" — *Tartakower, Polish/French Grandmaster*

(my comments: simply the simplest way to sum up the differences between strategy and tactics. Strategic planning and trying to get to the 'right' places, are best done when nothing much is happening and you set up what you need your way; when things are setup and in the middle of established platforms, things begin to happen. It is then the tactician pounces and can unleash calculated ploys to alter position).

11. Development, Open or Closed Plays

11.1 The Concept of Development in Chess

In chess, both sides have equal and opposite pieces. Further, the board as such does not favor any side (as might be in cricket or tennis, where surface of a pitch may favor certain players). The first and significant advantage in chess, is therefore for White– who initiates play and gets 'the right of way' to control the very first square, as per his choice. Black can reply to make White play according to the defences possible in reply to that move, to counter White's first move. The very first move (by White and Black's reply) is so important, that the broad nature of the game can be established right there. The subsequent moves from both sides, will usually follow a set pattern based on the opening adopted, since the opening sequences are so thoroughly tested in time. However, the idea from both sides is to retain control and to 'develop' pieces from their respective 'home' squares- to get them out actively 'in play'. It must be noted that an undeveloped piece also has an advantage being where it is, if it still performs a role from its home square. Bringing them out, just to ensure that they get active, is not always apt either as, an heedless forward movement will make that piece retreat just as quickly, thereby wasting moves and actually allowing the opponent chances to develop rapidly.

11.2 Control of Key Squares

Control of key squares and proper development of pieces to desirable positions is paramount in the opening phases. In chess, the central four squares are key squares (and those around these key squares as well), in the early stages, which both sides try to seize or prevent control. This is because once pieces are on central squares, they exert maximum influence to other squares, than they would if brushed aside on the periphery. This does not mean that pieces will not be placed off center—in fact they often would—since good opponents would prevent you from getting control of the center. So the next set of options for both players would be to explore non-center squares, but perhaps in a manner to support or eventually get to the center again, if possible.

This is somewhat like saying the bowler would like to bowl a particular line and length, to dictate the nature of batting. Batsmen can reply to equal (accept that line and length, but play relevant shots) or they can try to disrupt or be proactive to make the bowler alter the line length. Sooner or later, once both sides are doing well, the game may shift towards trying other options, towards a different line. As far as line and length is concerned, EAS Prasanna—legendary Indian off-spinner, puts it interestingly, as he reckons bowling is about 'length and line', where length has to be 'more' basic and line is optional. This is like pinpointing which of the central 'key' squares, in chess, must be focused on in a particular game, and which ones are then to be treated flexibly.

11.3 Activation of Resources

The other general thumb rule is that, minor pieces (knights, bishops) come out early– based on which pawns were moved first. This is done to reach or control the key squares. Since minor pieces have fair but restricted mobility, they need to get out early, as it may take more moves to get where they eventually should be. So activating minor pieces, with a few pawns, will be what you can see up front in most games of chess. Also, a knight usually comes out before a bishop, as it can jump over pawns and needs more hops to reach distant squares, whereas bishops can in one go, reach squares far away (although on its diagonal only). Gradually, as pawns move or get exchanged (open games) or remain interlocked head to head (closed games), the style of the game gets defined, since pawn formations dictate what goes over or between or around, and pawns cannot be retracted as other pieces can. The rook and the queen may then play defensive or attacking roles once there is purpose and mobility, since they influence many squares and can support pieces or target opponent pieces or squares. The whole idea is to activate your resources to the proper places, from which they can play well defined roles or be flexible as the game proceeds.

Development, is one the most interesting aspects of chess, since both players need their resources active or held back as need be. As far as cricket is concerned there is some interesting aspect to it. Even in cricket, players do not participate all at once (except fielders). As mentioned earlier, batting is highly sequenced (having two batsmen at the crease implies that another batsman who may be apt for a situation, can only come in, unless one of these goes back, and once out he cannot return). Bowling is quasi-simultaneous since bowlers are at least available for a few overs in between and can be taken out and brought back.

Chess is a perfect blend of simultaneous and sequenced play (since any piece can move or does exert influence on some squares, yet if you need to move three pieces, you need to do so in sequence). So cricket, though not entirely similar, does have a strong relationship to chess where resources get activated at different times and also do get out of play, for a given game.

11.4 Altering Balance

In chess, since the pieces are exact and equal at startup—and both players alternate moves—it means that each player has to try to get 'off' the normal paths, sooner or later, to create a sense of imbalance in the alignment of pieces. Only when some positional imbalance exists, is there a possibility to create an advantage in space, material activity or tactical ploys which tilt the board in someone's favor, perhaps at the price of some other 'acceptable' weaknesses.

It must be noted that in chess, any mirroring of moves by Black from the first reply, will fall apart as White has lead in move sequence, and sooner or later, one of the moves may demand another response due to a check or some capturing move. This means that once the control of central squares, is locked into equality, the focus of the game usually shifts towards activity which is conducive to a player style or along other 'playable' options. So the focus now shifts from center to other areas, as mentioned earlier, and in some cases you can have skewed positions or complex interlocking scenarios, which are enough to give a headache at first sight. But altering balance is key, and difficult to measure, since pieces can hop around and what looks imbalanced will soon fall into conventional or comprehendible positions.

Now in cricket, usually most of us measure parity by watching the runs–wickets and runs–overs equations, although differently in tests and ODIs. However, since we have so many other aspects which are already imbalanced at a given instance of play, there are so many factors that go unnoticed or can be tried out– since just about every format issue is different for bowlers and batsmen (Part I- Format Of Cricket).

> In a given situation, all the well known factors and
> common concepts, combine to create a peculiar in-
> stance of imbalance in overall position, which can
> be explored to convert into an execution advantage.

Modern cricket has explored a lot, yet I believe it misses many key issues, possible for exploitation. A simple example, is one of run-outs, and taking singles. These must be treated with different degrees of sensitivity, in different stages of a first innings of an ODI and the second, (or perhaps in test matches where a draw is attempted).

For example, when a team is in danger of getting all out in the first innings of an ODI, and the last few batsmen have some skill in slogging, perhaps they can relinquish a cheeky single, unless very obvious, when 5 overs are left. The fact that you do not know the target can be taken to your advantage! (by letting go some risky singles). Now once you establish that sneaking singles is to be avoided, unless 'earned', perhaps the non-striker need not take a start, and get run out by fluke (if the bowler got his hands into a straight drive). Likewise, from the bowling side, some in-fielders, not all, can then be placed even deeper to even prevent the 'well earned' single. This is a case where the peculiar balance of resources (few batsmen left; few overs left; first innings ODI; tail can slog a bit) has been recognized and converted into an execution advantage or an adjustment (run only 'earned' singles, no start by non-striker, save energy to slog, batsmen can pick their bowlers to hit).

The point is that there is 'the heat of the moment' and the 'overall balance', which influences what goes on in the middle. When to go with the flow, and when to assess the details, are both important.

12. Tempo, measuring beyond time

12.1 Tempo in Chess

In chess, one of the most important aspects that governs all activity is the tempo. As the term indicates it has something to do with pace of activity. But when a chess analyst says that by playing a certain combination of moves, it 'gains tempo', it is not how much was achieved in a certain amount of time in seconds or minutes, but how few moves were required to achieve a task, in relation to the responses possible from your opponent. So if you can achieve a combination of moves which, achieves a task with one less move (in relation to the opponent's replies) then you gain one tempo. In fact, you can often play a sequence of moves which are a bit convoluted (many more moves) but if it was what was needed to overcome the solidity of an opponent's position, it may be worth it, as gaining tempo after four moves or seven, will then not be of consequence- since being a step or two ahead of the opponent, is what the objective was. When you get ahead by 'a move' you gain 'a tempo'. White already has half-tempo advantage, at start of play, being the player to move first.

During development, most logical moves are those which do not lose tempo. This is why the general rule in development is not to move the same piece twice, as you are wasting moves- unless you move the piece to a square which would anyway not be accomplished in one move. This is also the reason why White has an advantage over Black, since it has a half-tempo advantage at the start. If you just play a move which had no bearing on what is happening, and say what is wrong about that? Well, it may look nice, but you may lose tempo, and eventually allow your opponent to either sneak in a combination, which just does the trick by that one move which went for a vacation.

Tactical players will invariably try to gain tempo after a flurry of ex-changes or some forced moves to get into a position which gets them a 'foot in the door' of the opponent's defence. **Positional players** may play complicated moves- shuffled around closed situations (pawns in-terlocked), and eventually gain even half-tempo– but a fair gain as they play with surety rather than experimental or adventurous uncertainties.

Every amateur or enthusiast can feel the loss of tempo, when you know that the computer or superior opponent with whom you are playing is making in-roads just that bit quicker, in terms of moves (to bring some pieces to defend a situation, you are just losing out by that one little move). Likewise, if you try to play a crazy sacrificial game against a computer (even an average chess program), and think that by firing many pieces to erode the pawns of a castled king, you can get through to checkmate the king, it might just happen that the computer gets enough pieces to add support or release space for the king to sneak out (by say moving a pawn to create space, which also leads to 'discover-support' from another piece such as a queen or rook, as the pawn movement cleared the path for that other piece. So a move, achieved two tasks- escape-space and path for added support).

The lesson to be learnt is that to gain tempo or to be able to sneak in activity which takes one move less to achieve a desired result, requires great effort. Usually you have to play some moves which sort of achieve one or two things on a move (in fact, every time a chess piece is moved, it effects new squares and releases support from squares which were covered prior to the move, and the same time releases the square for something else, and clears the path for yet another piece... many things happen on every move. However, which of the happenings, is relevant in a situation, and how they could in turn be countered is the tough part). This means, if your opponent makes moves which achieve multiple effects as well, he can cancel out your efficiency and there is no net gain in tempo.

But to measure any the pace of activity in terms of 'move differential' is simply one of the best lessons from chess. This is because in the real world or in other sports, the meaning of the word 'quickly' can be measured in terms of *activity in fewer steps*, not just *activity in so less time*. The biggest advantage of this way of looking at the pace of an activity, is that 'actual time' is not often in your control, especially when you have to wait for actions by other people. If you could achieve a task in the planned number of steps or fewer, you can pat yourself on your back, rather than feel bogged down due to delays and inefficiencies beyond your control.

When you are working on a project to develop a product- and other developments do not happen around you, say in technology, with supply/distribution issues, or finalizing partnerships, it means that your project is still stuck at step number 3 or whatever (not your fault, the ball is in someone else's court). If after two months developments do take place, you can now unleash step 4, and you proceed to the next step. If in case you finish your activity in the planned steps or in 6 steps instead of 8 (perhaps you did improve part of the product in the meantime), you still actually achieved the result in the required or fewer number of steps although over a longer period of time (sure, the loss of time was not worth it, but you can benefit by measuring efficiency this way, and it will often be more reflective of the 'pace' of your effort than actual time, which was not in your control– just like if your opponent took a long time to think in chess, and in the meantime you figured an even better way (fewer moves to earn an advantage, you still gain 'tempo' even though the game got longer in real time). Measuring tasks by steps in real world situations, is like measuring activity in chess by move-differential. Please note that 'actual time' does matter in chess, in terms of a player having to make 40 or so many moves per hour. Even if both players play at brisk speed (many moves in few minutes), none of them may gain tempo, as moves were all replied to counter and nullify each others strengths. It could be that the player who took more (actual) time on a given move—and came up with a plan, which eventually gives him a move initiative—was the one to gain tempo, as opposed to the opponent who has more time on the clock, who is now scrambling to catch up, in terms of move differential.

12.2 Applications in Cricket

Quick wickets slowly? Here is an aspect that modern cricket has sort of formalized, although I am sure it was just as much in use earlier. Let us say that in a situation where a team has lost 5 wickets for 120 runs in a test match, the normal (and meaningful as well) approach a bowling team would take, is to attack and put pressure on the batting side, especially if they had put up a decent score of 300 plus.

The idea is to just knock the batsmen off and wrap up the tail 'quickly'. The moment the word 'quick' comes to mind, we are naturally inclined to link it with real time (which translates to number of balls, since over rates/hour are are near consistent). However, if time was ample and a result was kind of certain, then we can interpret 'quickly' in a different way, instead of the conventional wickets needed in so many balls (overs). How about bowling in a manner whereby it is positively intended to take wickets, but with giving away few runs (maybe in-out fields to take the catches on defensive errors and stop boundaries off good shots). The idea is to think every 12-15 runs conceded, as 'a step', and if runs are made to be 'sparse' with a decent dose of dot balls, it would mean that when the next wicket would fall, the runs have not ticked as much. Essentially, your are measuring 'quickly' in terms of – these many wickets in so few runs given– instead of attempting—these many wickets in so few balls. It is about wrapping up the innings *quickly* per runs conceded although it may take a bit longer in terms of time.

Example of **wickets-per-few-runs tempo**: say in 3 hours or the next 40 odd overs, if we can 'wrap up' the innings from 120 for 5 wickets; conceding only 65-85 runs (trying near-maiden overs and covering big shots with sweepers; type 2 & type 1 bowling?), then we have achieved our runs/wickets for that phase of play, at about 1 wicket at 15 runs. You might take that perhaps. Tempo of 1 wicket per 'step' (where every step was 12-15 runs given)? The idea of this approach is that whenever a wicket falls, it was not many runs away from the last one that fell, although perhaps after many overs. The drawback is that cutting down chances on taking a wicket—due to some fielding & bowling being of containing type—may lead to letting the batsmen in, and they may score later anyway, because it was assumed that actual time is available.

Example of **wickets-per-few-overs tempo**: now compare the previous case to a conventional idea to 'wrap up', by good old aggressive bowling and more attacking fields with slips and other close in fielders. Absolutely nothing wrong with that, in saying that if we get 2 'quick' wickets, and then get into the tail, we have a good chance to wrap this innings up. But if after a dozen overs, wickets do not fall in this approach, there is likelihood that 30-40 runs may be conceded cheaply, on account of close in fields and due to the fact that wicket taking balls may go for runs (type 1, disadvantages, *Ch 6.1, p65*). Then batsmen back themselves and graft through, and all of a sudden 60-70 run partnership looks frustrating for the bowling side, howsoever attacking their attitude was. Then the tail comes in and has their share of funny shots... you may be in for 125 runs added by the last half of the team, if things fail (worse than previous case). If it succeeds then you may wrap up in 15 overs, & within 40 odd runs (better than previous case).

Needless to say, both approaches have their merits and drawbacks, but the options are available to think of 'quickly' as taking the wickets in so few runs or taking the wickets in so few overs– since the word *quick* implies activity in something fewer (as long as that 'something' has some connection with a progression or sequence over time).

This runs/wickets tempo is being addressed by modern teams, and it often baffles past cricketers as to why the fielding side is being kind of inactive, when they should go for the jugular. As mentioned, both approaches have their merits and it will depend on how a captain feels he can address it and how fatigued the bowlers are or how the pitch is– and he can also do a bit of both approaches to get the best mix and being right in between.

After studying chess tempo, it helps us formalize pace of an activity as related to fewer steps or moves. Just keep in mind that whenever you come across the word 'quickly', you must question yourself as to the pace of an activity in terms of what— lesser time (as normally one would) or in terms of reduction of another parameter (fewer runs, as described in this case). Usually such a parameter also changes or progresses over time, but perhaps not in linear fashion and, more importantly, it may be a parameter that can be controlled.

13. Chess Summation

13.1 Keeping options open and mixing approaches

I have tried to cover chess ideas in brief– those which are essential in chess and which will be required to understand applications to cricket in this book. As mentioned, I am not a chess player or analyst, but I do like to see games and the nature of activity that happens, and relate that to real world situations. There are many excellent web sites and tons of books, which can help you learn the basics. By and large, the chess community is astute and even club level players analyze positions with due consideration, not just on habit or legacy—which often happens in other sports. Often the overall picture or the probable reasons behind a specific approach of a team or player is not given due consideration in other sports, largely due to the amount of focus that goes into the shot execution and skills involved, with little time for why it was attempted that way (you may still disagree, but can at least look into what the players are trying). However, since chess is a pure mind game, the skills *are* about the attempt—why a player did or did not try something. You never get caught up as to how deftly a player moved his knight over the pawns, or which fingers were used in castling. So chess will help you to consider many things, even when your eventual choice looks straightforward or at times weird, when it perhaps wasn't.

However, to sum up, there are a few **important attitudes and a sort of maturity which develops within you by even just following chess.**

1. Ability to keep options open without personal preferences or prejudices– as games unfold and situations differ, one has to seek for options which may look less impressive, but are still viable on account of limited options available to you when playing a good opponent. You may have to consider options which may sound simple or uninteresting, but are potent on account of the peculiar situation. In the end it all comes down to options available, and although chess has unfathomable permutations, experienced GMs know when certain options are ruled out. It is just that those 'certain moves' may have to be arrived at totally dispassionately, arguably difficult to translate in other sports, because humans play shots well, only when they enjoy the feel of a good shot. But again, in competition, your opponent will rarely let you enjoy yourself, so you often have to be prepared to consider what is as such required, whether you like it or not. When sampling such 're-quirements' keeping your personal preferences aside, at least for a while, will help arriving at the solution.

2. Every action that has an advantage also has a disadvantage in someways– there is no such thing, as this type of move is always good or such a line of play is always bad. That is why chess players are masters of not just gambits and sacrifices, but they know when certain 'thumb-rules' need not be followed (for instance, there are times when a player opts not to castle the king at all, and thereby save a move) or certain weakness can be converted to a strength (double pawns on the same file, are seen as weak on account of disrupting a pawn chain, but they will after all influence some other squares which you can focus on or use the pawn ahead for activity and exchange it off).

3. Choose an approach not by past knowledge alone but by freshness of different situations, and giving due consideration to the drawback of something 'good' and value of something 'bad', as explained. Just when someone feels they have seen it all, the game throws in some new ways of doing things (reverse-swing in cricket) and you have to be ready to re-consider your past knowledge in light of the new ways available.

4. Forced sequences and natural moves: if you can force the opponent to respond in a specific manner, owing to the natural (logical) selection of moves, or allow the opponent to play moves which are even deemed good—but you know that they will be played— you can benefit. The fact that you are entering a 'known' condition is a plus for you, as you can then handle it by preparation or because it suits your pattern of play. You may even be able to take risks, as you gain time by anticipating, and can minimize risk by following up with certain other steps or releasing some.

5. To achieve desirable positions, you may need a mix of contrasting approaches- strategic, tactical and various in between 'shots', because when competition is at a high level, you will need to get your outcomes directly or indirectly, and may need to follow seemingly contradictory styles of play, even if it be just a move or two (such as retracting a bishop to defend backward pawns, may seem like letting off an attacking attitude, but the bishop still can control the diagonal from the back).

13.2 Recognizing when the 'chess advantage' is yours.

In the context of other sports, as has been mentioned, there will be a need to depend on skills triggered by passion (since humans are not chess pieces and go by mood, different each day) as well as doing things 'apt', in a dispassionate way, as the 'chess' dictates (where you are like a specific mechanical piece to fulfill a role). You need both, to enjoy the sport and be competitive.

But when should you go by passion and when by chess. One of the ways to find out, is to sample the available options for execution.

For instance, in a sport such as **table tennis**, it is possible to serve tight—so that the ball stays within the table edges and bounces minimally—that the receiver has to reply in a certain manner only, such as push it back and keep it compact. This kind of play is now in the domain of *chess*, as there is no way for your opponent to use passion and smack that serve, even if he anticipated your serve, as execution-wise his options are limited. So if you see the best players around in table tennis, they may never change their serve—maybe vary the degree of sidespin-underspin—but they will repeat that serve even if they lose points. This is because, they have worked out patterns of play for 'the' reply to that serve or at best few replies. This is the 'chess advantage' in table tennis, where the replies are few and known for certain serves– on account of receiver being forced to choose limited natural options.

Compare this to **tennis**, where the server has advantage due to power and angle, but if the receiver gets hold of it, he perhaps has options in space or depth of return, and deeper returns are good, unlike table tennis where a long return would allow for a third ball winner. So tennis serving and receiving, is in the domain of skill, (relatively speaking, as you need skill in table tennis to produce the tight serves), as there are more options to return, although getting hold is the tough part. I am sure, even in tennis, certain serves will perhaps have certain natural replies, but if the receiver is good enough to anticipate and get hold of the serve, he can hit winners in reply as well. In table tennis, even after anticipation it is mechanically not possible to hit winners on certain serves.

I can understand that it is not perhaps as straightforward in theory and practice, and players may server or bowl, with some degree of inaccuracy as well. But the idea is to understand that certain patterns are highly skilled, whereas some are more 'chess oriented' which work within a specific framework of possibilities.

It obviously sounds easier than it actually is, but as a junior table tennis player, I rarely recollect anyone advising me to focus on the limited pattern possible from a single type of serve- as a 'career' option, even if your opponent may be the best around. Surely, if I lost a couple of points, then instinct would be to alter the serve and do something else.

For that matter, take an example from another area of competition- as on the battlefield, especially in the bygone eras when wars were bloody and passion was a primary driving force for the warriors. Alexander the Great, was undoubtedly noted in history for his genius on the battlefield and intense fervor to win the world over. On one of his crucial battles in Persia, his **infantry had to face scythed-chariots** which had sharp blades attached and protruding out of the axle, on both sides of the wheel (which was known to Alexander). This meant that if the chariots charged into the enemy ranks, they would be ripping and spinning anything along the sides. Sounds scary but not for Alexander. Instead of trying to prevent the chariots from coming at his ranks—which he perhaps could not have anyway—he allowed them to charge into his outer ranks. Just that he punctuated his outer ranks with gaps wide enough for the width of the chariot and its axle protrusions. The other front ranked soldiers stood still with their spears pointed towards the charging chariots. Obviously, the horses would 'naturally' not run into pointed devices, but would rather go for the gaps. Since the gaps were wide enough, they did not cause any peripheral ripping, and as they chariots went a few ranks in, the outer ranks attacked the chariot from the side and behind, to nullify any advantage in design. **The lesson is that, if you can lead the opponent into something you know, and perhaps they do not, you can work out plans, to counter and even allow them to play to their strengths.** In this case the horses, were like chess pieces where the behavior would be sort of defined by their 'preset' nature.

The difference in both examples is that in the earlier instance (of table tennis service), the human player has the aptitude to try variations, but cannot owing to limited options in execution. In the other example, if the horses could think, they could perhaps charge into the ranks, ignoring the pointed spears, because with their immense force they could throw apart the outer ranks and create disarray due to chariot design. However, like water flowing where it finds least resistance, they were sucked in, and trapped due to their own strength of speed which prevented any other possible maneuvers. So it is all about what options you offer and how you prepare for the known factors.

Now in cricket, when the bowler knows something and so does the batsman know what is being attempted, there is an imbalance due to format. If bowlers can restrict options for the batsman, and since they initiate action, they know the variation they are trying to slip in, if at all (like the table tennis serve, you may not need to change it, if only few proper replies are possible). Besides, the batsman cannot counter it in a pre-determined way, by say adjusting where he stands or moves, since the penalty for being bowled is much more severe than a bowler losing runs. **There is therefore a natural bowler's chess advantage in**

cricket. As mentioned before, for a bowler it is like taking back a move in chess, whereas the batsman has to pass the test again (*Ch 9.2, p93*).

Further, this bowler's chess advantage gets deeper, if the bowler is a batsman who can bowl. Refer to the Tendulkar Dot Chess *Ch 21, p185-215* for how he has handled such situations and also his success as a bowler in this regard (not because he is an accomplished bowler, but **making the best batsmen think along with him in the same way, deepens the bowler's chess advantage**). After all, making the batsman expect something is a big step– as slipping in a surprise, or even touch of variety, needs a reference point. When both bowler and batsman, are batsmen as such, the options and expectations get just that bit deeper. Good for the bowler.

13.3 How much chess is good in human sports?

All this approach of limiting options and leading players into situations known and covered by you, and repeating it all again and again, sounds kind of dry and boring. Guess what, it sure can be! In a future book, I will try to show how rules can be adjusted and variety can be imposed by incorporating it in the format of a sport. **Just about every sport has reached a point where sameness, on account of planning a repeatable manner to accumulate advantages, has taken the variety out.** It is not the players' fault since their job is to win and get points, even if does not sound sensational.

This is the case with chess as well, where e4, d4 are replied by few set defences by Black (at GM level)– such as Sicilian, Ruy Lopez, (for e4); and Queen's Gambit (declined/accepted) and Indian defences (for d4). This has lead to Bobby Fischer's formalizing of **Random Chess** (*Ch 8, p82*). However, chess will take care of itself (let's hope) as there is always scope for permutations beyond what is believed to be indisputable or refuted, until a computer or some theory 'solves' chess like the Rubic cube, by giving a set of rules which always draw for Black or win for White?

However, in other sports, where humans replace chess pieces to form a team, there will always be a mixed possibility of skill-passion as well as logic-execution control (the chess). Just that players will, in their rightful desire to win, often explore the *chess* to compete in terms of preparation as clearly some opponents are way ahead in skill. It was done to Bradman (bodyline as well as by Sir Alec Bedser to some extent); and to/by Tendulkar in the past 5 years; and now to every major player.

It was interesting to watch Sir Garfield Sobers, recently on an Indian news channel, express his amusement over what constitutes an all-rounder, as he said that in his time an all-rounder had to put in a lot of work (to keep both batting and bowling going), whereas today Chris Gayle is seen as an all-rounder. Very relevant point, as he speaks based on measuring ability on skill (as he praised Flintoff and Kallis), as top all-rounders.

Sure Chris Gayle is not a genuine spinner, skill-wise, but chess-wise, in a ODI context he is more than an average fifth bowler. The West Indians can *dot chess* an ODI game with Bravo, Gayle, Samuels and the rest (they love to bowl first, and exploit the dot dilemma). So perhaps not by the standards of Gary Sobers, but from the purpose of a role, more like a chess piece, Chris Gayle is a tricky ODI bowler.

But the whole point is that eventually we need to address the format, every time players catch up with finding 'set' patterns to score points besides pure skills. After all we do not go to watch chess pieces but to see some passion and skill being unleashed. It is the format, which can impose a variety, and define scoring patterns in such a manner, that various skills are tested—and keeps the skill and 'chess' in balance.

14. Deriving Ideas from Tennis as well

14.1 Tennis analogy to sessions and matches of cricket

Tennis has an interesting format as a 'point' based game, since the accumulation of points is multi-tiered, with *sets* and then many *service-games* within each set. The advantage of such a format, from a point of view as a metaphor for other sports, is that one entire tennis match can be treated as a 'series' or 'tournament' in another sport—such as say cricket—with each set of tennis corresponding to one cricket match. This metaphor works since every set begins at 0-0 and so does every match in cricket. Within the context of each tennis set, there will be multiple games. So a tennis game can roughly be used to correspond to phases or sessions in cricket. Just as winning a game in tennis moves you ahead in a set, so does winning a session in cricket for instance (in ODI, you can see it in phases of say 10 overs per 'phase').

The only thing to remember, is that there is a limitation of this metaphor, as with any metaphor, since after all, tennis and another sport down to the details are different. In tennis, every game will result in a score, even if it goes into multiple deuces, since a game has to be played till either player wins it. However, in a broad context you can say that a session of cricket or say a quarter of basketball were nearly even, since it is a broad metaphor as such. Likewise, a 'session' can be so one-sided in say cricket, where many wickets fall for too few runs or if so many runs were scored quickly, that it would be like that session was more eventful than just one game of tennis and you can compare that session to multiple games with many 'points' scored, not just who won that session.

Another issue, is that serves alternate in tennis, but execution advantage in cricket need not alternate. There are some format based advantage for bowlers (new ball) and batsmen (power play; old ball in test cricket after 50 overs) and there are open phases where both sides do not have much advantage from the format as such.

As we will see, tennis is a good analogy to illustrate 'a match' and 'a series of matches' of another sport. You can use something like golf to illustrate well, but the problem with golf, as a metaphor for cricket, is that it is more of an *initiate and control* sport (*Ch 3.1, p42*), like playing by yourself– so a golf metaphor has to be used even more 'broadly'.

So here is what we can derive from a tennis metaphor:

1. Each session or phase of cricket can be seen as a tennis game– just that a session can be 'drawn' (ended at a deuce) or more 'points' can come out of it (eventful enough to be seen as multiple games).

2. When the opposing team has an execution advantage (new ball, wet conditions etc, or from a bowling context– batsmen have flat pitches..), and you 'win' that session, you can say you gave a 'break of serve', or multiple breaks of serve, if you got wickets in a bunch or smacked so many that the strike rate was propped substantially. However, if your performance was just about 'par', you can say that you 'denied them' since to be even, on their advantage is worth that much.

3. When you have an execution advantage in certain phases over the opposition then you are sort of 'holding on' to that phase, like you would 'hold serve' in tennis. Such phases are typical in test cricket, for batsmen between 50-80 overs, where bowlers are tired and ball is old, or in ODI when 5th bowler is operating (due to format, it is mandatory that 10 overs will be by weaker bowler(s)) and in power play overs.

All these expressions are a metaphor and must be used in a broad sense. But they are helpful, as often chess can be too complex for quick analysis, especially to assess advantages or disadvantages during play, rather than in planning or post match review.

So how does it apply to a 'series' in another sport? Well if you play a test series or an ODI series of 5 matches, your objective would be to try to win 3-0 or 3-1, as you would tennis. In context of a match, you should try to be sharp so that you do 'keep' deriving value from your advantages (hold serve) and find ways to break (deny or beat the opponent's advantage areas), at least once, if not more. If you can break your opponent once or twice and hold your serves tennis, you would win that set. So by doing your own bit well and sneaking or out-competing your opponent in their area, is a way to win for sure.

The lesson is that you never need try to win the set with crazy margins like 6-0 (if you do, incidentally, that is fine), and neither should you be indifferent and let matches 'drift' into tie-breaks, unless you are having a terrible day at the office or a very superior opponent, trying to hang-in is risky. As we will see in the match winner section, it is always best to overcome indifference and avoid uncertainties of tie-breaks. Also, winning 6-0 in one set does not give you the advantage of the differential in the next set, as it all starts from 0-0 again. So if you have a few tricks up you sleeve, it would be better to unleash them over three sets with a break or two in each set, rather than one set in record breaking fashion and lose the others even though you go down 'fighting' till the tie-breaks become like a lottery ticket dangling on a seesaw.

As you can see our tennis analogy of a 'set' as a cricket match, and the 'sets as a collection' like a series, works well in explaining how one must compete. Winning is about trying to avoid indifference (which lets a match drift into unpredictable phases) and also about not going crazy for some single-handed frenzy, which will win a set but never assure three or four well earned sets.

14.2 Execution Precedence over Match State

Another important lesson to learn from tennis, is that each game grants an execution advantage to the server. When you lead a tennis set say 5 games to 3, then it could be that you won 4 games on your serve and broke 1 game. This is a very nice way to explain to yourself or to others, who say that 'points are points' or 'runs are runs' no matter how they come—as when the total is done, you just add runs whenever and however. Sure the set score indicates 5 games won by virtue of 'addition', but ask any tennis player, they would easily say that a break well-earned was worth more than the other 4 held-games (which are also important, since you need to hold on to the advantage). So in sports which are *initiate-react* type (*Ch3.4, p44*), as in tennis, cricket and most team sports, the scores– runs, goals, sets are always in context of the quality of opposition. In such sports a 'score' can never be taken as an absolute measure (as we all know, but ignore). Tennis set scores almost always illustrate this fact very well, since everyone knows that breaking a serve to add a point to the games tally, is different from winning your own serve and adding to the tally, although it is by the same amount.

Another point to appreciate in tennis is that even if you are down 1-4 in a set, when it is your serve, it is up to you to not 'feel' the pressure, as the execution advantage is yours for that short span of a game. Sure, your opponent might have a chance to, say, attack your second serve or try some more volleys or winners being ahead, yet you can back yourself to win a service game, since what really happens on the court is how things are executed or can be executed. Since the service (execution) advantage is yours, you can focus on that, rather than the match score. On the other hand, your opponent can translate the 'lead' and 'pressure' into something that relates to tangible issues, as mentioned, by receiving the serve a bit more pro-actively.

The whole point is that execution advantage on account of format, will usually take precedence over other issues of score (as in serving at 1-4). Likewise, being ahead in the score (by a break or two), or even a set or two, can be translated to some execution adjustment, even if the basic execution advantage is with your opponent. **So the execution advantage due to format and execution effects possible due to match state, are tricky to balance clearly.** But as we can see the equations are about the execution issues—whether latent in the format or derived from match state.

Examples of Execution Issues taking precedence over Match State.

For instance, **Sehwag, in 2005-06,** was scoring 25-30 runs in 10 balls fewer. Since he opened the batting and played the top two new-ball bowlers of the other team, you can say he was 'giving a break' of serve. Sure India would like to see him bat along, but the fans could not bear it, that he was not 'converting'. Needless, to say, he could have done better, but his 'cameos' were not failures, but breaks of serve. It helped in flattening the strike rate, and bought more overs for others—to hold their serve. Interestingly, Adam Gilchrist does a similar job for Australia, but Aussie fans (I assume) somehow have a maturity to accept his role, and would take a 35 of 25 from him.

Another example, from **Tendulkar's approach in a test against Australia, in Mumbai, 2005.** In the first and second innings he came on to bat in the 3rd and 5th over, with less than 15 runs on the scoreboard, each time. The execution advantage is with bowlers (new ball) in both cases. Also, the match state (scoreboard) advantage is with bowlers, being 2 wickets down for few runs. However, in the first innings, it was worse, due to gloomy and overcast skies in November (bizarre for Mumbai), with showers stopping play a few times. Tendulkar and Dravid came in to bat a few times, and each time two or three overs were bowled. There were three execution advantages for the bowlers (new ball, wet conditions, frequent interruptions). It was hard work getting out of the first spell. Tendulkar was out playing 'too cautiously' in the 13th over (5 runs with 35 balls).

The second innings—again 5th over; 2 down for few runs— was not unusual for Dravid or Tendulkar. But this time there was no rain. The execution advantage for bowlers, was still there, but was 'usual'. Besides it was now clear that this was a low scoring pitch, in context of spinners not seam bowlers. So he played positively in general, and made a brisk fifty with some trademark lofted shots. The important point is that the in first innings the execution advantage was so highly in favor of bowlers, that it was not prudent to *just* go for shots. This time despite coming into bat at a poor match state, it made sense to attack, as the execution-advantage was much reduced.

This is a clear case that execution constraints should be given priority over match-state. In both innings the scores he came in to bat were similar–few runs; two wickets. To say he should have played his free natural game in the first innings as well, since even then two wickets

fell cheaply, in my opinion– have missed out on giving execution possibilities, a precedence over match-state.

PART III:
APPLICATIONS & CASE STUDY

15. Test Matches are limited over games!

15.1 110-170 Overs per innings!

Limited Overs Test Match !?! I am not recommending a new variant of classic test cricket. Rather, we need to recognize that test cricket is also a limited overs version of the game. There used to be timeless tests, a few generations ago, but since 5 day Tests have been standard with mandatory 90 overs each a day, we know the upper limit is somewhere close to 450 overs, if the match goes all the way. Although, each innings will not last an equal number of overs, the average innings can be considered about 110 overs (if four innings were to be played out). So about 100-120 overs are a minimum overs a team must target to play, if it wishes to last through a test match. And if you intend on winning or making the most of an innings, you are perhaps targeting about 150-170 overs.

So a test side must prepare to bat out anywhere between 110-170 overs, or else it would almost be like being bowled out without batting your 'quota' of overs, as in ODIs (although there is as such no stipulated overs in tests, but this is an approximate range for sure). There will be exceptions as in declarations in the second innings etc. But put this range of overs, in context of one day cricket era (or twenty20), it truly seems like a marathon!

Now let's see the key phases in the range of overs. Obviously, the first 12-14 overs are the new ball overs, where the best two fast bowlers are operating in tandem. Till 25 overs, the bowling team would most likely be in their first spells. Between overs 25-50 will be the second spell cycle (not in exact order but roughly since most teams have 4 top bowlers), where bowlers and batsmen will have to battle it out for wickets and runs as well, in a balanced way. Thereafter from overs 50-80, bowlers will be in their third spells– it is time for batsmen to enhance their strike rates and take advantage of an old ball and tiring bowlers. Then from 80-95 overs, the second new ball is available– perhaps not as potent as the first spells, but this is a chance for bowlers to revive their chances of picking up a couple of wickets. I guess this is kind of common knowledge to most of us who watch cricket.

Now if you see the crucial phases, where bowlers have an execution advantage- overs 1-14 and overs 80-95 are important. Every new ball bowler would wish to take at least one or two wickets in the 6-7 overs fast bowlers normally bowl in a spell. So each of these phases, can account for 2-3 wickets, considering obviously the pitch type and bowlers etc. So if you really intend to play 110 overs (to survive your test 'quota'). It is clear that you need 'recognized' batsmen when you enter the second new ball phase. And from a run rate point of view, you need to keep a wicket or two for the overs from the 50-80th over, to exploit the old ball. Since most sides have 6 recognized batsmen (give or take an all-rounder), it implies that when you enter the 50th over, as a batting team- you should ideally, not have lost more than 2 wickets– the runs could be at 2.5-3 per over (or even a less, but wickets are crucial). After 50 overs, if a team is say 125 for 2- does sound fair. But I can bet, that if you met the most ardent fans, it will surprise them, that you need to play almost the quota of limited overs cricket (ODI), for just two wickets!

15.2 50 overs for 2 wickets

Now just go back to the tennis analogy, the first 15 overs in a test, the batsmen are trying to prevent the bowlers from getting wickets, and the runs that are scored till 25 overs can be seen as "breaking runs", as bowlers have distinct and certain execution-advantage. From 50-80 overs, you can view batsmen as 'holding on to their serve", since it is their point of execution-advantage.

The days of Boycott and Gasvaskar as 'defensive' batsmen are far from gone. To be under 2 or 3 wickets at the 50 over mark, you need an opening pair to shut the possibility of a slide, in the first 12 overs. This is still a legitimate way to go about business. No great team ever succeeded without a stable opening pair, if not a world-class pair. India, although it has had the good fortune of a Gavaskar (and some sincere partners for short periods, like Chetan Chauhan and Anshuman Gaekwad), has not produced a stable pair since 30 years. Note: Sehwag deserves to be the top member of the Indian side, but he is not the one to think of 2 wickets at over 50! Unfortunately, the masses expect his trademark 170 plus and the pitch conditions often dictate playing out the first spells.

In fact, his opening knock in South Africa 2006-07, in the first innings of the Jo'burg test which India won, was not a total 'flop' as the media made it out to be. He made 4 of 26 balls. Rather he made 4 runs and played 26 balls! (Both Sehwag and Jaffer failed to score runs, but they got out around the 11th over. In the corresponding overs, South Africa lost 5 wickets and were all out in 25 overs, due to some exceptional bowling from Shreeshant and Zaheer Khan.

Yet, in India, we have a media which goes bonkers, when a tail-ender scores more than top order batsmen. If this bowler could make 20, why could not our legendary top order? But I have yet to see a placard demanding that India needs specialist opening batsmen to open the innings.

Tendulkar and Younis Khan have addressed this role in South Africa 2006-07 very well, with complete understanding that it will be possible for at least two or three of the remaining batsmen to 'hold on to their serve' after 40-50 overs. **Bizarre as it may sound, most of us look at the fall of wickets, in terms of runs, but rarely by over number.** Do this and it will get a little bit clearer, why 'just attacking' is not worth it, when the entire team can get a chance of getting runs 'on our serve', only if two spell cycles of the bowling team are through. To do this anyone who gets in to bat inside 10-14 overs, has to view balls left in that phase, as 'positive dots', and score off the bad balls.

I do not know how frequently the number 4 batsman, bats inside the first spell (12 overs), outside India. Dravid as number 3 does it every alternate time, but he is never expected to score quickly. Tendulkar does it perhaps more often, at number 4, then most others. Besides, modern bowlers exploit the fact that at 10 for 2, you are way short in terms of runs (you should perhaps have at least be 80 runs, refer to the tennis section, where match state can be translated to an execution issue *Ch 14.2, p132*). So mixing up defensive bowling, with in-out fields and few options for wickets is well worth it, rather than the good old days when bowlers would add more slips and try to knock down more wickets (trying to knock 'em in type 1 style, can also cost runs).

In my humble opinion, if India does not fix the opening issue soon, I would recommend that the solution can lie in Tendulkar to open (in tests). Then all the dot nonsense that may be thrown at him, will go waste, as the first 12 overs or till perhaps 25 overs, dot balls are positive for batsmen. Better to come in at 0/0 (at least it is a par score in run-wicket context) than be a middle order opening batsman! This of course is theory, how much age would be a factor we cannot say. But resting after fielding and still being padded to step in any time, can be more annoying than relaxing for sure.

15.3 Balls played by batsmen

In order to bat the (non-stipulated) quota of 110-160 overs, for a batting side to stay well placed in a match, we obviously need to begin to measure batsmen based on the balls played as well. Sure, the scores that matter are runs by batsmen and wickets by bowlers- but as mentioned, critical phases can wipe a team out well within a few dozen overs. Besides, by playing out spell cycles you push bowlers into more fatigue and even frustration, as wickets by nature are sparse. A spell cycle can be approximately 25 overs, since about 4 bowlers may bowl 6 overs each or a few more. Spinners will bowl longer spells but about 25 overs is about the time the other bowlers in the team will be repeated again, even if one or two spinners bowl long spells. After all, if you want to bat 110-160 overs, that can be about 700-1000 balls, and only perhaps 10 bad shots allowed. Players need credit for not getting out.

So to begin with, whenever batsmen play 30-36 balls, the innings cannot be totally useless, since together with a partner, they perhaps plays out about 12 overs, thereby pushing two bowlers out from a spell, and bringing in new bowlers. It sounds a bit far fetched, but it is not that insignificant- as runs are made off bowlers, and changing the context of bowlers by 1/2 spell cycles, does usher in fresh possibilities, because it is rare that all four bowlers bowl at the top of their potential all at once. Sure, runs matter as such, but when a batsman is out of form or just having an off day, if he can play at least 30 balls, it will be amazing to note how often the next batsmen go through with scoring runs very well, as just the bowling context has changed.

Situations when 'balls played' by a batsman will count as positive:

1. During new ball overs 1-12, thereafter, to a lesser degree, during overs 12-25 & 80-95.

2. Just after rain or morning dew, in case certain pitches are good as such but give a chance to bowlers in the morning.

3. When 2 or 3 wickets fall in a span of a few balls, and the bowlers involved will likely bowl more overs in that spell.

4. In the fourth innings, when a team can only draw a match, 'balls played' is the score that matters (batsmen may play defensively or play positively, as suits them, but the result from each batsman which needs to be seen– is the balls played).

Irfan Pathan made 0 of 29 balls in the third test against Pakistan in 2005, in India. He was a bit unlucky to play a good defensive shot onto his shoes and was caught in front. India did not lose the match by 168 runs, but by about 5 overs. This is an aberration in cricket—if you do have a concept of a draw—then a team which got out fourth, will lose by so many runs (losing the win) but they lost-the-draw by so many overs. However, the team which won did so by so many runs!

5. Skewed bowling attacks- where essentially one or two bowlers are key wicket taking bowlers- as in the case of Muralitharan for Sri Lanka. In ODIs, batting teams are often content not to give him wickets, than go for more than 2.5-3 an over. Balls played against Murali, in that case matter, but it may be a bit too complex to justify that from the point of displaying stats on TV. But the fact is that, the player who played out many Murali overs, does great service to the team, as we all know what he can do if the door is not properly shut (Australia 2003

World Cup semi-finals, their batting fell apart but they made sure Murali did not get a wicket. Andrew Symonds just played the innings of a life time).

Although, this is clear in ODIs as there is a maximum of 10 overs per bowler, this somewhat applies in Tests as well (both are limited overs games!), since a bowler cannot physically bowl 10-15 overs at a stretch without drop in performance. India exploited Murali on this count, by playing his overs, and attacking later in the innings and also sending Pathan to attack the pace bowlers, by opening (vs Sri Lanka, 2nd Test 2005).

15.4 Assessing the efforts as runs and wickets

As mentioned, in a Test match, about a minimum of 110 overs have to be played by a batting side to exhaust the span of 5 days. Obviously, this is a broad average range. Teams do get all out for 70-90 overs and still win, but then in those cases, there would be a lot of time left in the match, even after four innings.

So the phases which were tough for batsmen and bowlers, needs to be given due credit. How do we do it? I guess we can see when a dot ball is positive for a batsman and when it is positive for a bowler, and the phase where it is has neutral value.

Besides dot balls, there are other key elements such as partnerships and breaking partnerships, etc. **But how do we value such indirect contributions?** A brief explanation, with comparisons to chess, is attached in the Appendix (*Towards a formal assessment system, p274*).

16. The Great Dot Dilemma

16.1 The Dot State

Cricket is a game played around dot balls. As we have discussed, dot balls are not something to be ignored in any form of observation—but for appreciation or for assessment. From an execution standpoint, a dot ball is a buffer for both bowler and batsman to express and react to some sort of uncertainty or intent. Dot balls which are 'well left' are different from dot balls which are played defensively, which are different from those which beat the batsmen, and further different from the ones which were well played but to a fielder. So from the execution sense, there is already enough interesting things happening, even if no run or wicket went down.

However, from the match-state standpoint, the dot ball has a relevance too. As we saw, in test cricket, from a batting angle, dot balls are positive during new ball phases- since bowlers are letting go their advantage. Likewise, from overs 50-80, dot balls are kind of positive for bowlers, since this is a phase where the batting side can look to score off an old ball and tired bowlers.

What about ODIs? Obviously, dot balls are by and large positive for bowlers. A maiden over in an ODI, definitely props the bowling side.

About 5-6 quiet overs, even if wickets do not seem to be falling will have a great impact as that represents 10% of the overs, and can affect the strike rate significantly. Wickets are important in any form of cricket, since that is the best way to alter the resources that come into play. However, what if a bowling team were to only bowl dot balls? This is practically not possible, but if they can to some extent- it will be well worth it, as the final result which matters is runs and overs left. Wickets are needed to get you to tilt the runs/overs balance, and teams who cannot bowl out oppositions (from a test match ability) can still win an ODI, as long as the runs-overs equation is met with. Sri Lanka, who dominated One day cricket in the late '90s, struggled to bowl test sides out, until Muralitharan became prominent.

16.2 Dot Undefined

Let's look a bit closer at the ODI situation. In the first innings, a side which is batting has to set a decent target, which looks compelling on that pitch. They cannot be over-ambitious, as doing so they can lose wickets so quickly, that the team can fall apart like it often happens while chasing big totals. They cannot be too cautious, as there is no point intending to set even a slightly moderate target. The basic mantra is to play constructively, maintaining a decent run rate, by ticking away and picking the balls to be hit.. and keeping wickets.... and accelerating when the end approaches. Wait a bit... let's just see the method of maintaining a decent run rate—ticking and picking— it implies a 'steady rate' and rightly so. Essentially, you can have some dot balls, apart from many singles, twos and some fours & sixes. No problem with that, as it has always been like that. But as a first innings batting team, how many dot balls can you afford? what is the ratio of dot balls to scoring shots (since you do not know the target, you will take any scoring shots that come your way- be it singles or boundaries, to keep it ticking).

But in the first innings of an ODI, you do not know how many dots to wait for, before a bowler makes an error. So if a bowling team came up with a plan to bowl dot balls, and succeeded in doing so for even a few overs– a constructive batting approach is throttled for sure, as unlike a Test match, batsmen cannot wait more than couple of overs, or perhaps even 7-8 balls, without scoring.

This dot bowling will obviously be useful in the 2nd innings bowling of an ODI as well—dot balls are always good in ODIs. However, **2nd innings ODI dot balls are potent but are not a dilemma, as now the target is clear to the batsmen**–so they know how many dots they can wait and even if they wait for more dots than needed, they know how much is lost out, to be made up in last 15 overs or so, because they need not try to make any more than the target. So the rate of constructiveness is very clear indeed. In case the total is huge, batsmen will have to go for it pretty much from an early stage, no matter how the bowlers try to dabble around.

So in the first innings of an ODI, there exists are a Great Dot Dilemma, on account of not knowing the target, yet wanting to set an above par target (no one likes to set average or indifferent targets). And if the team is in a phase where wickets do matter, this dot dilemma is greater indeed. As a result, such dot balls cannot be easily given a value till at least 30-40 overs or so (strike rate & wickets matter till 40 overs, then the strike rate matters more and wickets less). So if bowlers can just address the strike rate issue with certainty and in particular string in dot balls, even without intent of taking wickets, it will pay strong dividends because wickets will fall indirectly (as batsmen cannot wait too long or rather do not know how long to wait!).

Which bowlers can exploit the Dot Dilemma? So this dot dilemma stuff sounds great in theory, right? Sure, it is always easy writing a book than bowling on flat tracks around the world!

But it sounds like you need Ambrose and Joel Garner who might be the only ones who can implement this theory, as they could bowl dot balls at will. Sure, they would be great to have around, but here comes Modern Cricket for you- this can be done by most good consistent bowlers and it has been done for sure, by most teams. In fact, Sachin Tendulkar is getting better at it as a bowler, in this regard, as he has been on the receiving end of such theories since the past 6-7 years. So why does it work, with bowlers who are just 'good' or part-time?

Again, let's look at the equation– bowlers want to bowl dot balls- but with certainty, and at the cost of perhaps not bothering about the wickets. Sounds risky for bowlers, because if the dot stuff fails, then it is not fun if wickets are intact as well. The secret is that if you are not uptight about taking wickets, then you can bowl with better focus on the dot ball (usually type 2/3), as you need not really 'tweak the ball or bend your back'- to bowl special deliveries as such and thereby avoid errors or even give a decent chance for batsmen to score off (no need of type 1 bowling). Obviously, bowlers can sneak in some surprise, now and then, since a failure (four or six, if at all) is no where as costly as a batting mistake.

There surely are different ways to bowl dot balls– with differing skills and plans. We will explore one of the ways of doing it with reasonable skill as a bowler, up next.

But here is something to verify what we are discussing. Australia have been doing it (exploiting this dot dilemma) to teams in the finals of tournaments, consistently since they beat Pakistan in the 1999 World Cup in England. If you observe their wins in the finals, when they bowled first, it has been weird, that on perfectly nice batting tracks, they have held teams for about 150, when bowling first. The interesting thing is that there were no (or few) knock out deliveries or special ploys to get batsmen out. Yet they did it to Pakistan; England & India in Australia, a few years back; and recently to West Indies in the Champions trophy 2006 in India. Most of us feel that batsmen gave it away- but it cannot happen so regularly. They did exploit the dot dilemma, and batsmen had to try something ever so often, usually getting little reward, and worst- they got out.

So is the Dot Dilemma an ODI phenomenon?

Yes, mainly so, and in the first innings, as mentioned, due to the unknown target– which needs to be good and the fact that bowlers need not really get them all out (they can wait with more dividends, but overs dry up for batsmen). However, it happens in tests as well, in certain stages. In tests, if after an innings from each side is over, and both have played quite well (almost no lead), then it might happen, that with about two days left and one innings each to go, it essentially is a two day match with one innings each—so sort of a limited overs match, just that it is of 90 overs each—if you intend to make a match out if it. This dot dilemma, now lurks on the side batting third in the test, as it is like the first innings of an limited overs match– since they do not know the exact target of declaration, yet need to speed up a bit. (see Capetown = Adelaide boomerang! *Ch 21.17, p214*). It can also happen in the first innings of the side batting second, since they are not sure of the target they may want to lead by as a first innings margin, and there is some need to score at some decent rate, (to get closer to a decent target). In the first innings of a test, it is perhaps least likely, even though you do not know the target, you need not raise the strike rate either.

To sum up the Great Dot Dilemma: If a batting side does not know the target, and has to show some intent on improving/keeping up the scoring rate, there will be a dot dilemma due to not being able to value the dot ball. Further, if the wickets, aspect is also delicately poised or matters on account of overs left to be played, this dot dilemma is great indeed.

Case Study, Jacques Kallis: An example of exploiting the Dot Dilemma and how to handle it. **South Africa vs India ODIs 2005.**

Here is an example of how Jacques Kallis was targeted in the ODI series in India, 2005. There were two ODIs which South Africa won, in good fast bowling conditions. In such matches, direct wicket taking option is the best way to go (type 1).

There were two other ODIs, one **in Bangalore and another in Mumbai,** which were like Indian tracks. Now South Africa have a decent batting line up, but they had few players with experience in India. So Kallis, who is the best batsmen on their side, now was perhaps the one who 'must' play. Imbalance in team composition? Exploit it. India just did that.

South Africa batted first in both matches mentioned. So the fact that Kallis 'must' play and the Dot Dilemma is 'on', was the key to India's execution plan. In the Bangalore match, they just bowled short and wide, without slips! Kallis was out trying to square cut. He could have glided the ball through the slips, but that is not how Kallis bats and not how a player who '*must bat today*', can bat. Taking out the slips, released a few fielders perhaps to save singles and sweep the only shot he could play in orthodox fashion- the square cut (pulling from outside off on Indian pitches is perhaps risky, as the ball stops a bit. And if he *must* play he cannot take risks early on).

The **next match in Mumbai,** South Africa batted first again. It was the same story by India. They did the same dot bowling outside off, inviting Kallis to nudge around, if he wanted to score. You could see the pressure—he must play, and this is a must win match—he cannot give it away. So Kallis played with grit and waited more than perhaps an ODI format allows (91 off 146 balls). Eventually, he was criticized as South Africa made only 222, which India chased. However, this was perhaps the only solution for Kallis to overcome the dilemma—of not knowing how much he could wait, in the first innings—was by not doing anything risky.

However, this was type 2-3, *one shot bowling* by India, where they relinquished their chances of getting Kallis out, but took away his constructive options as well.

So what is this one shot bowling? Read on.

17. One Shot Bowling

17.1 It is not so special!

As explained, the dot dilemma in first innings ODIs and perhaps 3rd innings of test matches, where the match is within balance but the target is unclear and yet run rate is to be kept up, leads to undecided dot ball value. At this stage, if bowlers let go the direct capture of wickets, and bowl dots with certainty, they have a great way to exploit this dilemma, as batsmen cannot wait (and do not know how much they can wait), neither is it prudent to just smack around. The modern way to go about it, is to bowl consistent and solid, without trying to get fancy or try special deliveries (bowling type 2/3).

17.2 but yet batsmen cannot just score...

But why would batsmen not score if bowling is less than special?

I call it **One Shot Bowling- where the reply possible is almost restricted to a particular shot or a restricted class of shots.** Such bowling, need not be special, but done with a planned line, length, and specific class of deliveries, with fielders set only for that type of ball, in full knowledge that the bowler will be accurate (since he is not experimenting with variety), and can be consistent (since he initiates action) and in case of occasional errors, it would be few runs and in worst cases a four/six. But for batsmen there are essentially 9 fielders placed for just that shot. It is a case where the whole is greater than the sum of parts, since every possible reply to these balls is covered– perhaps the lucky edges at times, and also the chance of losing his wicket in case of a failed defensive shot. Typically such bowling can be type 2 or 3.

One shot bowling still needs skill, but it is the quality of bowling not the speciality of balls that matters. Great strike bowlers of the past surely would not settle for an indifferent quality of balls bowled, and perhaps did not explore those options. They obviously could bowl dot balls but ever so often they would try to knock a batsman over with a good wicket taking ball, maybe twice or thrice an over (type 1-2). But on flatter tracks, batsmen usually score off these wicket taking balls as they are always bowled in and around them, and with attacking fields to catch errors. In One Shot bowling, even a good shot gets fielded (rather, 'the' good shot, as this is one shot bowling).

17.3 even if it is predictable

But then why don't batsmen improvise, since this is predictable...

Sure, it is predictable and yet every orthodox reply by the batsmen will be covered. And with fielding standards (in terms of athletic and acrobatic ability) improving, it is just a bit more difficult. Even getting a single will take some effort, if you play the proper shot for that type of ball. **So improvising with a great element of risk is one of the ways to go. And this is what bowlers want in the first place, to take the constructiveness out of batting,** This means that batting as an art of run accumulation, is now a run sneaking craft! Batsmen do know it is predictable, (but minor variations in speed or wobble are tricky), but if they in turn do something pre-determined the bowler can change the ball before release and perhaps target the stumps (if batsman gives room).

Options for the batsmen, when facing one shot bowling:

1. Trying big shots (if the kind of ball permits it) and risk getting caught if it is not a six.

2. Play unorthodox shots (as did Sir Don Bradman in the bodyline series- which is an example of one shot bowling, though allowing perhaps a wider class of shots, but covering them by packing most fielders on the leg side).

3. Alternatively the batsman can play the waiting game,

3a. till that bowler finishes the spell (if it is from a certain bowler such as Sir Alec Bedser to Don Bradman, incoming balls with a heavy leg-side field. (This was much after bodyline series). After getting out a couple of times, Bradman decided to see him off by padding or just blocking. Sounds mortal, but perfectly sound, if time is indeed on your side. Tendulkar has adopted this route, with mixed success- which is normal for such bowling).

3b. wait, since bowlers are not as perfect as may be needed. So wait and let them do this dot stuff, even when the run rate needs to be tracked. Keep wickets in hand and pick up whatever comes your way. Then bowlers might rue the fact that they let the batsmen off.

17.4 The chances for the bowler during one shot...

All this may sound like theory without practical basis. Not.

When we talk of the batting average of the best batsmen ever (except Sir Don), the numbers are around 50-60 runs/innings. This means that batsmen actually make a significant mistake every 50 runs or so (batting average is not about runs but about how often you make a mistake which gets you out, like a break in snooker is different from the total score in a frame, just that in snooker you do not get out). However, these 50 runs are usually scored with sound technique or at least a meaningful method, where runs were accumulated step by step (as in singles, and some orthodox boundaries). Even in cases of total attacking batsmen, such Adam Gilchrist, who likes to go for the big shots, the shots will still be well chosen shots, apt for the kind of ball, with quick footwork and timing etc.

So if a bowler were to force a batsman to play unorthodox shots only, taking out the frequency of singles and orthodox boundaries, you can see that a batsman would perhaps average much less than half, since the constructive component of the 'average' is all but gone. Besides, due to non-commutativity of good and bad *(Ch 4.2, p50)*, you could be gone very early indeed.

When can you bowl One Shot?

a. One shot bowling when dot dilemma is lurking– you can do this to any team or player.

b. One shot bowling in general- can be very useful but by targeting key players of the side, as giving away 20-30 slow and streaky runs might be worth a try. This is especially useful when teams rely more on key players such as Tendulkar, Lara, Inzamam (these teams have other big names, but those players favor a specific style of playing no matter what. With the dot dilemma, however those other batsman can be targeted as well, because of the run rate imperative). In general, it is not easy to do this to teams like Australia, where every batsman is above par, by world standards and with versatile skills– strike rotation and fair repertoire of few big shots. Giving away 30 odd runs perhaps slowly, is not fun, say to Ponting for instance, as every other bloke (Hayden, Hussey, till their wicket-keeper) is capable of brisk scoring. It is indeed tough to give anyone a single in the Australian line-up (one of the ways one shot bowling can be setup- is to give singles, and restrict fours, thereby deflecting the key player to the non-striker). Neither will it be fun, for instance to give Sir Viv Richards a single, and bowl to Clive Llyod or Greenidge/Haynes.

17.5 Light Gray Options for Batsmen

Solution to One Shot? Modern Cricket has a modern approach. Well, how about playing 'bad' shots– which look ungainly from the context of past eras, but are invaluable today. These are shots which rely on 'enough' bat or different areas of the bat which were never considered 'sweet', to get over infields. Risky shots but into safer gaps. It is not fun, but the best way to beat 9 fielders set for a particular ball would be to find a way to land into the gaps (apart from shots which go all the way for six). It sounds a bit unconvincing for sure. But today, you can drive short balls for six (using the upper part of the bat), pull wider balls with the toe end, and many other brute ways to go over fielders. It is not a solution, but one of the unorthodox ways to beat the dilemma, by striking and sneaking runs. Perhaps apt for bowling which is intended to take the constructiveness out from batsmen.

18. Draws in ODIs & Twenty20s?

18.1 Solving the dot exploitation

Since dot balls are extremely positive for bowlers in limited overs games, it encourages bowlers to explore the dot options often deeper in favor of wickets. This obviously refers to ODI and twenty20 formats (assuming that we ignore test matches, as a limited overs format of 100-160 overs per innings, for the time being. Later we can see, that to some extent what happens in ODIs can be used in tests, and vice-versa– perhaps at different tempos).

So bowling is likely to be passive towards direct wicket taking skills as compared to test matches (less of type 1 bowling). Further, with the Great Dot Dilemma in the first innings, this dot exploration can lead to exploitation, as superb dot bowling will result in wickets as well, on account of shot fabrication to overcome waiting uncertainty.

In my view, if the quality of ODI bowling drifts—as is happening—towards just focusing on the dots, it is going to have a different impact on the first innings and the second. **Further, since dot bowling will be usually in conjunction with reducing orthodox options, we are in for big hitting, as the only way out of dots. The results can be low scoring games or extremely big run plundering.**

In my view, this can be addressed by taking inspiration from test cricket. **Introduce the concept of a 'draw' in limited over formats, to ensure that only when a side is significantly better, they deserve to win.** But what would be defined as significantly better?

18.2 Wickets in ODI and Twenty20

Well it may well be worth to explore the wickets, side of the story in ODIs or twenty20. Essentially, the game is still the same, but for a team to 'win', it must take a minimum of a certain number of wickets. I know, this is not a popular option, as people want to see a win. However, winning and demonstrating the best skills in both departments would be worthy of a a true win.

For instance, if we have a clause that a team must take at least 3 or 4 wickets in an ODI (and perhaps 2 in twenty20), to count as winners, it might re-vitalize wicket taking patterns, and without making the game being taken for granted by batsmen—as just playing to hold 3 wickets is double edged indeed. Giving up a run chase and just focusing on a draw is not easy, when 3 wickets can be lost in a few overs.

So why is this aspect indicative of being significantly better? You can have a side score 400 in an ODI, but if they, as a bowling side, cannot take say 3 wickets, they are only half as good. Besides, wickets as in overcoming the defence will be worth it, either from quality of effort or even the entertainment.

This will prevent batsmen looking like bullies by big shot making, as their own bowlers then have to take wickets not just dot around. Likewise, bowling which gets away by sneaking dots here and there, especially in the first innings, will not be 'conclusive' if it could not take 3 wickets.

Also, this will make a series more interesting, as a hard fought draw in between will make the chances of a series being alive longer, and the winner will have to earn runs and wickets both, not just runs or dots. Then there is a great future for 'merit' based batsmen such as Rahul Dravid or Jacques Kallis, just as there will be hope for classical spin bowling, to really flourish with flight.

Such a concept is perhaps not admissible on account of spectator interest in the sport, which demands a result. However, a result is not just a win or loss—on runs alone— but how qualitative the wicket taking was as well. In tests, since draws exist, it forces bowlers to work their (type 1) skills to get 20 wickets, as the batting aspect alone cannot do the trick.

Even if a draw is not conceivable in ODIs or twenty20, they can use this fact of minimum wickets needed, as a way to credit points in a league table. I chose 3 wickets in ODI because it perhaps is a fair test for bowlers and cannot be misused as an easy escape path for batsmen either. Remember, that we had arrived at the fact that if a team is about 2 wickets down at the 50 over mark (*Ch 15.2, p140*), they are doing fine in a test context. So perhaps 3 wickets in 50 overs is what bowlers must be good enough to produce. If not, what good is it to make 400 runs and not have minimal capacity to take wickets.

Such a wicket clause in ODI or twenty20 can also prevent too many fringe bowlers or 'batsmen who can bowl' to overhaul classical bowlers. It will also keep the wicket taking bowlers going as well, and teams will also need some batsmen who can defend well enough for 25-30 overs, against classical attacking bowling, in event they have to settle for draw. If limited overs cricket is indeed a specific form of cricket, let it be a microcosm of test cricket, if not in many ways, then at least in terms of the basic aspects of batting and bowling.

19. Chess in Shot Production

19.1 Tempo within the context of execution/reaction

Now let's see how we can apply the chess concept of tempo, in cricket. As discussed earlier, gaining tempo is about achieving a task in fewer steps, not necessarily in terms of less time. In chess, it is about getting ahead in terms of moves. So how do we apply it in cricket?

To understand this, we need to see what aspect of cricket or any other event we are correlating, to chess. For instance, **if we consider the act of playing a shot in cricket as a 'game of chess',** then the parameters involved in that chess game would be judging the ball for line/length, footwork, bat movement, head position and all those finer points which are the key as well as minor parameters involved in achieving the goal. What is the goal when a batsman plays a shot? The goal is to middle the ball and get the timing right, so that the ball goes toward the intended direction. In short, let's treat the entire process of shot making from release of the ball from the bowler's hand till the batsman makes contact (and the follow through), as a game of chess– where each parameter has to combine in such a way, that it meets the target of making good contact with the ball.

And when parameters combine well in such a manner, that the batsman is 'there' to play the shot comfortably, we can say that the batsman has gained 'tempo', in a relative sense to the quality of the ball bowled!

Likewise, if we do the same for the bowler– treat the **act of delivering the ball as a game of chess, so that it is intended to beat the bat and threaten to crash into the stumps,** then the target can be seen as eventually getting an edge or getting through into the stumps. A ball which threatens to achieve such a target, by making the batsman not being 'there' when the ball is, would be seen as 'gaining tempo'.

So for the batsman, the 'steps' would be, say for instance, (based on my limited knowledge of the game) to judge the line & length, move your feet accordingly, getting your bat along the line, and then timing it with readiness for adjustments, in case the ball deviates after pitching. For the bowler the effort which goes into the 'steps' would happen before release, by ensuring the right line, length, flight/swing and the activity 'on' the ball is as intended.

Anyway, whatever the steps may be—perhaps different for advanced players—the concept of gaining tempo can now be understood as either side combining their 'steps' in such a manner, that they *gain tempo*, in relation to the combination of steps by the other.

A bowler can gain tempo by producing a delivery which finishes its 'steps' of release, flight, pitching and deviating – ahead of the batsman's sequence of steps of judging, footwork, and fine-tuning bat movement to make good contact.

An interesting implication of gaining tempo to get ahead in the steps, is that as a bowler you can make subtle variations, you can make the batsman 'lag' behind on one of the steps. For instance, a spinner can by subtle drift or dips in flight, make the step of judging the eventual landing spot of the ball difficult. This would then be gaining tempo as the batsman is stuck on this step, although the ball may take an eternity in the air (Bedi?). Or take the instance of modern day bowlers sending down many balls with a scrambled seam, needing the batsman to defer their last step of bat movement, even when they judged the length and had perfect footwork. So by disguising various parameters and subtle variations to be ahead of the 'steps' in a relative sense, is key to the bowler– and is also the reason speed is not everything for a fast bowler, as tempo can be gained in a relative manner.

Glenn McGrath is the best modern day example, of just getting ahead of the 'steps' by bowling with subtle changes in angle (but with similar line/length) and activity on the ball (usually seam movement, both ways, and at times a bit of swing) in such a manner that his in-between speed actually gives time for the batsman to read the ball, and often read it 'just' out of synch. One of the other things about McGrath is that on bouncy Australian wickets also, he somehow manages to keep the ball around the height of the stumps or just above- forcing the batsman to play in the corridor of 'height' uncertainty.

All this does not mean that speed is not necessary, as you can use speed to beat the 'steps' by bowling accurately and using good seam position or whatever other activity. It is like making the right moves in chess to gain tempo, and also playing quickly—in actual time—to push the opponent into double trouble. But when you do see that the fastest bowlers are not getting as many wickets, it is perhaps, that they are not gaining in tempo in terms of steps, as being just fast and predictable will be countered by good batsmen with a quick and clear mind.

I remember Sunny Gavaskar, once said that he regarded Andy Roberts very highly as he could manage to squeeze in something extra at any time of the day. This is perhaps not a statement indicating sheer speed, but about how Roberts can gain tempo by subtle variations from what looks like just another good ball (his run up could be misleading indeed as it did not give any clue of his intentions either).

Now let's see how some batsmen gain tempo.

19.2 Sachin Tendulkar & Brian Lara

It is very silly indeed for most of us (the fans) to debate as to who is better, as you can show various departments where each is a master and the tricky thing is that in every other manner, they are both world-class. Rather it makes more sense to see how they approach their batting differently, and why they are best at what they do.

First, let us see what a batsman is trying to achieve defensively. Obviously, if the ball is clearly not heading into the stumps, on account of width or height, the batsman can leave the ball, instead of playing at the ball defensively. But if it it is headed into and just around the stumps, a batsman would have to reply with the bat (unless pitched outside leg). Obviously good batsman, understand this difference– as the stumps are the 'king' when you treat the act of shot-making as a game of chess.

How does Sachin Tendulkar gain tempo?

Most good batsmen are good because they can accomplish the earlier mentioned steps (in a broad sense) with surety and brevity. Tendulkar is compact and a quick judge of the length, so he gets into the a defensive position very quickly. But then he uses different bat movements (wristy, straight, jabs, short-arm horizontal shots, etc.) where he is very creative indeed. This means that he is amongst the best in playing scoring shots off compelling deliveries, as he is quickly into a comfortable defensive position and then 'adds' a component of flair. When the ball is not headed into the stumps, he gains tempo by staying inside or outside the line and also meets the ball at in-between points (after pitching) at various 'gap latitudes'. In short, **while playing shots which are supposed to be error free, Tendulkar excels in adding a scoring component, due to tempo gain through compactness and positioning,** followed by creative bat movement. An advantage of this approach is that you can be in good defensive positions in case the ball is doing something unexpected.

How does Lara gain tempo?

Now here is an example of a truly advanced player. Many pundits point out that he moves too much (swaying movement, often shuffling), has a very high back-lift, and the manner he brings the bat down is perhaps too vicious. That makes three deviations from 'normal' batting, where perhaps one must move just enough, use a high back-lift only if deemed necessary (this is a Z-demand discipline, so you can often not compromise the defence), and bring the bat down in a simple and straight manner. **But this is Brian Lara and he is not normal, but advanced.** So let us take note of these points but see why he produces monumental knocks which are perhaps second only to Sir Don Bradman.

Surely, Lara has had his leg-stump knocked over a few times and is likely to nick a ball on the off-stump a bit more often than he would perhaps have liked. But in all this activity, when he plays the shot, he is amazingly very smooth and flowing, if not still. He does offer a drop-dead defensive shot, even after a super back-swing. So at the point of contact with the ball, if he can arrive at what cricket demands from batsman– some sort of stillness or clarity, it really does not matter how much activity happens before that moment (kind of like 9-ball pool players who are not as strict and still as snooker players, but when the cue goes through with the shot, it follows through clean).

Now the plus point of his activity. He uses the activity to actually get the intended good contact on the ball. The activity helps him defend well, as he uses the momentum achieved to make foot movements which are fully back and fully forward. **Initial activity, is Lara's tempo- gaining means, as he can reach where he wants to be, using momentum to cover space and make flawless contact with the ball.**

The next point is about when the ball is not headed into the stumps or it is within reach of his front foot– (and it is some reach!). **Now this is where Lara is ahead of the rest.** Since the ball is not going to get him bowled, he says 'let me just change the axis of the pitch layout'. Kind of like what we did in engineering problems of geometry– moving the origin of the axis to a favorable point, then solve the problem with a new origin (since equations may work better with say the origin at the center of some object), and then shift the axis back to the 'original' origin. Lara does not have to shift anything back after the shot, but what he does is that he literally moves about to greet the ball where he wants it, rather than play a shot to the merit of that ball (even if it can be scored off otherwise, since it is not heading into the stumps).

Brian Lara, controls the axis of merit. You can often see him end up on the '5th off-stump' and playing the ball on the on side. He also loves to attack spinners who turn the ball viciously for similar reasons. **When he does judge that the ball is not hitting the stumps, his initial activity helps him play similar shots to balls pitched in various areas, as he has just moved his point of origin accordingly.** It was interesting to hear Richie Benaud comment on Lara's 11,000th run in test cricket, as the ball was pitched outside off, but the ball being high, he moved further outside, and played it to fine leg, with all his three stumps exposed!

Most top batsmen will make room when the ball is not headed into the stumps. But converting initial activity into moving the very axis of line and length, is an act of Brian Lara. It is gaining not tempo but *tempi*, since he is now ahead in steps, of not just making good contact, but making altogether *another* shot– perhaps one which he would rarely falter on.

Well, all this does not happen when you play the first few overs or a session, but once he is in with 80-100 runs. Moreover, against the quickest bowlers, this may not be possible at all, as 'moving the origin' kind of activity is something that requires a fraction more of time, no matter how much momentum is derived from initial activity. All in all his shot-production, is based on hyper-activity which gets him to defend promptly by virtue of being able to reach and smother the movement. When he plays a scoring shot, he is eliminating chances of errors because of the manner or choice of shot he may be able to execute, due to position achieved by activity (which would have altered the effective line and length of the ball).

So why does Lara have a clinical ability to produce monumental hundreds? After all, most batsmen who have scored a hundred, will usually be defending well and see the ball as a football, as they say. But every batsman can make a mistake on a scoring shot, no matter how well set he is. This is just the nature of cricket, that even if you are defensively still impeccable, hitting a bad shot, to an indifferent ball can happen anytime.

But as mentioned, the point of eliminating errors in scoring shots is the reason Lara does it more often than others (except Bradman). The gaining of tempo and using it to shift himself to play shots he wants, is one of the ways he scores, as most balls are not off target by that much. But now his high back-lift which is perhaps a drawback early on, comes in– he will always be on top of short balls off the backfoot and on the front foot, he has the activity to reach the pitch of the ball and again smother it from an angle which comes down on to the ball. This means that if he middles the ball while playing a scoring shot (which others also perhaps might), any timing error will not result in a catch, as he is always 60° on top of the ball.

Folks, Tendulkar and Lara are the hyper-modern equivalent of chess players (Viv Richards could be from the past eras, and there might be others whom I have no clue about; this is from the modern angle). In chess, a hyper-modern school is one that encourages control of key central squares but without occupying them, as in a classical approach where you try to occupy the square to exercise control. Both of these great cricketers, control line and length aspects by various ways to be in and out and around it (except when the ball is really good, and you have to get in line and behind it). Their methods are different and in fact I would say complimentary.

Batting is a Zero-error demand discipline? Yes, both meet the demand, in their way.

Tendulkar is about adding a scoring component to shots which are required to be error free, whereas to shots which are supposed to be scoring shots, Brian Lara can eiliminate the chance of errors.

(by the way, I have arrived at the above description, by using an abstract system of sports expression—which I have been working on for quite some time—and then worked out details of all what you read on earlier pages, about Tendulkar and Lara).

This means when the ball is into and just around the stumps, Tendulkar scores on account of compactness and variety in bat-work, but on balls which are away and over the stumps or can be prevented from passing you, by footwork, Lara can ensure that the shot is impeccable and productive.

Tendulkar at his best, will be right on the button, scoring briskly without being beaten. Everyone begins with error free shots (defensive), just that Tendulkar adds a finishing touch of scoring flair. He therefore is amongst the best in combination of strike rate and batting average, amongst top ODI batsmen. His brisk scoring with minimal errors also gets him amongst the all time highest number of Test 150s. Tendulkar is about technique flowing into flair (which is why he perhaps gets out to wobbly bowlers—more often the he would wish—as his error free aspect precedes the creative scoring aspect).

Lara at his best, will convert his starts into monumental scores, in clinical fashion. Everyone plays scoring shots, once they are set, but Lara, converts his scoring activity into a flawless production. He therefore is amongst the highest number of 200+ test scores, as his full flowing shots can eliminate errors. Lara is about flair flowing into technique (which is why quick bowlers can get him early on—more often the he would wish—as his error-removal aspect follows the creative positional activity).

Tendulkar follows a snooker approach of exploring many opportunities without making a mistake– and can therefore reply based on others' demand (incidentally snooker has a similarity to the Z-demand of batting). Lara follows more of an English Billiard style of converting activity towards playing in his comfort zone– of playing and repeating shots, his way– almost in auto-pilot mode.

19.3 Releasing Tempo: Ponting and Hayden

When India toured Australia in 2003-04, they did experience pitches which were flat and with typical Australian bounce. Now it is understood in India, that to succeed in Australia, players need to have a good backfoot technique, on account of the bounce.

Amazingly, Ricky Ponting and Matthew Hayden had a different approach. They would come on to the front foot to fuller deliveries (which is normal) and would come to the front foot on short of length deliveries, and only if the ball was pitched way too short, would they play a backfoot shot. And even these were played without trying to back off into the crease. What this means for a bowler is that there was no way to push them back, no matter what. Even if they had to play a backfoot defensive shot, they would be emphatic, not to be dislodged.

It was not until Greg Chappell illustrated on TV, that in Australia, bowlers have to be very accurate in length, that one could figure out what was going on. The margin for bowlers is quite tight– slightly fuller and the ball comes on nicely to be worked away for runs, and slightly short would perhaps make the ball sail over the stumps. So what Ponting and Hayden were doing—coming front in a predetermined way— was to induce bowlers to bowl a bit shorter, which would then not crash into the stumps. So by coming front, and let's say the batsman gets kind of beaten, it can be fine, as long as you do not touch the ball—as it will not get you out lbw nor bowled. It would just be a dot ball, and perhaps look a bit dubious, but the idea was effective.

By not deciding whether to go back or front, the batsmen would simplify their mind. In a normal batting approach, deciding when to go back or front takes up considerable mental focus, and to do it every ball, can lead to an error in judgement, leaving you stranded in between or on the wrong side. By not having to make this decision, you reduce 'one step' and gain tempo! However, if the ball does get the better of you, when you are on the front foot you can 'release the tempo' you have gained, as it will most likely not be headed into the stumps.

However, to pull this theory off, Ponting is perhaps an ideal candidate as he is the best in pulling, off the front foot, and Hayden, during that period, was superb in slogging anything slightly short over mid-wicket. So lunging forward, irrespective of length would result in getting beaten—not getting out— or it would result in loads of runs if you could play big scoring shots which both Ponting and Hayden could. For instance, Adam Gilchrist and Damien Martyn, would go way back to such lengths, to buy time, as a conventional back and across approach– but could open up lbw, by allowing the ball more time to move or hold its line. From the bowler's point of view, the impact of Ponting and Hayden, not willing to budge, was in effect a story of frustration of almost bowling as if the stumps did not exist. You cannot checkmate an opponent who does not have a 'king' (the stumps)!

This whole approach, is like moving a chess piece into some intimidating position, and willing to retreat (batsman getting beaten), since the move was a bit premature—but without any loss—as the opponent is also not making progress towards your own king (ball going over the stumps in this case). You essentially reduce the chances of getting out defensively, if it is missing the stumps. The balls which you might get out, you might be beaten perhaps. This worked effectively indeed, as getting beaten 3 times and playing 2 scoring shots, is better than say playing 5 scoring shots and getting out once. Scoring shots and being beaten can be seen as commutative?! (unlike failures which result in being out; *Ch 4.2, p50*).

20. Chess in Team Roles

Now let's see how some ideas of chess work in cricket as a team game, with players assigned roles. In any sport, where resources (players) come and go (chess, cricket) or get active in certain ways (as in soccer, where a player may be on the pitch all throughout, but is active in different parts of the field), the concept of assigning a role is crucial. This is because resources have to be activated and deployed with a sense of timing, or have to be held back accordingly. To achieve this, the player will have to play a particular role to get the timing of activity as needed and will have to 'fit' into a role which compliments other roles or enhances the overall plan. As I will discuss later, we need better statistical measures to credit roles, as runs and wickets alone do not reflect their value, and yet such roles will create situations from which runs and wickets can happen.

To understand the significance of how roles can be played in a different manner, we can easily see examples from chess, where according to situation and nature of the game– open or closed, different pieces play a different role in terms of activity and purpose.

We are now comparing a 'session' or 'phase' of cricket to a 'game of chess', where the players will be like the pieces and the overall strategy and tactics, will be fulfilled by the roles played. In the previous chapter we compared the 'act of a shot or a delivery' to the aspect of *tempo* in chess (where the parameters related to execution are like the 'pieces'). Now, we are looking at the game it in a broader context, where the players are the resources or the equivalent of chess pieces.

20.1 Don Bradman sacrifices the tail, after counter gambits

Every chess enthusiast is aware and gets excited to see puzzles which involve sacrificing a substantial piece such as a knight, rook or often even the queen, to get various types of advantages. It happens in GM level chess as well, though not as frequently as one might want from the point of spectator excitement. When a player offers only a pawn, in exchange for no material but for a possible later advantage or enabling specific style of play, it is seen as a 'gambit' in chess. Such gambits are common in many openings, and the opponent need not accept the gambit (decline), and therefore deny the advantage that would arise— usually a clear file for activity (pawns get in your way, just as they help in shielding or in creating support for other pieces; at the execution level we can compare this to say a some slog-sweep when the batsman clears his left foot to make way for a shot).

However, what **chess teaches us, is that gambits and sacrifices, if they are sound, you will derive some advantage in return. However, they can often be countered by your opponent with similar sacrifices to nullify the advantage derived.** Another approach is to not accept the initial sacrificial piece at all, and decline it as indicated, if the presence of the piece on that square is not threatening.

Here is an instance which illustrates these chess principles very aptly. In an Ashes match (3rd Test against England, 1936-37), on a wet pitch, where we mentioned earlier that Sir Don Bradman sent his last batsmen to open, there was more chess earlier on as well. He informed his bowlers to defer bowling out the tail (a gambit?) for possibility of batting in drier conditions. Australia had already registered a low score and England was even less. In a low scoring game, where 10-15 runs matter, it is indeed a tough call to consider delaying any chance of knocking out the tail. But Don Bradman did it. Sensing this gambit, England declared as well, to be able to bowl at Australia (a counter-gambit to nullify the advantage). Surely, bowling at Australia in such conditions would be more rewarding than a few runs accrued by the tail.

It did not end there, as Bradman went deeper into chess, and sent his number 10, 11 to open (a sacrifice, since this clearly is loss of getting a good opening partnership, which is of high value in test cricket). Not only that, he also sent in number 9, since O'Reilly was out immediately! (*multiple attempts needed for a theory to work* as an implication of intention and execution uncertainty in cricket, *Ch 2.3, p38*). All these possible advantage gaining moves paid off, as he not only shut critics from commenting on his captaincy, but scored a double century to win the match, and eventually the series 3-2 from being 0-2 down. This is a case of multiple sacrifices, to attain a favorable position—dry batting friendly conditions.

20.2 Jacques Kallis plays the Defensive Queen

In chess, the queen is the most versatile piece, because it is mobile in all directions and also powerful in terms of reach, so long as its path is open (the knight is the only piece which can jump over pieces, an attribute the queen lacks). In cricket, truly speaking only all-rounders should be considered as the equivalent of queens–in context of a match– since they have the ability to make an impact with bat and ball, and in the context of impacting a result, both batting and bowling have to be potent. For this discussion, we can consider the most important or versatile batsman as the queen of the batting line-up, since the the context of analysis is batting (although Jacques Kallis is an all-rounder, this discussion is about the batting aspect).

In the second test against England (2004-05), in South Africa, Kallis played a great knock. England had won the first test, but in this one, they were bundled out for 139 in the first innings. However, South Africa's reply was not positive either as they struggled at 90-5 (considering the positive dots played by Gibbs and Rudolph till the 20th over, they had a fair start at 48-2).

Now here is one of the roles a queen might play in chess. Usually it is normal in chess, to support your important pieces with pawns (or pieces of lesser value). If the opponent attacks your supporting pawn you can in turn support that pawn by another pawn, or allow an exchange, as the opponent's attacking piece cannot be lower than a pawn. However, if you use a higher piece to support one or many of your other pieces, it is tricky, since a threat to the higher piece by a smaller one, will often force you to move off the square (as exchanging would result in loss of value for you). **However, at top levels, GMs will often use the queen as a supporting piece, using its versatile influence of squares in different directions to reach out and support other key pieces or squares.** They however are adept at knowing when they can do it and the queen will not have to move, and additional pieces are also available to offer stable support. So, the queen becomes quite effective in a defensive role by supporting other pieces, at least for a specific phase in the middle game, but needs to be dealt with care.

This match was a great example of that. At 90-5, with the main batsman at the crease, most other teams would then look ahead to wiping out the deficit. In this case Kallis played a supporting role, scoring only in orthodox manner, whereas AB de Villiers, Shaun Pollock, and Boje scored with some big shots to take the lead over 100 runs. This way the risk was taken off Kallis, who then switched gears and added another 89 with the last two. This is of course due to South Africa possessing a strong lower order. Kallis did assert himself as a 'queen' in GM style— superb in support and potent in attack later on.

20.3 Shahid Afridi, the Crazy Knight

We just discussed how versatile a queen can be, in attack and defense. Now here is the story of a chess piece which is crooked, since it hops two squares along a file or rank, and then one square at right angles. Yes, it is the knight— it always appears to be far away, since it does not move as long as a bishop, rook or the queen can in one move, but it can jump pieces, over its own, and also the opponent's. This makes it deceptive, since it can hop around in a weird pattern and finally reach further into the other ranks, before you can account for it, and often more effectively, than the other mobile pieces— which need clear paths to function.

As mentioned, a queen has attributes of other pieces, except the 'L movement' of a knight and also lacks an ability to hop over anything in it's path.

Take the case of Shahid Afridi— uncanny but effective, at least against India. His raw power in hitting sixes, is as strong as a queen in chess perhaps. But the way you need to handle him (not just his opponents, his own team as well!) is the way a knight might be used in chess, hopping around to just be of help at the right time. He may fail, and perhaps more often than not, but if you take him in the team, it is but worth considering what he might achieve if he succeeds, and when he can be deployed, not just as a batsman but as a bowler as well.

In the 2005 Test series of Pakistan in India, he showed his uncanny skills with bat and ball. He picked up Tendulkar and Sehwag in the 2nd test, although he went for more than 4 an over. In the third test, first innings, when Sehwag and Tendulkar were trying to reach faster to the follow-on mark on 370 and were set to score at a brisk rate, he got Tendulkar, who tried to hit him from the rough, over mid-wicket. In the second innings when India were trying to save the match—he just let himself go wild—by bowling sporadic line/length, as runs were beyond reach for India. He eventually got Tendulkar who dead batted the 'proper' bowlers for 98 balls, but there are no proper way to counter a 'crazy knight'– which Afridi was on that day. He also got Ganguly and Laxman. It was the case, when you forget the bad balls he bowled, but he did what Danish Kaneria could not do, to bowl out India on a spinning track. In that series, Tendulkar 'failed' with scores of 94, 52, 52, 41 and a 98 ball attempt to draw. Afridi was the unpredictable factor in 3 of his failings to construct a larger picture. Afridi can meet the X-demand of bowling (one of his freak balls will get the better of you, even if he can go for some runs) and also addresses the fact, that if wicket-taking process in cricket is by nature sparse, an Afridi can be used just to bring in unpredictability. India could not unleash such a knight when Pakistan were 60 ahead with 4 wickets remaining on the last day of the 1st test, (with India batting fourth).

There will be uncanny players like Afridi elsewhere (for instance Tendulkar as a bowler can be that way at times, and can be orthodox as well. In fact, he also got Afridi stumped in that match, as he lured him into hitting a six). But often, teams tend to assess such players on regular statistics. Rather they should be used in locked up situations, as knights on a chess board are most effective in closed games, with many pawns stagnant and pieces immobile behind the pawns. In such cases the knights can hop around in weird ways. **Afridi, even if his stats are**

not fulfilled, can always be seen as a knight and be used in short bursts, repeatedly, so that batsmen cannot construct and plan in a proper manner. As a batsman, he perhaps could be seen as a floating option, rather than debate whether he should open or slog later. He should rather be sent in, to create the imbalance needed in not just runs but also in the nature and mood of play. We can compare him to a chess knight, but in reality he can make a mockery of the 'chess' planned for him, as he is the least like a chess piece (which always behave the same each day).

20.4 Andrew Flintoff, Queen of the Ashes

From the context of a bowling attack or a batting line up, we can identify a bowler or batsman as a queen for that context of bowling or batting. However, the real queen (comparing to a chess piece) on a cricket field are genuine all-rounders, as mentioned, since winning a match involves both batting and bowling, and versatility has to be taken in that context, of doing just about both aspects equally well.

But the queen in chess, also has many difficulties, since it will be the first to be attacked by smaller pieces. A queen and a rook are likely targets for deflection, as moving them away from strong squares can keep them out of certain activity. The point we are trying to make is that even a queen, can only be expected to perform within certain parameters and cannot be expected to achieve anything single-handedly, although it can make an impact for sure.

Here is a series which belonged to Andrew Flintoff—the Queen of the 2005 Ashes in England. You can call him the queen as he was as potent as a bowler and a batsman. In the second test of that series, he made 68 and 73 (in the second innings he was brilliant with the tail, just as queens on a chess board are most active, when few pieces are there to obstruct mobility. He hit some mighty sixes, although all fielders were on the fence, to give a single. He made predetermined initial movement in the crease to counter their predetermined intentions (also no close in-fielders meant that he could somehow just tap the ball, if it got demanding on him). He walked across to the offside, to Kasprowicz, since he bowls a natural off-cutter and hit him for two sixes. Then he made a predetermined movement on the backfoot, to counter the fact that Bret Lee would perhaps bowl full. Two more sixes over long-on! Then when Lee dropped it short, he played it to third-man for four. **If you are not going to get caught, and are given so much space, this then is like an end-game in chess, and how a queen will be able to move and be potent.** If perhaps, they had maybe 5 on the fence and the remaining staggered in between, he would need to think more about what if, the shot was not working out. This was perhaps a defining moment in his path to glory (he had his slices of luck in both innings).

But wait, he also took 3 wickets in the first innings, and 4 in the second, which included Langer, and then Ponting for a duck in the second innings chasing 282. That left Australia struggling at 175 for 8, over 100 short of the target and no recognized batsmen left. Even on the last day, Flintoff got Warne, with 68 more to go and the last man coming in. Had Asutralia eventually lost by 2 runs, but this was too close for England. Had Australia won, would this performance by Flintoff been seen as a match winner? It should because you cannot expect any more in one match from a man, just as you cannot from a queen in chess (losing this match would mean 0-2 down and with McGrath coming back later it would have been all the more tough to win it from there). There are many implications of a queen and match winner, tournament winning and single-handed performances etc (*Ch 23–Ch 25*). This match was a great example of how one queen alone cannot do it (The 2 run margin is not what they would have targeted, when the last 2 wickets needed over 100).

20.5 Shane Warne as a Chess 'Shot'

We discussed how Afridi, would not be a bad candidate to fit the X-demand of bowling (where your best needs to be better than the opponent, and in wicket taking he can sneak in a few for sure). However, neither batting or bowling are as Z or X, since even in batting you need to get runs by doing the eXtra, albeit within the Zero-error scope. Likewise, in bowling also the error aspect has to be checked, else too many runs go away. But there has perhaps been no greater bowler than Warne, in the last decade or so, to be fulfilling the X-demand— his best balls will test every batsman, and he bowls many compelling ones each over.

Warne also has what chess players call a 'shot'—one little move which dents the story for the opponent. Obviously, such *shots* are possible for any bowler as taking a wicket or two can alter the picture (from a batting context, hitting a six or even 12-20 in an over can at best be useful but not lethal and cannot be seen as a chess 'shot'. Besides, batsmen trying to pull out a surprise is risky as well. **In the case of Warne—his one ball lethal blow—is similar to a 'chess shot', as it is a surprise for the batsman (and viewers) but he has it well planned.** This is unlike an 'Afridi chess shot'—a ball which perhaps surprises both the batsman and himself as well.

I cannot list or recollect how many times Warne has knocked over a batsman or two, even if those may be the only wickets he may take in an innings, but these are the equivalent of chess shots. Although, it takes only one ball to get a batsman out, Warne has a special skill to overcome the defence of a batsman, as a planned surprise. The Laxman dismissal *(Ch 3.4, p44)* was brilliant and has gone uncelebrated.

20.6 Jason Gillespie and pawn outposts

Gillespie, is no pawn with the ball, as we all know how lethal he can be. However, when it comes to batting, tail-enders are expected to offer support to the main batsman (or at times take chances and sneak in some runs, as we saw in the Kallis example; *Ch 20.2, p173*). However, there has perhaps been none more effective than Gillespie in recent times. He is the equivalent of a pawn which offers an 'outpost'– a square for a dominant piece to be posted and supported by that pawn (although in cricket, a tail-ender cannot 'convert' itself to another player, as happens in chess when a pawn promotes itself, by reaching the opponent's home rank– into a piece of the player's choice). However, a good tail-ender can provide support, as a pawn can, in chess.

And just as pawns which provide crucial support by not doing much but remaining where they are, Gillespie has the knack of hanging in. With almost no backlift, he stays back and just looks to block the ball, and often reading it off the pitch. He is essentially exploiting the aspect of a batsman's advantage of holding on (*Ch4.2, p53*; even though there is a Zero-error demand in batting, there is no need to offer an overpowering reply to each ball either). Gillespie, it appears, revels in this batsman's advantage of being able to offer a dead bat to the best of balls.

He has done it time and again for Australia, including a double ton against Bangladesh (not a trivial matter as Australia almost lost a test there). Against India, he helped Steve Waugh get a century and put Australia in the 'driver's seat' until they bumped into Laxman and Harbhajan Singh (Kolkata, 2001).

Later, in Sydney 2003-04 he supported Katich, against India, to have a 100 run partnership to bring Australia closer to avoiding the follow-on. India could have enforced a follow-on with five sessions still remaining, but opted to bat for two sessions, and could not bowl out Australia in the last three sessions. That is another matter that they did not take all the chances that came their way. But the thorn in the story was Jason Gillespie.

There have been tail-enders who have provided support in the past, but the **important aspect of Gillespie's batting, is his deep understanding of the batsman's advantage of not needing to offer a matching reply to every ball, when most of the world fears the fact of making the first mistake and you are out.** The similarity of his style of support, to a pawn outpost in chess, is that such a pawn is most frustrating to the opponent– being as it is a trivial piece, but being so effective that it enables the major piece (recognized batsman, in this case) to focus on its job. Another point is that pawn outposts in chess are useful perhaps at any stage, but in later-middle stages and end games they become crucial. Can we train tail-enders in a Gillespie-style to provide an outpost, and then often promoting them up the order, when one of the batsman is already very active and just needs support? Perhaps when two wickets fall in a bunch and we need to see off a spell cycle? The Gillespie style will not be as effective if no recognized batsman are available during the last phase, so such a tail-ender can create an outpost, in the middle for another active batsman.

21. Tendulkar Dot Chess

Sachin Tendulkar has been India's key batsman for well over a decade. Although India has had a Rahul Dravid, Virender Sehwag and VVS Laxman to bolster the test team in the past five years or so, and Saurav Ganguly, Sehwag, Yuvraj Singh and MS Dhoni to spice up their ODI, as a total effort in both forms he is still the wicket to get (this after being in his 18th year of international cricket).

Therefore it is no secret, that he will be the target for opposing teams—to either get him out early or somehow keep him off focus. As far as test cricket is concerned, India have had a dismal record overseas primarily because of lack of established openers. As far as ODIs are concerned, the middle order is good but often the ability to rotate strike has been ignored (though it has improved over the years). This means that when Tendulkar is out even with a decent 40-50 with a good strike rate, India have often struggled to followup constructively, in managing runs and the rate, without risks.

Further, is the difference in dot rate and strike rate. Even when players end up with good strike rates, if the dot balls eaten up in between are plenty, then it just allows the fielding side to keep going with plans or sneak in part-time bowlers, or forces the non-striker to take undue risks, when he gets strike.

It is no surprise that Tendulkar has been on the receiving end of the strategy and tactics laid out against him. Apart from being amongst the best in the world for quite some period, the gap between him and his teammates about 5-7 years back was quite significant. So it would easily be worth the risk to try out a ploy, and if it failed, he would get a fifty or an hundred (which he would get anyway every few innings if you do the normal stuff).

Tendulkar has in turn responded remarkably, over the years, as we saw it is not easy for a queen on the chess board to do anything single handedly. Apart from that a queen in cricket, as mentioned, would best refer to potent all-rounders, as you do need both departments (assuming the fielding is par) to get through.

We will see later, what makes a match winner—and Tendulkar belongs to the highest class—is one who keeps a margin for uncertainty and never lets a situation of indifference persist. In tennis terms he is looking for the 'break of serve' and can hold on considerably well too—avoiding a tie-breaker.

In ODIs he is perhaps the only batsman in the world to get ahead in strike rate and quantity of runs. He therefore reduces an ODI to test match strike rates, and with wickets in hand, (on account of the volume of runs he contributes). In test cricket, off-late he has played 'positionally' to reduce test cricket to first-class cricket—as that is what happens to bowlers in overs 50-80, in their tired third spells and old ball. Batting at 15 runs for two wickets is not fun, and it is worse when you come in during the first spell (under 12 overs), as attacking is not the need of the hour (unless the pitch is too uncertain to play orthodox shots).

One of the criticisms he faces is that he does not win many matches, but just accumulates runs! Well it is not that the runs do not go to the team total. Another gem, goes as follows– 'so what if his averages are high, what matters is winning'. As we all know, the way to winning is to post a bigger total than your opponent—so if averages do not matter—do we, frequently propose to play more players in a team? And admittedly, often the phase in which runs are made (or even balls played, as we saw earlier), can have a different impact. And now when he has played a crucial role, 2 down for a few runs (perhaps a dozen times in a year or two) can those who take a shot at his average, recognize the indirect 'role-based' contribution?

If there was any meaningful reason as to why India with Tendulkar have not won as many matches as they might have, it is because he is not as good a leg-spinner as Shane Warne!

It may sound surprising but it is a fact, that he has made a difference in both Tests and ODIs with bowling. In that famous Laxman match where India fought back (Kolkata, 2001) after following on, against Australia, and went ahead over 350, you can say India had earned a draw, as Australia had to be bowled out in about two sessions. Harbhajan was the 'terminator', but guess who Tendulkar got? Adam Gilchrist and Matthew Hayden, and Warne of a googly!

He has later picked up Steve Waugh, Damien Martyn, Kallis, Jayawardene, Attapatu, Brian Lara, and Inzamam (quite frequently).

All this indicates, not how good he is as a bowler but how he has exploited the *bowler's chess advantage* in cricket– if the other batsman is made to think along the bowler's line of thinking, the bowler will win more often than not, as the bowler controls the options possible by initiating play (*Ch 13.2, p126-127*).

Before we explore Tendulkar and chess, be reminded that I have arrived at such observations because – I have watched him 'as if playing him', over the years. The second reason, is how I try to learn from other great players– be it Jan Ove Waldner and every Chinese in table tennis, every analyst in chess, GM or otherwise, Steve Davis & Stephen Hendry in snooker, Earl Strickland and Efron Reyes and other big names in 9-ball pool, Geet Sethi and Mike Fereira in Billiards (from India) and today Roger Federer in tennis— whosoever are great in their sport, you study what their intentions are. They will rarely be 'wrong', even if their execution fails (which is bound to happen in any competitive event, especially those which are reaction-driven). And assuming, that their plans were not totally right either, even then they would have found a way to address a situation—which is not worth discarding– rather put them in your 'options' repertoire. You may need them sometime.

So let's explore some of the chess that has gone on between Tendulkar and the rest. Just to remind you, 'applying chess', usually involves following a path of restricted options for both parties, wherein certain known replies are the only ones *naturally* possible. Applying chess is usually different from unleashing skills, as we compared earlier.

21.1 Nasser Hussain in India, 2001-02

One of the hallmarks of Tendulkar, is that in his prime and even today, he does not get beaten that often, even when he scores briskly. During his best years, it would be interesting to see how he fares amongst the other greats, in terms of the number of times he is beaten inside a score of 10 runs or say in the first two overs. I would guess he would be very good, and considering his dynamic approach to batting—his not being beaten defensively— is something to fear.

England captain Nasser Hussain found a way, along with Ashley Giles, their left arm off-spinner. Hussain has been criticized for negative tactics (it really falls under the category of strategy, as that line is part of a long term plan, perhaps not to get him out but reduce his options). However, to be fair to Hussain, he said that just reducing his rate of scoring was a boost, and perhaps their best chance to do well in India. Although Tendulkar scored fairly well in the series, Hussain did prove a point (though it can be argued that letting Tendulkar play himself in, is perhaps a poor attitude to begin with). Hussain also tried 7-2 fields bowling outside off, but Tendulkar did manage to work the fast bowlers, quite squarer than the on-side fielders.

Hussain had now opened the doors to others in the world, that targeting a key player, and perhaps giving singles does have an impact. The batsman on the other hand can play unorthodox shots, but for how long can he do that? Sehwag did come down the track and won a battle or so. But Tendulkar knew, he was now going to be targeted this way– *one shot bowling*, with few orthodox options for runs. He cannot just hit around, because this is how things were going to be for a long time to come (as mentioned earlier, you cannot do this to every batsman, as wickets need to be taken and everyone cannot be given singles).

Tendulkar, on the other hand also understood the advantage of waiting in such defensive strategy. Your run-making options are reduced, might as well feel good that their wicket-taking options are reduced too! England lost perhaps on account of the fact that they were (at that time), not good enough to beat India in India anyway, but Hussain must be credited for making an attempt to try something different, and not abandoning his theory on first attempt of failure. After all, he did not have Shane Warne on his side, and even Warne had not seen many bright days in India.

21.2 Tendulkar Deflected at Natwest 2002

If Hussain could not succeed with Giles in India, he did to some extent have a limited gain in the test series in England. They did draw the series, in spite of the fact that many key players were missing.

But this leg stump theory did work perfectly in the Natwest ODI finals. England had posted 325. This was the beginning of the many instances, India would concede 200 runs for 2 wickets in ODIs from that point on. Since India won that finals, this fact never got media attention. Anyway, Ganguly came in and played brilliantly, smacking AJ Tudor over the off-side, by moving away outside the leg stump. Giving himself room was a safe bet, since Tudor was trying to bounce him, and the balls would go over the stumps. His 63 of 40 balls almost brought the match back in parity (since this perhaps was a run a ball pitch). After giving India a 'break of serve', Ganguly could have perhaps held on, since the equation was already altered. However, he went for one shot too many and fell to Tudor in the 15th over with India strong at 106-1 (trying to maximize on the 15 over field restrictions then; however he would be most useful if he had kept himself for Giles, as hitting sixes of left-arm spinners is Ganguly's forte).

From then on, what India needed was efficient strike rotation. And when Sehwag left soon after, Tendulkar had come in when constructive play from then on could have been the bulk of the solution. But soon Mongia (9 of 15 balls), Dravid (5 of 12) left, with India at 132 for 4 in 21 overs (needing 194 of 174; 20 runs lesser than balls remaining). The hard work of Ganguly was erased along with 4 other wickets.

Tendulkar had a bad day against Irani for sure, but he made 12 of the 10 balls he faced from Giles. Then why did he play a risky shot to Giles? (down the track to lift inside out over extra cover). Because singles alone might not do any good in restoring the strike rate. Tendulkar was out for 14 of 19 balls (of the 48 balls bowled during that phase). **Hussain had succeeded in deflecting him, through one shot bowling from Giles– by allowing a single but perhaps forcing an unorthodox shot for a boundary**— which was much needed with the fall in run rate. By the way deflection is one of the common ways of diverting a chess piece away from a valuable square (the striking end in this case), by involving it in other tasks (in this case, available singles).

We all know the end result was a famous win, but it should have been won with holding wickets and rotating strike, after Ganguly and Sehwag had gotten off India to near parity. In my view, Tendulkar still did the right thing, after India fell back by 20 runs (to balls available), as making a nice 40 of 50 balls would have left India worse.

21.3 Pakistan loses on type 1, World Cup 2003 3

Need a bit of break from chess? India needed it then. Australia had exploited the first innings dot dilemma against India, in World Cup 2003. No devastating balls, but just superb dot bowling resulting in a wicket, since batsmen could not wait anymore (Ganguly 9 of 21 balls, Dravid 1 of 23; Kaif 1 of 16; Yuvraj 0 of 8; Dinesh Mongia 13 of 39). Tendulkar made 36 of 59, and for most of his innings had received less than 30% of the strike. This is dot exploitation at its best.

To get away from dot chess, consider what happened against Pakistan, who batted first and posted a decent 273 batting first. Saeed Anwar, in his heydays, would perhaps have had a better strike rate, but with 3 of the best pace bowlers in their era, it looked like wickets should be kept intact to begin with, as this was a good track to score on.

Tendulkar and Sehwag unleashed some skill that day against strike bowlers looking for wickets. You do no expect Waqar Younis, Wasim Akram and Shoaib Akhtar to dot around. This was type 1 bowling, to try to get early wickets and make in-roads. However, Tendulkar is also amongst the best at scoring against wicket-taking bowling.

Early wickets needed? Well here was a case of Tendulkar and Sehwag getting 3 bowlers out inside 5 overs! Refreshing game– skill vs skill. This was indeed a great knock from Tendulkar (98 of 75), with great strike rate with orthodox shots off good balls. Remember, type 1 bowling has its shortcoming, that a wicket taking ball can also concede runs in an orthodox manner. Perhaps, such type 1 bowling and scoring briskly is perhaps not going to be common in ODIs (?).

This was also the match where Tendulkar was beaten in defence by Akram, cut in half but the ball sailed over. Tendulkar also had a narrow missed shot at mid-off.

Just another note: Tendulkar and Sehwag both hit sixes over third man to short and wide balls. What if the bowler repeated that again and again—type 2, one shot bowling—how many such shots before it could go to third man, and perhaps an extra third man or behind point on the off side fence?

21.4 Offside Defensive Tactics, Melbourne 2003-04

Tendulkar did not have a good start in India's series in Australia– one of their best chances to do well, considering that McGrath and Warne were unavailable, and Bret Lee missed the first two of the four match series. Tendulkar started the series, being lbw to Gillespie of a ball which never looked like coming in as much. This was in one of those rain affected matches, when India's first innings essentially began on day 4 (Australia batted first and posted about 300 plus). Nobody read anything into a match which was perhaps headed to a draw, as India needed just over 100 to avert the follow on.

The next match was at Adelaide. Australia had put up a huge score of 500 plus, with India perhaps missing a trick or two, as Katich was not attacked enough when Australia lost four wickets for about 250. In reply, India began well, and when Tendulkar came in to bat, they had an off-side field setup for full and wide deliveries, which is what Bichel did. The Aussies were not going to let Tendulkar play a natural game and take wickets with type 1, beat-your-defence-type of bowling. Just make run making tough, by bowling sharp (not the Giles stuff) and wider on the off. It just took few balls, Tendulkar tried to drive Bichel of a wide ball.

Was he out of form? In my view one could not say for sure, as he had faced just a few balls till then. His second innings was positive for sure as he had a good 70 odd run partnership with Dravid to take India closer to winning.

Then to Melbourne– out in a bizarre way again, of an innocuous ball down the leg side from Bret Lee. **Is he really out of form?** His stats show that, but defensively he has not yet been beaten by much, so far. Nonetheless, the situation was getting to everyone.

In the second innings, we did find out that he was struggling, as Australia had offered him a refreshing variety of dot-chess. **Giles had been doing defensive, dull and strategic bowling on leg stump, now he would face defensive bowling, but intriguing and tactical (since it was forcing in nature and had sporadic threats).** Essentially, Nathan Bracken bowled left arm round the wicket into the off-side rough, from wide off the crease, with most balls definitely not going anywhere near the stumps—but you would never know which ones would—as the rough is filled with uncertainties (outside the leg stump rough can be padded, but not this). The result was a bucket full of dot-stuff (acceptable to the bowler as they were dots) with a few nasty ones shooting back into him. I was watching-as-if-playing Tendulkar then. It was difficult to think about runs, as you could never know which ball to really leave; and playing them was perhaps getting you a single, square on the off-side? He managed a forty, with almost one chance going down behind the wickets. The Aussies had exploited the fact that he was under pressure and would not be in any risk taking mode to score. Defensive tactics was the way to go—forcing defensive response to leave and play a times.

In chess, there is often confusion as *tactics* refers to attack and *strategy* refers to defence. This is true to quite an extent, since tactics by and large are active ploys and strategy is about arranging resources to meet long term plans. But tactics & strategy need not be interchangeable with attack/defense respectively, since the purpose of forcing-activity can be to achieve a defensive goal, and something well planned can often be just as penetrative.

21.5 Tendulkar Karpovs the Aussies, Sydney 2003-04

Melbourne, I can tell you was far from fun 'watching-as-if-playing' from my living room. Exploiting the rough outside off-stump (for fast bowlers) was something I had not seen in my limited cricket observations, at least not as a repetitive, calculated ploy. How would he counter this in Sydney? I usually do ask such questions many times in various sports I watch, so that I can learn a thing or two, next time the same teams match up.

Australia had retained Bracken, and Greg Chappell said as a commentator, essentially for a defensive role. This time around Tendulkar had plans as well. Not to play a single scoring shot on the off-side! But to achieve this defensive strategy (since it is a long term positional approach), and score runs as well, would indeed be weird. Also, since you are really not as open in shot making, it is like a closed game in chess, where pawns interlock and restrict options. In such games, a fair amount of shuffling of pieces goes on behind or around pawn formations. The end result can be that activity happens off-center, as the focus shifts elsewhere (the center is most important in chess but is perhaps already deadlocked in a close game). Shuffling pieces around, often for the heck of it, and making weird moves and getting obtuse replies is normal. Anticipating abnormal patterns is normal in such games. Anatoly Karpov and many other positional players will often make a game of chess look like this (normal step-by-step games can be analyzed by opponents who are just as good, but shuffling around the 'norm' perhaps allows you to squeeze in some value in between the steps).

The important point in this approach from Tendulkar was more than just 'not playing' offside shots. This was the equivalent of the abnormal shuffle type of moves here– he would leave balls precariously close to the off stump, and often play balls outside the off stump, on length, but into the leg side. This is confusing to a bowler, since if he bowls on the stumps, he either leaves the very close ones or Tendulkar works it to the on-side, when it did threaten the stumps. The moment it is bowled slightly wider, he would leave most, except a few which, out of anticipation of fuller length, he works to the on-side. The key was that once the ball was surely not heading for the stumps, he could defer his shot making intentions, till the ball had come closer to him. If he felt that it could be worked onto the on-side, he would, else leave it with surety. **If you want to bowl dots with sporadic and weird threats (as in Melbourne), I can likewise play dots as well, with sporadic shot making and in an unconventional but sure way** (by and large dots are par for both in tests, so why should I be the one who suffers a dot-ploy– you can too). He had managed to out-shuffle the Aussies, like in a complex closed positional game of chess, with waiting but never letting the bowlers know exactly which balls he would leave and which he would play.

This is different from a normal strategic approach by batsmen such as Gavaskar or Dravid, where they also take matters step-by-step, wait, and play according to the merit of the ball, but based on correctness of where it should be played. Tendulkar was also playing step-by-step and working himself into the game, waiting, but by 'shuffling the merit of each ball'– many which could be played were left, many which could be left were played, some on the stumps were defended or worked to the on-side. You may be tempted to think that this sounds like an exaggeration, but when someone scores a double century with only one or two scoring shots on the off-side, there will be some plan behind the approach, and obtuseness as well– in this case to counter the weird ploys he had faced.

In my view this was one heck of a chess reply, as a closed positional shuffle. Tendulkar, as such would perhaps be closer in style to Kasparov (dynamic but willing to work out complications thrown at him). He did work out the complications, shuffled his intentions, and squeezed potent moves in between– replying Karpov with a Karpov.

They say Laxman played better in that innings. That is true, when you consider the quality of shot making, as such. But if you treat it as a reply to what went on earlier in the series, to the obtuse events he went through, this was a brilliant equal and obtuse reply. Last time 'you were well off, with many dots off which some of them being threatening (but not knowing which one, since it was from the rough), this time around I will offer the dots (batting first; no rough), but will not let you know which ones I will score off.

This may all seem equal and opposite, but it is tough for batsmen to pull off, as bowlers initiate play as such and batsmen can make that one mistake needed to end the plan.

For those who think that India still did not win, just remember that about four chances were dropped by the keeper, one of the spin bowlers was not quite there, and there was 100 run partnership in the Aussie tail– and yet you were in a position to enforce a follow-on with 5 sessions left. You cannot as a batsman, do much more than put a team in this position. That Sachin was not used as a bowler, as he was effective in the series, was perhaps a different matter (he did eventually bowl after tea on the last day, but it was too late).

21.6 Aussies take revenge, ODI Final 1, 2003-04

The dot drama, ended with parity in Sydney, as the series was levelled– perhaps a fair outcome to a series where the bowlers had taken all the heat on flat wickets.

However, in the ODIs, it is the bowlers who have a clear dot-ball advantage. In tests, it can be seen as equal (except certain phases), and rarely would it be worth getting out to a ball which was just worth an indifferent dot ball.

When Australia bowls first in the finals of an ODI, they are masters at evaluating the 'great dot dilemma'. Batsmen do not know the target, and hence cannot value a dot ball. Yet they know they need to provide momentum, but cannot just lose wickets.

The first ODI final was at Melbourne, India batted first. Tendulkar would now look to playing a constructive, positive innings– keep a good strike rate, with risk-free scoring shots, an art in which he is best in the business. But the Aussies knew that, so why allow him any constructive options. At the other end however, Sehwag was never going to play in this manner or that, he knew only one way to play– destructively. So the solution they reached at was alarmingly simple– exploit the variation in bounce due to morning dampness, forcing Tendulkar to pull from outside off-shoulder height, and bowl into Sehwag's shoulder.

Tendulkar was well aware that smacking two or three boundaries to Gillespie and Bret Lee, was not going to solve it, as they would persist (can they take a 30-40 from Tendulkar; they would for sure). Sehwag although powerful on offside short balls, was not quite a natural puller.

So both Gillespie and Lee got into the act straight away, not bowling a single ball which was headed into the stumps– all short and shoulder height, mainly just outside off stump. Moreover, the height to which each ball came up, was varying, but was always chest height or more. What the heck, if one of the balls went over, it would be an extra. Tendulkar read the plan early, and had prepared to dot out the first few overs, until he could read the bounce. Gillespie was simply brilliant, as he varied his angles by coming close to the stumps (over the wicket) but sending it like a little bit of a 'round the wicket' angle. They got Sehwag defending, as he gloved a rising ball into his shoulder. Tendulkar was looking to get back and across, but was bowled as Bret Lee bowled one which took the top of the stumps. Tendulkar appeared to crunch down, as if it stayed low. Well guess what, it did, as the stumps are much lower than his chest and shoulder. This was the Aussie revenge. If you plan a constructive and dynamic game, we will force you to play a destructive one, but with some options of failure. This was great-one-shot-bowling, with subtle variations.

In the recent South Africa ODI series 2006, India faced a similar barrage of short bowling, since the bounce is like Australian pitches. The ODI rules have changed since a few years (well before this Australian series), allowing one ball over shoulder high per over (less than head high). However, this means that fast bowlers can bowl outside off, shoulder high and make it difficult to pull. Forget the no-ball, bowlers will ball 4-5 in an over, as a sure dot ball is a winning weapon in ODIs. It was good to see Tendulkar, revive his backfoot game (as he had in the 2003 World Cup), as he earned a brilliant 35 in the first encounter (the first match was rained away). No opening batsman from both sides could register more than a twenty, in the three ODIs, till the series was alive. Tendulkar was out cheaply once thereafter, and then chasing a huge score, pulled one of Pollock from off-stump to be caught at square leg.

This is why the loss in the ODI, was not quite a proper predictor of Indian batting in the tests. South Africa lost the first test by getting carried away with shorter length– dots are in fact negative for bowlers in the first 12-25 overs of a test.

21.7 Deflection Continues, Sri Lanka Asia Cup Finals 2004

India were under pressure to perform in the finals of tournaments. This was their chance, in Sri Lanka, as conditions are similar to those back home. Tendulkar and Kaif, had somehow managed to sneak India into the finals, by getting some bonus points against Pakistan (by scoring a certain % of the total, you got bonus points even upon losing).

India did well when they bowled, with Tendulkar bowling a harrowing one shot line, round the legs from a wide angle, (around the wicket).He got Jayawardene out for a duck, and ended up with 40 for 2, in 10 overs. Sehwag also bowled 10 overs giving 32 runs for 1 wicket. Harbhajan bowled his 10 overs for 48 runs and 1 wicket. This indicated that the pitch was a slow and tough track to bat, as part time spinners had bowled twice their quota. Sri Lanka ended up with 228 in 50 overs.

When India batted, it seemed like the story of lack of strike rotation repeating itself. Sehwag (5 of 12 balls), Ganguly (4 of 20), Laxman (12 of 34), Dravid (16 of 28, fair enough), Yuvraj (8 of 29), Kaif (5 of 15). Tendulkar top scored with 74 of 100 balls and the other batsmen combined had 50 of 138 balls. Tendulkar was eventually out trying to force the pace and India eventually lost by 25 runs, as Zaheer Khan smacked a few in the end. Sri Lanka had managed to keep Tendulkar off strike (100 balls from 236 balls bowled in that period).

Tendulkar topped scored from both sides, with the highest strike rate amongst batsmen from both sides, ahead of Attapatu- the man of the match (65 of 87 balls). Some bowlers did whack around a few runs quickly though, as it happens in ODIs. And the public conclusion was that Tendulkar let the team down, he did not finish! I do not think that with the rest of the batsmen making 50 combined in 138 balls (a strike rate which will help you chase a score of 108), it even makes any sense analyzing why we lost. No point criticizing the other Indian batsmen, as there can be a collective failure (not by this strike rate though), but it is pointless trying to blame Tendulkar for playing 'slowly', when in fact he had read the conditions the best, as a batsman and bowler as well. The real secret of Sri Lanka's success was again one of deflection– and bowling at the other batsman.

21.8 Tendulkar Walls, but Afridi gets him, Pakistan 2005

As mentioned in the 'crazy knight' discussion *(Ch20.3, p175)*, one of the ways of overcoming 'chess' on a cricket field is to have a player, who cannot ever be defined as a chess piece. Afridi fits that perfectly, nobody ever knows what he might achieve, including perhaps himself.

In the third test against Pakistan in India, Bangalore 2005, India were given a 383 run target on the last day. Except for Sehwag, nobody had ideas of a win, especially when a draw was needed to win the series, and a draw was evident. The positive approach however helped India get a good start, which ended with Sehwag being run out in the 24th over, with 87 on the board. Another 300 odd needed in about 70 overs. Rahul Dravid stepped in and saw the session till lunch and by the time Gambhir got out, the 'asking rate' had jumped up to 4.6 runs/ over, with 275 runs to get in two sessions. Tendulkar and Dravid, sensed the fact that a draw was the only meaningful option. They began to drop their bats dead on whatever came their way. The other two recognized batsman, Laxman (had an average series) and Ganguly (had a tough time), but you could hope that they would be able to defend, both being good players of spin. If India could reach tea time with two of the four recognized batsman, they would have been home.

So Tendulkar began playing every ball as if a dot was worth its weight in gold. Should he have played positively? Even a four every over would not get India to a win. **But by playing positively, at least the fielders would be pushed back and chances of getting out would be less. Wrong,** because there is no law in cricket which forces the opposing captain to do so, and if runs would not matter, he need not (cricket has weak phase-connectivity! *(Ch 3.5, p44)*. And this was a must-win match for Pakistan, no matter how you play there will be close-in fielders. If the pitch is demanding but not that bad, blocking was a valid option. But as Javed Miandad pointed out, you cannot block like the way Tendulkar did for more than twenty odd overs. Well, that is what he was perhaps intending, to reach tea-time, by playing twenty overs that way.

This situation of drawing in fourth innings, when the target is unlikely in the time-frame, has been an unsolved riddle in cricket. Collingwood was recently criticized in an Ashes loss in Adelaide 2006, for playing slowly. However, that was a third innings draw attempt, where adding runs reduces the chances of achieving a fourth innings chase. Nonetheless, in the manner English batsmen got out to Shane Warne of balls pitched outside leg, it was tough to be harsh on Collingwood. Playing positively, needs a lot of luck, as your first bad shot will nullify the runs scored for sure, which were of little value to begin with. Likewise, Gayle was criticized for batting slowly—that must be some hard work folks—and West Indies managed a draw with last men in, (India in West Indies, 1st Test, 2006). Ponting did play one his best knocks in the Ashes 2005, to save the match, playing positively, but the fact that McGrath had to bat out the last overs, indicates that there are no clear answers. And if Michael Vaughn ever needed an answer as to why England failed to win that match, one of the answers lies in Afridi! (when Gilchrist was out, Australia needed more that 250 runs in about 50 overs. That is demanding in ODIs as well, and with 5 wickets gone, and in my view, Vaughn could have propped the attack, and tried a few extreme out-of-the-norm ploys, as Afridi did to India. But to be fair to Vaughn, in that series he had the toughest role as captain– whom should he not bowl!

In context of the Indian match, if anyone thinks that India did not fight hard enough, they are mocking themselves, as we saw how the other draws were achieved with the last men saving the day. India did not lose shamefully by 168 runs, but narrowly by four odd overs (losing the win and losing the draw need a better definition in cricket). And India did not give Kaneria, their strike spinner, a wicket, (till he did get a tail-ender out). It was Afridi who had gone crazy for sure. He knew that he needed 3 or 4 awkward ones to beat the impeccable wall which Tendulkar had built around himself.

Whether to play in a run-scoring sense and or in a defensive sense, being positive in either of the methods, is perhaps the key to a draw (an explanation given by Michael Slater!). Yet when to apply which, is a fact nobody can tell (especially on fifth day Indian tracks)—as nobody can tell the best way to not make 10 mistakes over 540 balls. In an assessment sense, it is best to measure batsmen in terms of balls played in such draw attempts, whichever way they achieve it. Then Pathan's 0 of 29 balls will indicate the fight was a bit better.

21.9 Tendulkar vs Inzamam, Recognizing the chess

We have discussed that there is a *bowler's chess advantage* in cricket (*Ch13.2, p126*). This is essentially because they initiate action, they know if they will bowl as per plan or throw in some surprise. If it fails for bowlers, they can repeat their ideas, to quite some extent, like taking back a move in chess, unlike a batsman who walks back upon a silly shot.

And this becomes all the more advantageous when one batsman bowls to another, both who can think along the same lines. Because part of the tentativeness and caution in execution arises because both know the depth of the matter, and scope of the sticky options, which perhaps a bowler—who cannot bat—might know, but not to a great depth.

This is best explained over Tendulkar's bowling success over Inzamam in ODIs, as both play similar roles in their teams and have a depth of experience. Obviously, Inzamam is a great batsman, and as such need not fear Tendulkar's skill as a bowler. However, Tendulkar probes along what both know, and exploits the *bowler's chess advantage (Ch13.2, p127)*, that he can make a mistake– especially being a part-time bowler– whereas Inzamam's wicket is precious and giving it to a 5th bowler would be a waste.

In the first ODI in India, 2005, he bowled round-the-legs, sharp leg spinners, much as he did in Asia Cup Finals in 2004. This was almost one shot bowling as the angle only allowed shots behind square on the leg side. However, he had left no slips for Inzamam, and after pinning him, he slid a straighter one, which Inzamam tried to glide to third man and was bowled. The length was key as it took the top of the stumps. It was neither driving length nor for a firm square cut. He went on to take five wickets in that ODI, including Afridi, the danger man who can make a mockery of any chess planned for him.

Three matches later, India batted first and posted 315, with a Tendulkar ton and Yuvraj Singh cameo. The above 300 score was quickly nullified by Afridi, who finally batted up the order and smacked 40 of 23 balls– 'breaking back a serve' to draw parity. After that, India let the match amble along with Pakistan 'holding serve'.

Tendulkar was brought in to bowl the last over, with 3 runs needed for a win. What would he do? Tendulkar figured that just a straight approach, such as bringing in all fielders, will perhaps not win such a battle. He decided to bowl round the wicket, with many fielders on the off side and have a couple of fielders *outside* the circle on the on side! That would give a single for sure, if Inzamam played it there. But that is what Tendulkar wanted! He knew what ball he would bowl, Inzamam did not, yet he sensed it. Tendulkar bowled two balls sliding towards off, with speed difference, and had Inzamam fallen for the bait, he could have got out, nicking it. He managed a couple and eventually then played two more dots, and scored the winning runs of the last ball. This was not a case of Inzamam keeping his cool, as you never want to win of the last ball of the match when 15 runs of 18 balls were required. Pakistan should have won the match earlier. But such is the pressure in Indo-Pak games, that a power player such as Inzamam could not just finish it earlier, as the blame for the loss would entirely come on him, when uncalled for run-outs were the reason a bit earlier (a 35 of 36 balls; Younis Khan and Kamral Akmal were run out).

But when a batsman bowls to another, assuming he is a decent enough bowler, he can create a doubt by hinting at patterns of play, which both know, but can sneak in a surprise, since bowlers initiate action. Such bowlers can make batsmen expect something, and then just deviate a touch differently.

21.10 Undriving Vass- winning a wait

Tendulkar had returned from an injury, and he came back to rejoin the Indian side with the Dravid-Chappell combination, being tested out against Sri Lanka in India 2005, for a 7 match ODI series. And Tendulkar was back with a bang and made a huge impact in the first two ODIs, to give India a much needed win over Sri Lanka in some time. India won the series 4-0, with MS Dhoni coming of age, as the dynamic keeper for India. Vaas had Tendulkar playing two forcing shots, to an angling off stump line (being left-handed over the wicket). Tendulkar was caught of a full-wide ball. This was to perhaps disrupt the one-shot line which Vaas would now use to stop Tendulkar. He perhaps tried to force Vaas out of that line early up. Incidentally, Dhoni launched a smacking 183 in this match, and incidentally got away edging a similar ball past second slip to third man, to start off.

The next match, the same thing was repeated to Tendulkar, full and wide, to invite a drive but with a packed off side field. One-shot bowling of type 3! The targets being over 250, there was no time to wait (this is not a dilemma but a forced situation). This time he came down the track, to hit him over mid-on and was bowled, with the ball knocking the off-stump bails. Not fun, as this should otherwise have been a safe shot, since the line was as such, wide. But Vaas cashed in the *bowler's chess advantage ((Ch13.2, p127)–* that a predetermined move by a batsman cannot counter a predetermined plan (his line). He could switch the line straighter, the batsman would at best connect for four. But the ball was well 'aimed' by Vaas, to crash into top of off stump.

The fact that Sri Lanka was not trying to get Tendulkar out by type 1 bowling (to beat his defence), was in itself a sign that they had had enough of him from the first two games.

However, in the last match of the series, Sri Lanka had made a moderate 244. Vaas was back to bowl his full-wider one shot line, allowing Tendulkar to drive, but with a packed offside field in front of square. These balls were of driving length but of square-cutting width. Best left alone in test cricket. However, in ODI they are useful but more potent in the first innings when the dot dilemma is strong.

This was evident, as Tendulkar could wait for sure, or rather knew how much he could. This was a model way to beat one shot bowling by waiting and then choosing the boundary attempt. The number of fours he managed to squeezed through point and extra-cover was delightful indeed. Finally, Vaas pitched one a bit closer to off-stump. Tendulkar had waited for that one, and he just held his bat still, with face pointing to fine-leg, which is where it went for four. Vaas had a grin on his face as both Vaas and Tendulkar knew a little bit more of what was going on there. This was a well crafted 39 of 48 balls. Dot balls are obviously potent in an ODIs in both innings, but not as lethal, in conjunction with the dot dilemma of the first innings.

21.11 Murali Exploited on a Skewed Attack, 2005

Muralitharan, by now a legend of the game, was to try to achieve glory for Sri Lanka on Indian soil. He is the main bowler for Sri Lanka, who could be instrumental in bowling sides out twice. He does have good support today, with many more bowlers– Vaas and some good spinners. But however potent the others are, Sri Lanka are a skewed bowling attack, with too much tilt towards Murali. Now this being test cricket, any singles gambit against Tendulkar as an ODI player, will not be as effective. On the contrary, Murali was now singled out– not by hitting him out of attack—as he will soon be brought back on any- way—but by ensuring he does not take quick wickets; and to be worked to a point of fatigue of the bowling team (yes, he does tire every few hours, and so do the others).

This was evident as Laxman and Tendulkar, made sure that the Indian batting can have resources left to score against the others (2nd Test Delhi, 2005). They played him out from the 13th over till about 40 overs, with great care. Just how lethal was Murali? Well he took 7 for 100 runs and bowled about 40% of the Sri Lankan overs. But he did not 'run through' as a fleeting glimpse of the scorecard would indicate, since Laxman played 117 balls, Tendulkar 196 balls and Ganguly 129 balls. The dots in these were 'positive' for batsmen, all through the innings. Murali would bowl from one end. Putting dots in between his wickets, meant that runs could come from the other end. India made 290, when Murali had snapped up 7 for 100. The news was about Tendulkar's 35th 100, but they forgot to emphasize the balls he played! This is a strategic way to overcome a bowler, apart from hitting him out of the attack, (which Tendulkar does more often in ODIs and some test situations). On a tactical note, Pathan opened in the second innings to pinch a 93. India perhaps did not need that much, but the reason for this is to score in the initial non-Murali overs.

The potency with playing out Murali, was shown again in the third test, when Laxman and Tendulkar played Murali from overs 12 to 31 (he came in early on), till Tendulkar was out 'cheaply' for 23 runs but with a precious 66 balls, (23 with 66 balls, not 23 of 66). It was Lax- man's turn to come good with a century.

Punctuating Murali's initial spells, did show results later, as the Indian lower-order, with Dhoni, Pathan (when he batted lower) and Agarkar all were amongst runs in the series. Murali was over-bowled as you would expect, but his other innings just fetched wickets like other test bowlers do. There is only so much you can do if you bowl 35 overs or more each innings.

21.12 Exhanging Queens, vs Pollock in India, 2005

Here is an interesting match for dot-chess analysts. South Africa in India, Bangalore ODI 2005. South Africa made just 169 with brilliant exploitation of dot dilemma by India. This is what Aussies do to teams in the first innings of ODIs. But chasing 169, offers no dilemma as the required dot rate is known and you can wait to advantage.

That is exactly what Tendulkar and Gambhir did. Tendulkar waited for the 8th over, before he tried to launch Pollock out of the inner cricle and was caught for 2 of 22 balls. However, waiting to see spells from big bowlers is not anything new. Teams have done that to the West Indies with Garner or Ambrose etc.

This however, is a prophylactic case for the Nimzo-chess freaks. It goes this way. With 169 on board, South Africa can only win if Pollock and Ntini grab about 3-4 wickets in their first spells of about 5-6 overs each (since the other bowlers are not exactly ideal to get an Indian team all out, Bangalore). The next point is that a bowler can only take a few wickets, if they take the initial one, in the first place.

So, if this is seen as the only way, (which may be debatable, but it was so in this bowling attack for a Bangalore track), then the objective is to make sure it does not—even if it be improbable anyway.

So the objective of the Indian openers was to ensure that they do not give even one wicket. Doing so would take away the only option for

South Africa. The beauty of it is that South Africa were also prepared to try something different, as getting 3 wickets as such is not really likely by conventional fast bowling with slips. It might, on another pitch, but perhaps not here. The result was that they bowled to Tendulkar without any slips, when they had to attempt to get a side all out under 170! Pollock bowled just short of length and straight with fielders in a ring– to make sure that there is no orthodox way for Tendulkar to get a single. He would have to go over the circle. Gambhir waited for a few overs and then began flashing around trademark style, with some streaky shots. Fair enough.

The important thing was that Tendulkar had his focus, about the fact that the objective was not to give a wicket till 8 overs or so, rather than runs. **Wickets was the score that mattered.** If India achieve it, the only chance South Africa have is gone (due to limit on overs per bowler, and typically a bowler will bowl 6 in one spell). Pollock did bowl immaculate-wicket to wicket, and Tendulkar resisted going over.

Just for those who think I am pushing a Tendulkar chess story too far, since 2 of 22 can never be given credit. Well they have always missed what I learnt from the masters. The intention of top players are always to be studied, as execution can fail. It was not as if Tendulkar was trying to hit around, and missed 22 times. He never attempted to fabricate a shot (he perhaps would have scored in an orthodox manner, if Pollock bowled a bad ball; but to good balls they had set a field which demanded fabrication). It was clear that shutting the doors would rule out the only chance South Africa had. This was evident as Pollock and Ntini did not even finish their quota either, once the first 10 overs were through. Tendulkar did not win a match here. It was already won by the bowlers. He just took out the last option from South Africa. India were home in 35 overs. **This is a case of prophylactic moves in chess, to eliminate the few possible options the opponent may**

have, however improbable they may be, as options is all one's got to explore. In the context of roles, it is similar to a chess player exchanging queens (Tendulkar; Pollock-Ntini; in this context) when he has a strong advantage (in this case India's bowling effort), so that the opponent has only few minor pieces to pull off something special (South Africa defending about 160; needing 9 wickets), has no chance of being caught up without their queen (in this case, without Pollock-Ntini, as their overs are nearly done).

21.13 Shoiab Akhtar Deflected on Skewed Condition, 2006

Cricket teams, unlike a team of chess pieces are rarely equal and opposite, and further, never equally strong, as there are bound to be weaker and stronger areas in each team composition.

Just an imbalance in composition, translates to execution advantage. Take for example Adam Gilchrist in the England Ashes Tour 2005. He had quite a poor series by his standards as a wicket-keeper batsman. However, he had a role in the great Ashes match which was drawn by Australia– just being in the team! (3rd test, in England, 2005), although he made only 4 runs (*with* 30 balls). This is not a case of psychological impact of his 'being' in the team. Sort of, but it does translate to reality, as it impacts the score at which an opposing captain declares. At 423 runs in 100 overs, Michael Vaughn perhaps declared with enough margin, to account for a Gilchrist-based Aussie team. 380 or so might perhaps have been apt, for most other teams. You can say Gilchrist was only good on 'paper' as far as this series goes. But you can never know when his paper turns to wood.

Take the example of Brian Lara in the Champions trophy in India, 2006, in the finals against Australia. His importance in the team had an implication of execution advantage for West Indies, even though he got out early. Glenn McGrath was 'deflected' to third in the bowling order, to counter Lara. This was an advantage for earlier batsmen—which incidentally was the time when runs came in—and to the point that Gayle was unstoppable and smacked McGrath as well. It took a brilliant ball from Nathan Bracken to knock out Gayle's off stump- type 1 special.

This is like a major chess piece such as a rook or queen, which even if not developed (yet on its home square), already exerts influence by being there, and thereby attracts some amount of opponent resources to begin with (deflecting it from other tasks).

Now take the example of Tendulkar in Pakistan 2006 (second test). The first test was such a run fiesta that not even an innings from each side got over, with over a 1000 runs and only 7 wickets. India lost only one wicket, after Sehwag and Dravid had a partnership of over 400 for the opening wicket. The second test was another flat deck, and if I remember right, the only ball which really troubled the batsman was Zaheer Khan getting Inzamam from round the wicket. Finally, after 7 days of test cricket, Tendulkar, would get a turn in the middle. Dravid and Laxman had a solid partnership overnight, and Shoiab Akhtar bowled a few in the morning on the 3rd day. They added over 100 more runs, but Akhtar did not come in before lunch to break the pair. he did not come back after lunch, and eventually came in when Tendulkar came in, allowing a two hunderd partnership to floursih! Another case of deflection!

If this match would have a result, then Akthar was perhaps the only bowler who could run-through on this pitch, from both sides– so skewed towards him it was. He promptly took the new ball and just began banging every other ball short to Tendulkar, who made no attempt to score off him, but scored off Asif, who was bowling a more orthodox off stump line. Why score of Akhtar, as he was going to bowl

5 overs anyway. Playing him out almost ensures a draw. Besides, the balls being bowled were defendable by leaving them, but hooking could give him a chance to grab a few more (incidentally Yuvraj was out hooking to Asif). This is another case of chess prophylaxis– if there are only few or only options for the opponent to make in-roads, however remote, it is best cut off. And with Shoaib, remote run-through probabilities are more possible. Tendulkar however got out to a short ball down the leg side, but had left Shoaib only an over more to try anything. Sure, India would have liked to see him bat along, but again, if you see the intention, it is clear he did not want to hit, unless it was a constructive option. It was not an End-ulkar innings, as Moin Khan would like the world to believe. In fact, Tendulkar perhaps played a role in ending his career, in Multan 2004, getting him bowled on the last ball of the day, between all three devices a batsman has to prevent the ball from going into the stumps (a bat, and 2 legs).

21.14 Accepting the singles gambit? Pak ODIs 2006

India batted first in the first ODI, Pakistan 2006. Tendulkar made a 100 of 113 balls (of the 270 balls, during his stay at the crease). Looks like the same old singles gambit? Yes, but this time it was accepted and accounted for brilliantly. Although, Sehwag left early and Tendulkar was bowled on a no-ball, trying to work it to the on side. This was the break he needed perhaps in Karachi, where also he was looking good.

The solution was superb. Instead of solving the singles issue, by sudden improvement in strike rotation, they made sure that every wicket that fell at the other end brought a player, who was capable of unorthodox or risky shot making (Pathan, Dhoni) and thereafter a player who may not like singles as much, but loves shot making– Yuvraj Singh. So giving singles to Tendulkar, always brings in a player who is looking to score freely than be concerned of strike rotation. This also addresses the dot dilemma problem, as Pathan and Dhoni can explore light gray options for sure. Its like strategy and tactics going hand in hand. India posted 328, and considering that they had gone in with 5 bowlers, this was compelling indeed.

Despite a huge score, India eventually lost, as most of the Indian bowlers were indifferent and Murali Karthik, the fifth bowler unfortunately had a bad day with four wides and a no-ball during the last few overs. Sehwag was forced to bowl, giving 11 away in an over. India lost on D/L method. However, India would soon fix the bowling problem, with Tendulkar later in the series, who got Inzamam out twice, and bowled outside the off-stump swing bowling, end exploited dot ball pressure in the middle overs.

21.15 Overcoming inswinging one shot, Pak 2nd ODI 2006

Pakistan made 265, after recovering from an early 4 wicket loss. The ball swung in the initial overs and after Salman Butt fell, the other middle order batsman, could not sail past into the 5th bowler stage (Tendulkar/Sehwag bowled as India played 4 bowlers). India could have knocked more wickets, but perhaps Dravid would in the end take the 65+ runs given by the fifth bowler- as India played Raina and super-sub Powar.

When India batted, Pakistan had a good plan for Tendulkar but forgot about Sehwag (who was having a bit of a tough time in the swinging conditions). However, they bowled all over the place to Sehwag, who cashed in on balls which were either short or full, some outside off and some into his body.

But for Tendulkar, they did a *type 3, one shot bowling-* with fielders in front of square on the leg side (two of whom were between the non-striker and mid-wicket). Pakistan read the situation quite well as they anticipated Tendulkar to play straighter to the incoming ball, which was getting him bowled (as he usually works them to square leg). So they kept it simple- bowling slightly full and at a wobbly speed- just enough to nip back. He also played a false shot, when he tried to slash-drive a ball outside off stump and got an inside edge which missed the stumps. But such one shot bowling in the second innings, with not too big an asking rate- is effective only to a certain point since the batsman can wait for the bad ball or wait to be proactive (unlike the 1st innings, where you do not know how to evaluate a dot ball). This was evident from the fact that Tendulkar could find the right mix of waiting and attacking– he first hit a fuller off stump ball over mid off, then waited till he pulled a short one on the leg stump, then a straighter ball not quite as full, he worked it off the back foot and managed to find the gap through mid wicket. Pakistan had a good plan, but as we've seen, such one-shot bowling becomes more effective in the first innings.

21.16 Waiting on Nimzo-Pollock, 3rd Test Cape Town 2006

This was the third and deciding test of India's test series in South Africa. The series being level at 1-1, this was the chance for India to create history, as they had never won a series in South Africa.

India had posted a good score of 414 in the first innings, with South Africa replying with 373, thanks to some good lower order batting.

So it was day 4, with India ahead by forty odd runs. With two days remaining it was a good chance to convert their first innings advantage and 'stretch their lead'— to declare in the evening giving South Africa about 275-300 to chase. The target was perhaps right, but it was the wrong assessment! Firstly, a forty run lead, although handy, cannot be considered an 'advantage', as it is marginal in a test context. Then to say that a team batting third is 'stretching the lead' is all the more dangerous, as the other team has not yet batted again! For instance, in the first innings of a test, if a team is batting with 120 on board, would you say that it is a 120 runs 'lead', since the other team is on 0 (having not yet batted). Now, just think of this as a two-day, one inning a side match— with India batting first. Even if the first team is batting with 120 or whatever in the midst of an innings, it is not 'stretching the lead', which is still the marginal 40 odd run minor-advantage. The match is in parity– just as India can win by declaring and getting them all out in a day, they can be all out and be chased.

Now the next major point. Here it comes—the Great Dot Dilemma— of the first innings of an ODI and in such third innings, where both runs and wickets matter (on account of near-parity), yet the first team is looking to push scoring– without knowing the exact the target. It is very difficult to value the dot ball.

At lunch, India were 70 odd for 2; in 25 overs. The lead was still 40 runs. After lunch Ganguly, was out to a full and wide ball from Kallis (he had come in at number 4, since Tendulkar was away from the field and the openers lasted within those 7 minutes or so). In came Tendulkar, and so did Pollock. All that was needed was a positive 35-45 runs and a partnership of another 80 odd would take India to a solid 150 plus (but the lead would be still 40). **And did you think South Africa would just try to get him out?** *Nimzo*-**Pollock had different ideas. He instead choose to exploit the Dot Dilemma.** He bowled reverse-swing, full and straight, but with an in-dip. He had more fielders around and in front. This can be classified as a mix of type 1-3 balls, since it can get you out being straight, and also allow you to drive it mildly, but with a field set for only that ball. He was well supported by Paul Harris, at the other end bowling left-arm off spin, over the wicket into the rough, with a packed leg side field. South Africa's plan, was to reduce their options to take wickets but cut off the runs as well (when most would have thought that they needed 'quick' wickets). Well the tempo of 'quick' in this case was in terms of runs.

Tendulkar was immensely criticized but let me tell you— his assessment to wait was spot on. In such a dot dilemma phase, in an ODI you might lose your wicket in trying to fabricate a shot. Now it was not the case in test cricket to fabricate, and there was no reason for India to lose 4 wickets in that session (as Ganguly rightly pointed out in an interview, that the problem of that phase was that they lost wickets). Even if a batsman did fabricate a few fours, Pollock would have continued the full (or length, but not short) and straight line. It is like 'overprotecting' the strong point of reverse-swing and tricky line– to dot for sure or get a wicket perhaps— in a situation which the other team needs prompt runs but cannot lose wickets. Since all fielders are set for that line only, and with due dot-support from the other bowler, this is a case of focusing all your resources on one point— probing dot ball line with a chance of wicket.(In chess, Nimzowitsch, has a concept of *overprotecting* your strong points, by developing and engaging the opponent to put his energy on that strong point, and eventually the battle tilts in your favor as you keep other issues at bay (inducing a prophylactic) and also it unfolds with your plan developing, not the opponent's.

So why was India right, in not attempting to fabricate? They could have at best picked up about 25-30 more runs, and with more chance to loose the wickets (as said except for Tendulkar's lbw, which although marginal, was kind of fair, all three other wickets were uncalled for). Also, KD Karthik, the keeper, did not break the 'shackles', as the pace bowling to him was to get him out directly—and runs can flow in such bowling—but Harris continued the negative one shot line. Karthik, of course, reverse-swept him once for four. I cannot dream to imagine

Dravid or Tendulkar getting out trying to reverse-sweep, and not being criticized later – 'as there was the need to try that type of a shot'.

The match state was at parity, and not with India 'in lead', as discussed. So if they did not lose the wickets, and went into tea, with just fewer runs added, then the game was heading into 30 more overs, with India either drawing or winning. Now the dot dilemma is gone, as India cannot be bowled out (like the slog overs of the first innings of an ODI!).

In my view, **the way to analyze this waiting game would be like– had this session not existed, who would benefit?** I think India would, as then it would not be easy to bowl them out, and the runs would eventually come in the last 10 of the 30 odd, overs after tea, with all other fielding quandaries on the other team to save runs.

For India, it was a case of not reading the fact that the situation was one of parity at the beginning of the day, rather than one of advantage — and that India was yet to earn the advantage to then force a declaration. Going with Sehwag to open and thinking of declaration from the onset was a bit ahead of the steps. But Pollock was brilliant and so was South Africa's converting the dot dilemma into an execution advantage. For Tendulkar, it was a case of Adelaide boomeranging his own ideas back at him, after the famous win for India down under.

21.17 Adelaide Boomerangs in Cape Town

Remember India in Australia, in 2003-04, second test at Adelaide? Australia amassed 500 plus, with India replying back with Dravid and Laxman, to give Australia a 30 plus lead (similar to the pervious example. Australia made the same mistake—call it over-confidence—when some of their early batsmen tried to force the pace. It was too early to call for declaration, as there was no real 'lead' as such. When Steve

Waugh (who batted very well in that innings, in an otherwise indifferent tour), and Damien Martyn were batting, Tendulkar came in to bowl. This was the same case of the dot dilemma now being on Australia—runs needed at some pace yet their wickets in precarious balance, it was not easy to evaluate the dot.

Tendulkar latched on, and lured Waugh and Martyn into false shots, by bowling leg spin, full and wide, and turning further away. They both drove and edged it to first slip. This was type 2-3, one shot bowling from Tendulkar, as the batsmen perhaps could have waited easily in defence if they chose too. Ajit Agarkar also had Katich out, going for the hook. This was the case where Australia did not play the waiting game and perished and lost easily.

However, back in Cape Town, Tendulkar waited hard to avoid falling into his own trap, he had set for Australia! This time it was made difficult by Pollock's superb one shot bowling. What India had gained in Adelaide—a win, when they had earned themselves a draw—they lost in South Africa, from a position of parity, by losing 3 unnecessary wickets and Tendulkar who was out defending his own dots, which boomeranged through Pollock (obviously more lethal than Tendulkar's bowling in Adeliade, as he also had a compelling wicket taking option of a bowled or lbw).

Just as a comparison, **Tendulkar's bowling, was a tactical ploy to take a quick wicket or two, by forcing batsmen into a false shot. On the other hand, Pollock's bowling was one of deep positional play,** of persisting with a probing spell to squeeze options, and keep a wicket taking option open.

21.18 Out-dotting West Indies in ODIs 2007, India

The recent ODI series against West Indies in India, January 2007, is perhaps an indication of how the dot ball exploitation has been maximized by teams. It must be said, in context of the forthcoming World Cup 2007, the West Indies are going to be a force to reckon with, not because of the likes of Marshall and Garner but because of wobbly dots from Bravo (he has half a dozen varieties), and other support bowlers such as Chris Gayle, and Marlon Samuels, who cannot be treated as spinners, but as crafty bowlers who mix speed, trajectory and overspin or get bounce out of a scrambled seam.

Yes, these guys love to exploit the dot dilemma, as they chose to bowl first in India, no matter what the pitch was like. Surely, they were perhaps experimenting a few things about chasing or some other issues, and may perhaps not *always* bowl first in the World Cup, but they are beginning to like bowling first for sure.

Likewise, from India, their fifth bowler in Tendulkar has what it takes to dot around. In the first ODI in Nagpur, after India amassed 338 (being put into bat), the West Indies made their attempt to chase it but after Gayle departed, Chanderpaul and Samuels got bogged down with some good bowling from Harbhajan, and Tendulkar bowling round the wicket to the left-hander, wide and turning away.

Eventually, Lara came in and had to go for it. He had an edge to third man of Tendulkar and also an inside edge of Harbhajan. But he hit a few splendid sixes of both bowlers. If you allow him to get to the pitch of the ball, he can make a 10 run/over target look silly in the slog overs. Tendulkar could not just dot around against Lara. But Dravid persisted with Tendulkar, even after being hit. Figuring that he cannot beat Lara in flight, with his brand of part-time off spin, Tendulkar came over the wicket, and skid it wide and flat, to get him stumped.

The tricky thing about this dot stuff, is that Tendulkar knows when the batsman is in constructive mode (where dot balls are most effective, as batsman cannot play unorthodox shots). In the first innings, dots are potent, due to the dilemma of unknown target. In the second innings, they are useful, but batsmen will have to go for it, as the target is known, and they know how many dots you can wait. In this case, Lara could not wait, so he switched his focus to actually trying to pass him, rather than wobble some wide off-cutters (which may work in a middle phase of a 2nd innings, where some consolidation is needed).

Tendulkar does bowl wicket taking deliveries, especially in his leg-spin brand and some in his in-swing slow seam bowling. This is very useful when you cannot just dot around, as he can look for wickets as well.

In the second ODI, in Cuttack, India were all out inside 200 runs on a slow pitch, with the West Indies bowlers enjoying their pursuit of bowling dots in the first innings. However, this pitch was too bowler friendly, and it helped spinners to cause confusion between dots and scoring shots, even in the second innings– even when batsmen knew the target was low. Tendulkar persisted with off-spin, from round the wicket to left handers. There was a mix of clear dots (fuller and wide) and some closer to the bat, with some flight, since wickets were also needed. The pitch did the trick—earlier big hitting danger man Dwayne Smith was out to Tendulkar— then the ball stopped on Bradshaw and was caught at short cover.

Once the tail was in, Tendulkar just focused on bowling full and wide, seam bowling instead of spin, over the wicket to the right handed tailenders. He perhaps got away with a wide, but he was targeting to bowl it that way, and sneak in the last two overs, without giving Chanderpaul much strike. Eventually India won by 20 runs, but Tendulkar, switched his bowling, based on the best dot options to each batsmen.

It was interesting that a spectator from the public outside, when interviewed on TV, was bemused at how Tendulkar got the results but was not bowling 'well'. Sure it was not 'good' balls (like type 1 stuff) but apt bowling – a mix of type 2-3, which prevents the batsman from scoring or allows specific shots only, and on this pitch it was confusing indeed to even classify it discreetly.

Considering that the West Indies pitches might be kind of similar to Cuttack, we can look forward to interesting dots from part-time bowlers from various countries. Tendulkar has expressed his eagerness to bowl. It will be an interesting World Cup for sure. Dots & big sixes are perhaps the prime candidates for match winning. A variety of dots, makes dot-chess exciting for sure.

Final comments on Sachin Tendulkar, *the Dot Chess Player.*

Tendulkar has seen it all– **direct type 1** bowling which gets you out, as well as dominating such wicket-taking-bowling. He receives less and less of such bowling. **Type 2 bowling**, which tries to prevent a batsman, is what every bowler will bowl, to every batsman, as that is the direct way to a dot ball. He garners runs on such bowling as well, but short and shoulder height, type 2 has contained him lately, on account of fewer horizontal shots. It is no wonder, that type 3 bowling is frequently resorted to him, as he still has scoring options for type 1 and type 2, with fair chance to hold his wicket. From **type 3**, he can be allowed to play shots, which are well covered, and perhaps be given a single when he plays the proper shot.

Further, type 3 and type 2 **one shot bowling,** which essentially takes out the constructive components, and forces risky shots as the only option, is the way to go against him. Whereas most top batsmen in the world, still face type 1 & 2 bowling which tries to get them out or prevents them from scoring, he is up against type 2 & 3 one shot, often with little interest in getting him out– lots of dots, then giving him singles, or forcing unorthodox shots.

As mentioned,

> a targeted batsman can be restricted in terms of scoring rate or batting average—by nearly half—if the team is willing to give singles, and bowl dots by letting go some chances of getting him out. This approach, however, can cost some runs, but will usually reduce the potency of the targeted batsman significantly.

> Further, with one shot bowling, you can exploit any batsman, in a phase which needs consolidation of holding wickets—since batting has a non-commutative nature of good and bad shots– making batting risks 'more risky' than bowling experiments.

Tendulkar is doing fine folks, his biggest drawback has in fact been his ability to play scoring shots and a brisk constructive game on wicke-taking bowling. If he actually gets beaten in defence a lot more, you might see the Tendulkar of 'old' more often, as bowlers will then try to get him out directly. Till then, there will be selective exhibition of skills, but stay tuned to **type 3-one shot chess, with GM Tendulkar**.

And yes, watch out, he bowls with a lot of chess as well!

PART IV: ASSESSSMENT & STATS

22. Team vs Individuals

22.1 Cricket as a Team Game and Role of Players

They always say that cricket is a team game- the team comes first then the individuals. Fair enough. But the team depends the of quality of the individuals, and their quality on a given day or series depends on many other factors, personal and professional. So the quality of the team will also be well served, by taking care of the well-being of the individuals. Why do we count the individual runs or wickets at all, if the team score is what matters.? It's because we want to see human (individuals) achievements—the team is not comprised of chess pieces- which perform like robots no matter what. So the well being of individuals cannot be ignored, and we need better assessment methods, to measure individuals.

There is needless pressure and often disrespect to players because scores often show up enough holes for the media or even some experts to revel in. It is the nature of cricket, that batting or bowling, will produce some poor results, even when a player is doing well, due to the Z and X aspects as described. I have however rarely seen a system of TV stats, which gives an allowance for this. Unfortunately, players become punching bags of sorts, for not performing for their country. The country comes first, the team is more important, so why are players not able to do their job? How do we assess the performance in a better way? Wait for my next book!

22.2 Then assess the roles, with different stats!

Firstly, if players play within a framework of roles— for the cause of the team— it is but right to assess that role with statistical tools which better reflect that role.

Here is an example from Indian cricket.

When we say that the team matters more than players—and most will agree to that—it also follows that we assess the merit of a player effort based on the role that was assigned 'for the cause of the team' or the role a player had to play on account of the manner in which situations unfolded on the pitch. **It is wrong to talk of the team and then measure a player with conventional stats, which are not apt to measure the role assigned.**

For instance, India has always struggled overseas and one of the (many) reasons is the lack of a reliable opening combination. During their **Australia tour (2003-04)**, they were well served by Akash Chopra and Virendra Sehwag. Sehwag was already an established player, though not a conventional opener. Akash Chopra was untested, but seemed a straight and compact batsman, and was asked to see off the new ball as the top priority. It worked, and Indian batting finally came good in Australia. Now if we look at Chopra's stats (as a *runs* average)—which was perhaps still good for Indian openers overseas—it makes little sense, if he was assigned a 'role' to dot out the new ball. He made no hundreds or big 50s either. But he should have been measured on balls played, and then the runs as an addition (I will propose an assessment system which will address such issues, but nonetheless he should not have been measured by conventional averages, if he was asked to play a role in a certain fashion). Next time his grandchildren ask him how many runs he made in Australia, he can reply it in terms of balls played —or well-left—instead, and be proud of his fulfillment, even if it cannot be rated as an achievement in terms of runs.

Another example from Indian cricket.

Sehwag's scores in context of ODIs, in 2005-06 began to bother the media and analysts, even when India were winning and doing well. Whereas there is no problem with studying the performance of a player, even when the team does well, we should also be sensitive to the fact that Sehwag would be wary of his scope as well. The point is that, he was getting out between 25-35 runs, however with 10 balls less. His strike rates were well over 100 and in Australia they would take that, as they accept Adam Gilchrist for his strike rate boost, often with scores in the 30s. However, rather than see the value of what he did in the 'team' context (India were getting off to 50 odd runs in 7-8 overs), he was grilled for getting out 'cheaply'. Sure, we would like to see him make bigger scores, which he is well capable of, but the fact is that he was not getting out cheaply. The kind of role he was playing, could simply have been well illustrated by displaying his strike rate- and the effect it has on the 'team score'. He was giving India, the first 'break of serve', since the first 3-6 overs can be seen as execution advantage for bowlers, even in an ODI.

It is not fair to talk about the team, then single out a player and then not use a team parameter (score or position)—which the player altered or affected—as the reference point for his contribution to the team.

23. Match Winner vs Fighter

There is a lot of confusion and misconception in the world of cricket about the concept of a match winner, a fighter, a single handed performance, a finisher, a man for the crucial moments...

However, there is a way to demystify such issues by recognizing what constitutes good competitive cricket, what makes a contribution valuable, how well certain roles were fulfilled. If players did what their role demanded or what the situation demanded, and if it was a job which requires skill and application, they need to be given due credit, rather than see how sensational or memorable their performance was, which although great for the fans and the history of the game- is never in the hands of a player (if he out-competes and makes the match one-sided, then it will rarely be seen as memorable). So how do we assess or analyze good competitive performances.

In my view, chess players are the best at analyzing match situations, since chess is a game of exact logical outcomes. However, the depths to which good chess players (let alone Grandmasters) can analyze the possible lines from chess positions is quite remarkable, and just about every sports person can benefit by simply understanding how they analyze positions. Chess players look for the slightest imbalances even when both material as well as position are equally poised, and then find ways to capitalize from such imbalances.

Then at the other extreme are individual sports– such as tennis, where the individual *is* the team. There is also a lot to understand what goes into a good performance, from individual sports, since they have to play all the different roles themselves, and they know what was tough or crucial.

Let's see if we can offer broad definitions or explanations for such competitive aspect.

23.1 Match Winner- as keeping uncertainty away

The best or proper way to win, is to ensure that a team tries to win with a reasonable margin, which accounts for the uncertainties of the game. For instance, in **chess,** a player could have a pawn advantage or even equal pieces with a passed pawn (no opposing pawns), and can win right at the very end of the end-game. This is because, chess being an exact game, a player with experience can convert a miniscule advantage to a win right at the end, because things do not suddenly fall apart if you had earned a winning position (unless you blunder).

In a sport such as **tennis,** you would always want to break your opponent's serve at least once in each set, or perhaps twice, since you can hope to hold your own serve to win a set. If you just hold serve and cannot break your opponent, then you may get into the tie-breaker, which is too short a format to really decide the worthy winner (though not quite as cryptic, considering that an entire table tennis game is almost like a tennis tie-breaker with an 11 point format or a penalty -shoot out in soccer). **Snooker** is a good example of why players concede when the frame has reached a point difference of 60-75, and there are not many balls left to score off, without forcing your opponent to foul through snookers. The best way to win in snooker, is to play safe and stitch one strong break of say 70-80 or make mini-breaks and mix it with solid safety- because the unpredictable part of snooker is that even a decent club-level player can knock 30-40 point breaks and a mistake or two, may not allow even the best in the world to out-snooker an opponent, when the reds are cleared, and only a few options remaining.

Now talking about **cricket**- it is truly a game of uncertainties, and more so when you consider that 3 wickets can fall in a span of 10 balls, especially if there are tail-enders involved. Likewise, when 6-7 runs per over are needed in ODIs (even for a few overs), you can see the lottery unfolding for both sides- a couple of inside edges or top-edges can get you there, and perhaps good cricketing shots will find fielders. **So it is prudent that teams work out the runs, wicket and run-rate equation in a manner so that you win by margins, which take these uncertainties out of the very equation.**

In my experience of watching cricket since the 70s- I have seen three sides dominate cricket- West Indies (late 70s-80s), Australia in the past decade, and Sri Lanka (as a one day team) for a brief period in the late 90s. The reason these guys dominated, was not because of last-over histrionics, but because they were better enough to win by calculable margins (again, you need not try to win by crazy margins either, like you would not in tennis, try to win every set 6-0 in tennis or plunder chess pieces and then checkmate).

The benchmark of a winner is not how they fared in un-predictably close encounters, but how they kept such uncertainties away—the kind of situations which nobody would like to be in, in the first place, as they do not have any meaningful latitude for competing on skills.

For instance, Roger Federer won the **2006 Wimbledon** with dominance without losing a set till the finals. In the finals, against Rafael Nadal, he lost a set in the tie-breaker, the only set he lost in the entire tournament. His greatness was that of the 18 sets he won, 16 were won outright and only 2 were won in the tie-breaker. Tennis tie-breakers are in fact quite fair—as fair as tie-breakers go—since you still have to win 7 points and each point is still played with the same parameters as any other points (unlike soccer, where the penalty shoot-out is a different discipline altogether, and now in twenty20 cricket, they intend to have bowlers take aim at the stumps). Ask any great tennis player, if they would like to play in a tournament of only tie-breakers—to really test a player in 'close situations'—the answer will most likely be an emphatic 'no'. Ask the same to the lower ranked players, they will perhaps say 'yes' just as emphatically. **Who would not like competing against a Federer or Sampras, with only tie-breakers? They have many chances to swing the unpredictable in their direction.**

In general, matches in most sports which go 'down-to-the-wire' are filled with errors (and often blunders) on both sides or at least one side who did not push to do better. History of every sport is filled with such matches, which were clinched on the buzzer. Obviously, these games would be indicative of intense effort on both sides, but need not be the best contests or for that matter.

For instance, everyone remembers the Borg vs McEnroe **Wimbledon finals (1980)** as perhaps the best ever classic, which without a doubt it was. McEnroe dominated the first two sets, winning the first easily. He also won his service games easily in the second, but Borg managed to hang in and broke McEnroe at the end of the set, and immediately broke him again at the start of the third! Wily old man. Then it was the turn of Borg to not convert over a dozen break/match points in later sets, to let it go all the way to the final set. Sure McEnroe played out of his skin, but had Borg converted one of those (which you would expect from Borg to do so from a dozen attempts), the match would not have been a classic. The brilliance of the match was not how it took so many twists & turns and kept millions glued to their TVs, but how Borg went ahead 2 sets to 1, even when McEnroe took more points as such (since Borg won his service games with difficulty). The next year's final ended with McEnroe winning 3-1, but it was a good contest nonetheless, which very few remember.

Likewise, in snooker, World Championship Match, 1985 finals was rated as the most memorable ever, featuring Steve Davis-Dennis Taylor. This was a match where Steve Davis, already the Borg of Snooker, was supposed to win easily. He did start off well and led by a big margin and then somehow Dennis Taylor came back. This match went into the last frame with 17 frames each. A single frame to decide the world snooker champion is way too close to call. But the drama went the full distance, and after many errors from both players, Dennis Taylor managed to clear some of the colors, and brought it to a Black ball (the last ball left) game. Whoever tips the last ball in, wins. There is no science in this, since you have to take your chances at potting, as playing safe may not ensure much of an initiative either. Steve Davis was clearly affected and nervous as if he was playing his first ever match (at least this was perhaps the first such final). He was expected to win. Taylor, on the other hand smiled after every miss which landed safe, until one of them ended up a foot away from the pocket. Steve had the last shot, —so it seemed—a thin cut (bit tricky but you would take it for a world cup shot). Well he missed and Taylor had the last laugh, to win the championship. **So was Steve Davis of weak competitive character, because he let the situation get to him?** Ask any player in the world, they will tell you what he is made of, even in the 9-ball pool arena (which is not his game as such). Full credit to Taylor, for beating

Steve Davis in the finals—no matter what the errors are—it is a super achievement. But wait, the story does not end here. The very next year, Joe Johnson reached the finals against Steve Davis and beat him convincingly– playing aggressive snooker in such a fashion that Steve was outplayed and he did not even feel bad about it! Johnson bettered what Taylor had done, but most of us do not even remember his convincing win. Tip: next time you lead in a match, you might want to slow down a bit, so that it goes down to the wire. This may be the road to glory...

Now, take the world of cricket– the **great test between Australia and West Indies (1960) which was 'tied'**. It is perhaps one of the most memorable in the history of cricket, culminating in the run-out by Joe Solomon aiming at one stump from square leg. If you ever see footage, you will note that the match went up and down a bit, but Australia should have won, had they not blundered so many run-outs, which perhaps was the right assessment for the match. But it became part of cricket folklore on account of the errors. Spectators always like such dramatic endings, as even Sir Don Bradman (not a player then), told Richie Benaud (who as a player, sat dejected, since he knew they should have won), that this was great for cricket. Sure, this was so for spectators, but not for the side which should have won—especially when they knew that one of the shots in the last over should have gone for four, had the tuft of grass been cut near the fence!

Likewise, India suffered psychologically for quite some time, when Javed Miandad hit that **last ball six in Sharjah (Aust-Asia Cup Finals, 1986)**. It sure was a good innings, but to say that Miandad did it all, would be unfair, to say Abdul Qadir who got Kris Shrikant the danger man out and also smacked a cameo to actually alter the situation of indifference into a tangible one for Pakistan to approach. Talking of blunders, there were 3 in the last over. The first was when Miandad hit a superb shot, to be equally well fielded, at square leg to stop a four. The flaw was that they ran a single and got the last man on strike! The next shot, they had to run a single, but the ball went straight to Azhar(?), who could have ran out the batsman by running to the stumps instead of throwing. The last ball as we all know was the full toss from Chetan Sharma, which has become part of his player profile (wrongly). The fact is that when chasing about 250, if you need a six of the last ball, you have done something wrong as such. Although, not entirely Miandad's fault (though they blundered in the last over), he did mention that blaming Chetan Sharma for that full toss, was being too harsh, as Pakistan losing early wickets was the big mistake. Miandad is a champion because he knew that there was a proper and better way to win such a game, rather than hit a six off one ball that was left (no player can really say that he can hit a six on a given ball, because if they can, they should have hit it a few balls or overs earlier, and perhaps avoided such a blunder-full scenario).

Not that every extended contest has to be that way, because you may see some games going a longer distance with high quality and no errors either- especially in chess, where top Grandmasters will give perfect or sound replies to their opponent's moves. Again, in chess, such games which go well into the end games, are sound because of the exactness of the format, but in most other sports, where there is some scope for players to play by mood or a bit of a different role (which chess pieces cannot do)–great teams will squeeze in something compelling, well before it becomes out of hand.

The whole point is that winning that 'down to the wire competition' is good for sure, but it should never be given a tag of greatness, without careful inspection, as to why it went to that stage of unpredictability in the first place. Moreover, for a team or player **to achieve a position, from which winning is possible by doing regulation methods, since**

the uncertainty is reduced or out of the equation, it is worth a lot more than making the day a memorable one for spectators.

The Art of War, Sun Tzu (*Chapter IV on tactical aspects*)**,** the old Chinese manual about principles of war fare (applied in management and sports as well) puts the matter in perspective,—**the best warriors are the ones who put themselves beyond defeat (by avoiding mistakes), but they neither get credit for their wisdom nor their courage.**

23.2 Fighter— up-front and fight-back

So what about fighters? From what we have discussed, it appears that players who fight hard and 'come from behind' are not to be applauded, since the best way to win is to keep a margin which makes a predictable sense. Surely, winning by keeping the right margins and eliminating uncertainties is what one must strive for, but reality is not always ideal. So what about those who fight-back in a game?

Well, there is another fundamental confusion of what constitutes a fighter. There is this notion that when someone is 'down and out' and rises again, can be referred to as a fighter. Surely, that is so. **But you have to be a fighter at every phase of the game, as you do not get freebies up front or in the middle.** To be down and out, usually implies that your team fought poorly to begin with. This is so, because in sports, everyone starts with the same bank balance– unlike real life.

A fight exists at every point, shot or ball played qualitatively (as long as the match is not in an irreparable or totally drawn state). It is far from easy to score a goal in soccer when the game commences or to even leave the deliveries bowled at you by an attack such as the West Indies of the 1980s. They do not bowl trial balls upfront.

In any contest, you can perhaps ignore the match state to a degree but it is indeed difficult to ignore the basic execution advantages. Scoring off your opponent's serve in tennis is tough no matter what the match-score, since the execution advantage is not with the receiver (although the match state can be converted into some execution effect (*Ch 14.2 p132*).

So the truth is that fighting up front to eliminate uncertainties is the key. Fighting to make a comeback in a match has its merits, as human events are not always ideally executed. And if you had learnt the virtues of winning with margins, then, when you are down, you can treat the remainder of the match, as a fresh match which needs to be won by margins which were your plan anyway. For instance, if you are 1-2 down in tennis, you try to find a way to win the remainder of the match 2-0, as if it was a new match from that point (to win 3-2 eventually). Again fighting back is about how you would try to win by clear margins, just that there is a different starting point.

Fighting back as a test of character...

As mentioned, a fight exists at every qualitative stage of any sport. To fight back and take the game down to the wire, is cool, but when you fight up front, it indicates that you have done your homework down to the wire, before the match began. The moment a match commences, you are in a sense fighting back from what someone had seen of you in an earlier match. Can you say that Federer lacks character as he rarely has had to fight back (and in cases where he did and lost closely, it was because that was his bad outing - since it went down to the wire!). In fact, he has such a stature, that he would have fought so hard on match preparation and strategy, that he can fight up front and win by desirable margins.

23.3 Why it is natural to be a fighter in sport

If winning with an approach of making sure that you take uncertainties out of the equation is the best way to go about business, why try to make fight-backs—let's just concede—because when you put yourself in a mess and be the first to admit that things fell apart.

Sure, this is done say in snooker and chess, where it is considered disrespectful if you continue beyond a point from which it is simply prolonging an obvious result. But again, in such games, execution errors from an opponent need not be as common as other sports, as there is a certain sense of exactness of conditions and format of such games (chess board/pieces, billiard table, balls etc.). This is not however the case in say cricket or soccer (to a large extent), since goals or wickets can happen due to reaction errors.

But there is major reason not to give up in a match. There is simply nothing more to lose! If in trying to go for an unlikely win from a hopeless situation, whether caused due to your own fault or by virtue of a strong opponent, you lose badly or you lose by a some closer margin- you lose anyway. Whether you try or not, the worst you can do is to lose that set or match. So you never need give up.

But compare this to a real life situation. Say, you need to put more money into a project which got stalled. Should you put more money into it or just agree to shut it and let go whatever went into it? Because by fighting to turn around the project, the additional money that you may lose (if it were to fail), would leave you with less money for your next project. Whereas in cricket, the runs or wickets which fell apart in trying to salvage a lost cause, will have no future consequence, since the next match would begin from scratch (an exception to this is when run rates or some scoring aspect from a lost game are counted towards ranking in a league phase). So usually when you fight in a game, you can say that the worst I can do is lose a match, so I might as well fight. Fighting back in sports is a very natural thing, whereas fighting back in life is a real challenge, because the poorer the outcome— the more is the loss of time, money and well being. So when you assess fight backs in a sport, you should still be able rate the merit on the quality of the performance, just as you would measure quality of performance, when a player fought to keep adversity at bay.

This is one of the reasons, when someone fights-back 'from the jaws of defeat' and eventually wins, it may not be the end of the world, as if some savior has arrived. Because from such situations, if you cannot win, it is understandable, and often pressure got released from both sides (those who were ahead, may not tweak their strategy as sharply as they should and those who are all but lost, have nothing more to lose and can take their chances, as they may lose anyway).

Take an example from the **2nd Test, Ashes in England 2005**. Australia had all but lost the match with 2 wickets left and over 100 runs to make. However, Bret Lee fought back to the very end and never gave up, and in the end Australia fell short by 2 runs! This does not mean that Bret Lee was a great fighter— rather, like most Aussies, they are remarkable competitors and they realize that fighting back is the natural thing to do. But the important point is that after the match, although they perhaps felt 'so near, yet so far' they were well composed in accepting that they had lost the match much earlier (as Ponting mentioned in his post match interview). Fighting back is natural to all competitors but what makes Aussies a notch above is the fight up front which prevents them from getting entangled from such matches which twist and turn—more often than not.

Just as I write, we have been privileged to witness a brilliant performance by **England to beat Australia in the first CB final of the ODI**

tri-series in Melbourne 2007. This was Paul Collingwood's day- a catch of Ponting at short cover, run outs and then coming in the fifth over to make a fighting century. This was a great fightback for the simple reason that the quality of the innings-, was as constructive as it possibly can get. The important thing was that Collingwood did not tumble away to glory upon victory, firstly because this was the first match of a 3 match series and the Aussies were still perhaps the favorites to win two in two, and secondly he has a balanced mind to appreciate the other pluses in the game- restricting Gilchrist to just 10 balls in the first 5 overs (taking him off strike is important), then getting back into the game after Ponting and Hayden had set up Australia for a big score, and then the support from Ian Bell to reach 140+ with 7 wickets remaining at about a run-a-ball in 18 overs, and then Flintoff getting the run-a-ball strike rate with a good 35 to get near the Australian total (after Flintoff fell). Collingwood's knock was excellent, but England's result as a whole was not a model for a match winning team but one of a good fight back— to allow your opponents 170 for 1 in 33 overs, was not fun for sure and then giving in 3 wickets in 5 overs, (not counting the catch McGrath dropped off an Ian Bell hook), when chasing 250 (the best target you can possibly try to get against Australia), is a matter of concern.

What does *not* constitute "jaws of defeat"

This is one of the many aspects, which gets blown out of proportion nowadays. There is often a lack of differentiation between 'down and out' and a 'sticky' or 'poor' situation. Many fight backs are not really lost-causes (although it may look like going nowhere), simply because of the fact that there may be a lot of room for regulation-play and still getting close to the target. This is the reason Collingwood's attitude in the first ODI finals at Melbourne 2007, must be applauded, as he could have sensationalized his story. Sure 15 for 3 is a cause for concern, but when chasing 250 and with 3 batsmen of quality left (with Bell and Flintoff), it is not hopeless, especially when the strike rate could be managed. Rather one good partnership and decent contributions should get you close, since good batsmen can be expected to score 40-50s and one of them a bit more. This is how Bell and Collingwood went about it, because had they assessed it as hopeless, it would indeed get worse and land them in the jaws of defeat, for sure.

So here is a way to define a good fight back-

> a performance wherein the team or player is aware but not affected by the probability of success due to a below-par state, and is focused on making best use of the available resources to attain parity or advantage.

This means that a mature player will know how to assess weak starts, indifferent states, bad positions, lost situations, and search for options accordingly be it defensive or positive or proactive or attacking. Sounds a bit tedious? It sure is, which is why you should plan for the best winning approach—to target margins which keep uncertainty away (that will be tedious as well, but worth it).

23.4 Evaluating Match Winning Performances

There has been some flawed ways of doing stats of match winning or potent performances, by seeing the final result of the match. How much does such a batsman or bowler average, when the team has won? This is most unfair since it is rare that single-handed performances could win the match in themselves.

In the great comeback by Botham **(Botham's Ashes, 3rd Test 1981 at Leeds)** after being made to follow-on, was indeed remarkable, but Bob Willis's 8 wickets for 43, was special, to knock Australia out under a target of 130 runs. In the **Ashes match (2nd Test, in England, 2005),** where Australia were down and out then just lost by 2 runs, instead of at least about 100, Flintoff did everything any player could do with bat and ball, as discussed in the Queen of Ashes (*Ch 20.4, p177*). Had they lost, would that performance not have counted? He put the team in a position by which the match could be won by doing expected things. That is what was is needed to be looked at, as all a player can do is put a team in a better position than what existed.

So doing stats this way is simply unjust, as we have seen double centuries, end up on the losing side or matches being drawn because of lack of bowling depth. Likewise, if bowlers may knock teams over, and get little support from batsmen, the stats will be worse, as such matches will reflect a loss, rather than a draw, because it will be result oriented when bowlers outperform.

For instance, Subhash Gupte, the legendary Indian leg-spinner, once took 9 wicket for about 100 runs in the first innings **(against West Indies, 2nd Test Kanpur, 1958)** but India lost that match! You cannot say that was not a match winning performance, because of lack of support from others or a great reply from the opponent in the next innings (by Sir Garfield Sobers in that case with almost a double ton).

So such stats, which rate an individual by the team result, end up nowhere, and in fact they may often show up - fringe players, since when they played, many others might have played as well to win the match and when they failed, their failure was so bad that the team perhaps lost from a good position. So their failure itself alters the criteria of the statistics and does not get sampled in! (their bad may be so bad that it was responsible for not winning and hence was not a valid sample).

I have heard such silly things for **Gavaskar's centuries and India winning.** Unfortunately, he did not bat from both ends! Ask any fast bowler in the world, and they would vouch for Gavaskar in their team not the other (and he was also amongst the best players of spin!). The fact is that in matches that were won when the other players excelled, strong players may have provided some valuable support runs (even if it was not their day), but on other situations when strong players excelled (perhaps more often), the other players perhaps were so poor that the match was lost due to lack of support runs. So doing stats of when this player did this, you either have to get into more detail of what the others did or did not, and what is the pattern of the team's winning strength as such. If the team's wins are sparse, then stats just won't do justice to strength of a player, anyway.

Or for that matter, consider **a hypothetical case of Don Bradman playing for a weak side such as Zimbabwe or Bangladesh** or even some other teams which are not on the top today. Surely, he would score the double centuries (that too every 3rd innings, not perhaps more than that!), but if his bowling attack could not get teams out twice, he would end up on the losing side very often with perhaps a few draws!

It was interesting to see an article online (perhaps cricinfo.com), on the **winning-est players ever— how many times (percentage) did their team, as win to loss %, when they played? No, it was not Bradman or Sobers, it was off-spinner Rajesh Chauhan from India!** He played about 20 odd matches, and has never been on the losing side of a test match! This was because he was perhaps good enough to be India's third spinner, and was taken to play in the sub-continent (where India rarely lost) and would not fit into India's team, on tours overseas, where India lost more than they won. His not being able to make it into the team (with due respect) in conditions where chances of losing were high, was a plus in such stats! (granted the numbers of tests is low but it illustrates the flaw in the process).

So let us move on to the issue of when a performance matters, and which performances to sample.

In my opinion, such confusion exists in cricket, since it is a team sport with sequenced-performance by players. So it makes it easy to see what an individual did, but yet very difficult to assess the impact in context of the team equation, since there are too many factors which are critical (and come and go in their own sequence). As was mentioned earlier, averages matter— because totals matter—but only when taken over a large number of samples, as in a career or over a few dozen of matches. But in 'a given match', we need to see crucial roles as well.

For instance, in a game of **chess** where all pieces have to make positional sense- even if the game was made interesting by a few pieces such as a bishop-pair or knights which hop in weird manner- it is normal for chess players to analyze positions in detail and not see snapshots of a phase or certain piece-activity to make a sensation out of the brilliance of that phase alone (even if it was that phase which did the trick). You never hear of a chess player saying that the bishop knocked the rook off, when it mattered! Likewise, in a sport such as **tennis** where it is a total individual sport, a player knows how to assess his performance at the crucial stages, because he is in it 100% of the time. Even if he fired in an ace at the right time, he knows just how valuable his service returns or baseline play was, without which he would not be in the race at all.

The point is that a thorough analysis in games of simultaneous participation, is normal, as analysts are forced to look at the overall context, as in chess or soccer. In an individual sports such as tennis, the player is responsible for his own undoing or victory. **Cricket, being sort of sequenced, the individuals get measured, but often wrongly,** as they are still fulfilling a role for the team.

24. Playing when it matters

24.1 How often can it work out?

This concept of playing 'when it matters', has reached such silly proportions in the media (in India), that it has affected the psyche of the fans, experts and also ultimately the players. **One might say that players must not be affected by external pressures, but it is never possible to ignore the spectators for whom cricket is played for in the first place.** In India, after every match there is an analysis of who is in form and who let the team down. If a player cannot perform, he should be replaced, since the team is greater.... it goes on and on.

The fact is that in cricket, an 'in-form' player can get out (because of the Z-demand and the fact that he does not know when his next mistake will happen) and an 'in-form' bowler may bowl brilliantly and yet not get wickets (because of the X-demand and the fact that conversion between beating a batsman and getting the wicket is never an exact science).

24.2 Understanding the Natural Pattern of Success/Failure

For instance, in a span of 5-6 innings, let's see what kind of break up is 'normal'. About one in six innings can often be part of drawn situations or those where the tempo has set in, or result is but a formality, or those which need a crazy strike rate inducing batsmen to fabricate shots. These should be out of statistical considerations from a short term perspective, (though not from a career angle, as overall records should include whatever is fair in international cricket). From the remaining 5 innings, even world-class batsmen may produce 2 failures (below15-20 runs), 2 decent knocks (25-50s), and perhaps one excellent performance (80 plus). **They may have in fact played very well in each innings till the ball they got out, since the Z-demand spares no one.**

The only exception was Sir Don Bradman, who would have 2 out of the 5 knocks as big hundreds. In fact, Sir Don averages in the 30s for his non century innings– which is about every 2 of 3 attempts! If thirty is a failure, then the mighty Don failed way too often (from the 2 of 3 times he failed to score a 100, he would have some 50s, but it just goes to show that about 30-40% of the times he failed to make any notable impact- from a media point of view. But if someone considers 30 as a good innings (which it can very well be, if you see the quality of shots till the shot you got out on), we can just about see that Bradman was averaging ahead of most great all-rounders of the world, even if you exclude his centuries! As far as his centuries go, his average hundred was worth about 230 or so! His successes are best ignored, when studying what is 'normal' in cricket.

The whole point is that for any batsmen to produce an innings of notable quality more than 2 of 5 times is perhaps beyond personal control. It can happen but cannot be assured even when in form (when in form, you can make many more flawless 30s or 40s, but you do get out often due to many factors, often even beyond the bowler's control). You can perhaps make contributions of some constructive value perhaps 3-4 of 5 times. But 1 or 2 failures in 5 is normal, for any batsman. This is the nature of batting.

Likewise, in bowling, if you take wickets as the benchmark, which in Tests one must, there will be 1 in 6 innings, not much to bowl at or the pitch just favors another kind of bowler in the team. The moment your colleague knocks over a few wickets, the pie is reduced (unlike batsmen, bowlers on their day can share from only ten wickets, whereas batsmen can pile up more). Now, of the remaining 5 innings, bowlers can bowl well in all of them, since they do not get 'out' on the first or few bad balls. But since there is an X-demand, the 'well bowled' spells may not be good enough to get wickets. In ODIs, even on a good day, just an over or two of inside edges can spoil your economy rate. So statistically, bowlers are a mirror of batting, with 1-2 of 5 as notable; 2-3 of 5 as well-contributed; and 1-2 of 5 as an indifferent innings. But bowlers need not be total failures, since the regular bowlers can be assured 60-90 balls a day and getting even one crucial wicket or one good dot-over in an ODI can be noteworthy (which unfortunately does not come under statistical radars).

Just a note: this natural pattern is a broad generalization, and real outcomes obviously vary from series to series, but nonetheless this natural pattern over 6 innings is a good reference point. Someone can come up with another natural pattern over a different number of samples or based on different ways of categorizing performance into more categories than three— failure, decent or exceptional. On an assessment system I am working on, I intend to consider balls played, positive/negative dots handled.... but for now let us see how/when to use this natural pattern as a reference. If you come up with your own way of classification and have a different pattern that can work fine as well, so long as it does fit the general pattern of scoring and wicket taking.

Also, this natural pattern has been taken in such a way that the excellent or good scores can be relative to player strength. The 'excellent' for a top batsman would be 150, whereas for other good players it could be 75.

24.3 Comparing Performances to the Natural Pattern

Based on the above natural pattern of outcomes in cricket, we can now compare performances a lot better, especially for short spans of a few innings or even a year (2-3 test serieses or 20 odd ODIs).

Considering one particular innings

If you consider any one particular innings and rant over why someone did not play an innings of some merit, well the answer is that no one is yet born to say he 'will' perform in a given innings. This may be different in 'balanced Z-X' games such as tennis, where the much better player can claim to win with certain surety (since the first double fault does not end his day, neither does not serving so many aces or winners lose it; as explained earlier it does not make tennis easier but the uncertainty of cricket, can make a batsman's innings shorter than a tie-breaker, and the bowler's best balls could be unfruitful, although as good as an ace. (Note: tennis is an individual sport so certain margins of error have to be allowed. If a tennis player can make a few double faults or miss volleys, it would be like a team in cricket being allowed 6 blunders or so — which is why there are about six batsmen, not one).

Considering a few innings

If you consider a few innings (3-4), well, it is worth considering. However, it is better to measure quality based on balls played, as that could be in hundreds of balls, or even dozens of balls in case a batsman got out early. Just count the frequency by which a batsman bungles up, that is—the percentage of balls being beaten. Another indicator of quality is frequency of scoring shots to dot balls (not the runs, but % of balls which were scored off). Likewise, for bowlers, count the % of balls he beat a batsman and percentage of dot balls bowled to non-dots. **You will get indicators for the defensive and scoring form of a batsman or bowler—in a much better manner, since there are enough samples and cricket is played ball by ball, anyway.** Taking averages over too few samples is not meaningful in a statistical analysis, especially in cricket, where the standard deviation (of runs/wicket) would be huge—unlike say, measuring the average bowling speeds per innings, could still be an indicator of 'speed', since the speeds have minimal deviation and there will be many samples, as we measure based on total balls bowled (the slower balls which were clearly intended, can be discarded from the sampling process).

Considering a series or two

It is best to consider 6-10 innings of a series or immediate past series, to make any statements about performance. Even on 10 samples, averages can at best be rough indicators. Every century will add 10 points to the average. A double century would add 20, and if you got a 40 not out, you add 4 points straight. **So a bowler or batsman with one or two exceptional innings, will throw the average off in such a way that you cannot call it an average.** The best way, in such sampling (about 10 innings) is to follow the pattern which indicates the nature of outcomes, as discussed- 2 failures, 2 decent outings, 1 excellent. **Rather than take averages, see how the player performance compares to this natural pattern.** If in 10 innings, there were 4 failures (0-20), 4 good innings (25-60) and 2 excellent ones (85-150s)— the player is doing just fine. Obviously, actual patterns may not follow the above and the mix is likely to be different, but you will at least find out by how much which aspect differs. Did the best scores of the batsman not reach expected heights (failed to convert starts). Were there many similar scores, but no failures? (consistent but indifferent). Or many failures and one or two big knocks or wicket hauls (inconsistency).

24.4 When does it matter, and filtering it right.

How do we say which match matters?

Well, most of them do, else they would not be playing and we would not be watching. So it is perhaps better for us to recognize—and exclude—the few matches which do *not* matter in a competitive context. Record-wise, every international match should count, since it was a worthy appearance, representing a country and the game.

However, there are matches which are clearly competitively meaningless, such as those, where the series result is already unchangeable —dead-rubbers and left-over league matches—which will have no effect on the positions of the next stage. Teams play to win a series or tournament, and once the results are out, the exam as such has ended. Such 'dead' games did not matter from ball one, from a competitive sense, not from a sense of record or as a test of skills as mentioned.

Such matches which do not have any effect on the tournament, can be safely kept aside when evaluating competitiveness. This does not mean that such matches may not have a sense of seriousness or playing with passion. However, strategically and tactically the team which has won the series or qualified will usually never be as sharp, and if at all may seek to experiment new combinations or rest players partially or completely. Likewise, players in the team which has lost the series or cannot qualify, will have nothing more to lose and would perhaps take any risks along their way without much worry- and it may fetch rich dividends.

For instance, it is no surprise that Australia has remarkably lost many of the dead rubber encounters, after winning the test series in past years. This is indicative of the fact that they have been either experimental or just taking things as they come (rather than dictate proceedings from the onset, which is what the Aussies normally do).

Then there are 'certain sessions', which matter less.

Next up are sessions, which are already headed into a draw (tricky to decide when it is headed for a draw, but possible to work out). However, draws are never a foregone conclusion, as it is easy to lose quick wickets for sure. So the probability of the result may be a draw but players still have to *make* it a draw, however evident it may be. However, there are ways to find out such sessions—from which a draw is likely.

How do we tell when a draw has 'set' in? In my view, you can compare wickets remaining in the match and sessions left (Test matches). For instance, it is very rare that a cricket match gets over in two and half days (8 sessions). This averages 30 to 40 wickets divided by 8 sessions= an average 4 to 5 wickets per session for a 'rare' result. We can now have **a thumb-rule to find out which session of a match a 'draw' has most likely 'set-in'.**

1. At the beginning of a session, find the number of sessions possible in the match.

2. and *estimated* total wickets left for a match to be completed. This total will be (wickets left in the current innings + (10 x minimum number of innings left)). The minimum number of innings will be based on the follow-on or innings-defeat criteria. If any of these is possible (based on run-differential of 100-200 runs), then it could be a 3-inning match. If not, then the match is a four inning match.

3. Now we can compute a wickets/session ratio. If more than 4 wickets/session are left, there is a fair chance of a draw, 5 wickets/

session are left, the chances are better for a draw and if 6 wickets/ session are left, it is almost certain to be a draw. The only thing to keep in mind is that this formula is considered over at least 2 or more sessions. If only the last session is left, and 6 wickets to go, it still is a live match since in one session these many wickets can fall. Also, it might happen that in the remaining innings one of the team does not bat for all 10 wickets, owning to declaration. Nonetheless playing a session or so to declare and set a safe target eats up time worth the 5 odd wickets which we have accounted for.

So as a general thumb rule, if an estimated 5 wickets/session are left in a match (with two or more sessions remaining and run chase non-obvious), we can perhaps take those sessions out of competitive comparisons for 'when it matters' (or give such sessions lower weights of 0.33-0.5). **However, the sessions before the draw had 'set-in', must be given full weight (1.0), as the competition was just as relevant as any other result based game.**

In ODIs, every phase matters, since draws are only possible when minimum overs are rained out or cannot be completed for any reason.

Matches against the 'minnows'

Much is usually said about playing teams such as Zimbabwe or Bangladesh, against the traditionally recognized teams in world cricket. These matches are trickier than they seem, since a loss to such a team would be an overnight entry to the 'media hall of shame'. Australia had a tough time winning a match in Bangladesh (albeit that they claimed fatigue). They perhaps do not spend sleepless nights over their dead rubber losses but this would not have been fun, after a loss in the Ashes 2005 and once to Bangladesh in the ODIs in England. They were tactically at their sharpest when the situation went out of bounds– Gillepsie bowling sharp in cutters to a 4 fielders in mid-off, mid-wicket to try to get a few wickets.

Nonetheless, these matches are arguably not the competitive benchmark. It can then also be said that Australia, when they play most other teams, besides perhaps South Africa and in the sub-continent, are usually like they are playing with minnows. But this is hard to define, as Australia still need to work hard to achieve a result, whereas teams playing Bangladesh or Zimbabwe, as they stand today, are closer to an assumption of victory, at least after halfway into the match. But these are still live competitions and cannot be treated as dead rubbers (weight=0) and draws (weight =0.33 to 0.5). These can be perhaps weighted just above the sessions where draw 'set in'. About a 0.66 weight on such games for the major team and a weight of 1.0 for the lesser team.

Must-win matches

Those matches in which losing, results in the conclusion of the team's participation (knock-out or league endings) or end of the tournament (the final), are obviously important. You may be tempted to give a higher weight to such matches, since it is the 'crucial' match. But we must also keep in mind, that when a team plays a must-win match in between a series or tournament and comes out triumphant, it is worthy of merit, **but was the must-win situation as a result of the format (knock out) or because of the lack-luster performance of a team in the earlier stages,** which puts the team in the 'must-win' situation in the first place. This situation will be similar to the earlier discussion of match winning and fighter, where we saw the virtue of eliminating those uncertain situations are the best way to win.

So in general, most matches should matter just as much—to avoid must win situations when possible.

The only matches to be excluded are those mentioned earlier (where the rubber is already decided and league-matches which are formalities on account of the next stage setup already).

> In short, all matches matter just as much, except those when the series or tournament outcome would remain unaffected. Must-win matches matter and so do matches which could avoid the must-win situations.

But if we do want to select must-win matches for stats, here is how they should be filtered—we must consider unavoidable 'must-win matches', because of the nature of the format—such as knockout and finals.

When you bring it upon yourself to be in a 'must win' match in the middle or end of a series or league, this is not to be treated as a 'must-win' for statistical filtering, as doing well in your pervious matches could have avoided such a must-win situation. These must-wins are 'bad must-wins' as they could be avoidable. To credit a player or team 'more' accolades for a doing well in must-win match when say, you are 1-2 down in a 5 match series, would be disrespectful to the other team's earlier performances, (which won 2 matches), and they in fact did things right to avoid a must-win situation. Also, the one match you did win, was in fact more crucial as it gave you a chance to avoid such avoidable matches.

A match is unavoidable must-win, if losing or drawing it, ends your chance in the tournament or series and such a 'must-win' match, should be due to the format, not for bringing it upon yourself to be in a must-win situation.

The Finals are a case of a unavoidable must win-match for both sides, and winning it wins the tournament!

Obviously, the finals as part of the format are to be included. This does not mean that the last match of all two-team series encounters, if the series is not yet decided, are as good as the 'finals'– due to reasons mentioned earlier.

A point to note: if the 'finals' of a tournament is a three or five match series (like in Australian tri-nation ODIs), are in fact not finals, as it is a series of 3 matches—matches may not be a must-win, or could be avoidable must-win. If such games are treated as 'finals', then every other two-team series should be treated as a finals as well.

The Finals issue in case of India

Surely, one would like to perform well in the finals, and Sourav Ganguly's team was seen as chokers on account of losing so many finals. It is true to some extent, but the results were not as alarming, if you see the basic nature of the winning pattern as such. Ganguly had a good team, with 3-4 stars in batting and 1-2 in bowling. The team was as such good to win about half of the ODIs they played (and to be fair many of the finals were against Australia). Now it so happens that India almost played half their ODI tournaments, as a league of teams followed by a final, and half the tournaments as a series of 5 or 7 ODIs against a specific team. They perhaps won about half their ventures (as expected), but it just happened to be more of the series-based tournaments, not the league-final type. So if you see the nature of their expected winning pattern, it was not that bad about losing in the finals as such, but rather a story of winning percentage being just about par, not any better.

Summary of when it matters: to keep it simple, it is best to just exclude those matches which did not competitively matter (once the rubber is dead or next stage positions in a league, are already set), because these matches did not matter and everyone knows that the result is of no consequence to the tournament, before the match begins.

For an academic exercise, the discussion on when a draw has set-in and giving lower weights to 'minnows-matches' can be done—but with careful observation since—draws have to be achieved and wins against minnows are far from a certain outcome.

25. Match Winner vs Tournament Performer

Now that, we have explored what is a match winner, a fighter, a performance 'when it matters' let us see how these concepts can be taken ahead in context of the tournament.

So we have seen what a match winner is- someone who can put the team into a position from which regulation play can win a match, since the margin of unpredictability is well kept. If someone cannot do it this way (when bowlers have to defend low scores or batsmen have to face a target which is ridiculous in terms of strike rates or wickets remaining), they can fight for sure and pull off miracles—as Herschelle Gibbs did against Australia's mammoth 434 to win an incredible ODI (Jo'burg 2006). However, there is no human way (as of today) of defining how to chase such scores methodically. Sure that was a great performance, but we are trying to decide on terms which there is a way to work out a plan (with scope for flair and regulation play). In fact, the Man of the Tournament in that series, Shaun Pollock did not play in that game! This was the 'final' ODI, but an avoidable 'must-win'— as had Gibbs or Smith done half as much, in the middle of the tournament, it would have not gone into the decider in the first place.

25.1 Learning from Tennis

So winning a tournament is a lot more than winning a match, just like winning a set in tennis and winning three sets to overcome your opponent is different. Actually let's study the analogy of a multi-match series (assume a 5 match cricket series) to one tennis match of 5 sets (has been discussed *Ch14.1 p129,* but we now look at in a specific context). The first common fact is that the each set starts at 0-0 and likewise, the each cricket match starts fresh without deficit carried over from any previous matches. The 'momentum' and confidence factors do carry forward and can rarely be ignored, since good players or teams can then experiment or take a few chances as the lead increases on the 'set score' (or matches won). But the fact remains, that being good or even great in one set, is only one-third of the job, since the next set starts afresh. A tennis player needs to win 3 sets, each from scratch, so winning the first set 6-0 or 6-1 with three breaks of serve, the lead does not carry over to the next (you might incidentally win a set with such a margin, but you cannot be obsessed about winning with such margins). So if you do have many plans to break a serve, you will perhaps be better served by unleashing them in different sets. Similar things can be said about cricket, since three matches have to be won to win the series. You may have to play different roles as the situations will vary and sometimes you can be a dominant winner, sometimes supporter in terms of runs, or play out crucial phases or take out certain bowlers to upset a spell cycle.

25.2 When can match winners win tournaments?

However, there is some difference in a team game vs tennis. The individual has to go through all the 'roles' in an individual sport. For instance in cricket, if you can have a match winning performance one in five times (which is the best someone can achieve, after Don Bradman and is discussed in the natural pattern earlier) and play a supportive role, when you have to work hard on other days, you can be useful in the tournament context as well. Sounds like the tennis equivalent where you win one set and lose four? Not exactly, since there are other 4-5 batsmen or bowlers in a team game—who can be winners on their day as well. Like in tennis, some sets could be won due to baseline play and in others you might volley a bit more, and then at times you use aces or winners. The 'variety of shots' *is* your 'team' in tennis and all of them need not be as active each game or in each set. **So in cricket, we can say that if an individual has a huge impact on one game in a series, and with purposeful roles in other games, you are contributing to the tournament.** But there is a key point to remember— you are assuming that the other players will put up a match winning performance in other games, as individuals or as combined efforts. If the others do not, then one in five match winning effort will indeed be like winning only one set in tennis and losing the rest. Worst still, in trying to force a match winning performance, you might end up as the tournament loser, as you can fail when trying to excel too much, and fail otherwise because of the *natural pattern of outcomes (Ch 24.2; p241)* which keeps the frequency of performance in check anyway. In short, **match winners can be tournament winners, provided you consider what the rest of the team members are made up of** and what can be expected of them in a given situation.

25.3 Consistent above-par outcomes impact a tournament.

You can often see in long cycling races, such as the Tour de France, where the ultimate winner never won a single phase but was above average in each (Lance Armstrong did win one his tours, quite like this). The day's honors go to someone different each day, but you keep your overall contribution ahead.

A good example of this is Shaun Pollock, who rarely bowls badly and is usually more than useful with the bat. He has often won tournaments or many a series, with few or no man of the match awards in that series- and yet being the man of the tournament. This is one reason all-rounders can make an impact on the tournament, by putting forth good performances with bat and ball, rather than excel as a match winner in one of the matches.

This also explains why Tendulkar and Inzamam are exploring different ways to contribute to the team- to win the series or tournament, rather than being a match winner and often face problems as described, when match winners cannot be tournament winners. Sure, given the chance, they would unleash their skills freely, but they have recognized that if they still have a good enough team and if they use their experience and versatility, they can ensure the team benefits largely (Tendulkar has been making his best effort to make sure the team reaches 50 overs in a test with minimal wickets lost, just about every other time he has batted last year or so, whereas Inzamam has come lower down and managed the lower order and the tail, not without criticism though). This does not mean that either Pollock, or Tendulkar or Inzamam would not be interested in plundering more, just that they first ensure that the best role for a situation is fulfilled and then can try to push ahead.

25.4 Winning Single-Handedly? Handle with care...

Single-handedness is tricky for sure. Match-losers are tough to define, as the *natural pattern of outcomes*, where few failures are normal, is seen as an excuse that everyone fails sometime. Since you have other team members, it is best to assess what would be needed to enter the next phase of play—more runs, keep wickets, manage strike rates, etc. Nobody ever won a team game single-handedly, and trying to would be imprudent.

26. Presenting known ideas in a better way

26.1 Sunday Stats

The manner in which samples are selected for statistical evaluation, by media as well as the public at large, are often very ineffective in arriving at the real story. In many cases, samples are chosen or omitted in a manner to suit a cause or motive. Often the result of such stats, is almost as if you could see which days of the week, a player or team played poorly and proclaim that in recent times a player did not perform well on say, Sundays! The fact is that there will usually be cases of ups and downs for every player or team, pegged to the *natural pattern of outcomes*– sometimes better or worse, and it can happen that an outcome pattern may coincide with occurrence of certain events– which may have no correlation.

However, at times there are genuine ways to filter, for instance, on pitch conditions or type of bowling attack. We discussed issues of 'when it mattered' and when it does not. Even then there will always be a need to take precautions in filtering samples, as players unfortunately cannot tell their captain, that today they will play in such a way, that they wish it could be filtered out from their record.

Let's see how things can get flawed, even when we have taken care in being fair to players or teams by considering relevant samples

1. Too few samples: it is quite common sense in statistics, that any 'average' should be based on a sufficient number of samples to really indicate anything. Also, on account of the huge deviation of scores across innings, an average is perhaps one of the most *average* tool to measure either bowler or batsman. But even as a tool which does indicate how players have contributed, in a broad sense (not in a comparative sense), even a dozen odd samples may not work out. For a batsman, one score of 120 will prop the average by 10 points. Likewise a bowler who went wicket-less in an innings for a hundred odd runs but bowled very well in a series or two, the average will look poorer by 10 points. This will further be enhanced if a batsman or bowler gave or lost a 'chance' in their innings. We had touched upon this point earlier, and will address it by taking a ball by ball approach, if it is important to consider a few innings perhaps during a series.

2. Better attempts get on the better side of the filtering criteria: here is a good example which will illustrate the point (since it involves Sir Don Bradman, it cannot be disputed!). Don Bradman, averaged in the 30s in his non-century test innings. This sounds 'mortal' at first glance, and I am not sure, there perhaps might be many other batsman who average in a similar range, in their 'non-century' innings. The flaw is that, Bradman scored centuries at such a frequency, that for this kind of sampling, his being better gets *outside* the filtering criteria, which has been selected. What if a player existed who scored 7 centuries and failed once few times to get out for say 3, 7, 11. His non-century innings would then be averaging 7!

The above example indicates that it is **tricky to filter based on criteria, which could have been bettered or taken out of the equation.**

The *avoidable 'must-wins'* were a similar case, when you could have done better and avoided the possible avoidable circumstances.

Another such case, for instance, is comparing 2nd innings performances in tests. Every player has good and best test matches. But when a player comes good in a match, and actually scores heavily in the first innings, the second inning may often not exist for him or it may be a forced issue (declaration) etc. So being efficient in a match, could mean that there may be no second innings and hence your good matches get excluded. Virendra Sehwag is one such case, where the media loves to remind that he averages in the twenties in his second innings. If there was a second innings he perhaps had an indifferent match (when in form). Sure he would like to play in any innings, but the numbers will not reflect it, because his better samples got the better of the criteria.

3. Your poor attempts actually affect the filtering criteria: what is the average of a player each time the team won? As discussed in the Match Winner discussion, this is another flawed way to go about things. Firstly, an individual performance is best evaluated as—did it happen 'when it mattered' *(Ch 24.4, p246)*—and if so it counts as an individual performance in a competitive sense. The team winning has many other factors to the story. Again, the best recent example was of the Flintoff match (2nd test, Ashes 2005) where he did everything and England did beat Australia but by just 2 runs. Had Australia won, his strong performance and in a good competitive situation, would not count!? Whereas another player, may have many more failures which actually affected the filtering criteria (losing) but those weak samples got left out, when in fact they were one of the reasons a team may have lost.

4. Comparing by career matches: when we talk about a batsman's performance over say 50 matches, and say that in a similar number of matches he was better than an ex-great player or current player for that matter, it needs to be qualified with years as well. If someone played 50 matches in four years, which were his best, and some former player played 50 matches in a career spanning 15 years, then it will not be an apt comparison, for obvious reasons. Perhaps you can take the best four years from the 15 year career, but that may not be apt either, as we may then run into the problem of few samples, due to frequency of matches in that era. There are a lot of players who look as good as Sir Vivian Richards, by batting average over a 7-10 year career. Cannot compare this way!, since his career was much longer. Moreover, it is tough to compare eras, but I have a way to perhaps work this out (comparing eras and situations).

26.2 Short term indicators: based on Dot Aspects!

The best idea is not to do statistics with few innings, but when it needs to be done during a series or tournament, here is a better way to do it Rather than taking averages across innings—as there will be too few samples—take a look at the number of balls bowled or played, as then you will have dozens or hundreds of samples (you need to see the match, not just the scorecard).

Form for batsmen: just count the number of times the intention and execution had a gap. You need to do it differently on defensive shots (it is called being 'beaten') and attacking ones (where some tolerance for the intention-execution gap may be acceptable). As a batsman, since you play in a Z-demand format, somewhat beaten is beaten, because you can never complain that you were *marginally* lbw or *just* out by the ball brushing your glove. Your percentage of balls being beaten while playing defensively, is the first indicator of form. Then the same type of analysis can be done to measure 'attacking form' by taking the number of scoring attempts and on how many of those balls did the execution fail (ball going to fielder with a proper shot is not a failure, as that is natural in cricket,. The dot rate will address this issue). Also when a batsman attacks simply to get out of trouble, this is a case of being beaten in defensive.

So based on the percentage number of balls a batsman's execution failed on defensive and scoring attempts, will give you a better picture for the short term, on the 'basic form' and 'run-making form'.

Form for bowlers: since there is an X-demand on bowlers– an extra effort which must be good enough to get the better of the batsman substantially (to get a wicket), you need to change the definition for bowlers a bit, but we are still looking at execution percentages on a ball by ball sampling.

So for bowlers, it must be seen how much 'well and truly' they beat the batsman. They may not often get a wicket, but there is no exact science between totally getting a batsman out and 'just about'. So 'well and truly' beaten can be perhaps defined by closeness to the edge of the bat or the stumps. From a defensive angle, dot balls which the batsman played and missed or edged in trying a scoring shot is a type 2 bowling measure. When batsmen played a shot but it went to the fielder, it is a type 3 bowling aspect.

Strike Rates: batting strike rates can be a fair indicator even in a few innings, since these are samples based on ball to ball anyway! As far as bowling is concerned, balls/wicket strike rates cannot however, be derived from a few innings since wickets are sparse and not as regular compared to scoring runs. However, the economy rate (runs conceded per over) by a bowler can be a fair indicator even across few innings, as there will be adequate samples and also there are many methods to prevent run making consistently (more regularity than wicket taking)

Yet, if you consider a few innings, a better economy rate measure would be to consider ratio of dot balls to balls scored. This is of significance, more so in ODIs, as hitting one or two big shots after a dozen dot balls, makes a strike rate look good, but even if you are good at big shots, it indicates lack of strike rotation, and a burden the team has to face due to eating up dot balls—in event you get out before any big hitting and as the non-striker watches as well.

Of course, all this is assuming that that the batsman did play enough balls or the bowler did bowl enough overs per innings, for the sampling to be adequate.

Negative Phases in ODIs– any dot ball pressure and reduced strike rate for an extensive phase is not desirable, since it leaves the task for others that much more difficult. So the strike rate at the end of the innings is not the only one that must be noted, but perhaps after every 25-30 balls. **How many 30 ball phases did a player have during which the strike rate was below par for that pitch.** This is tougher to decide in the first innings of an ODI, since the target is not known. However, a minimum of about 4.5/over for tough pitches and 6/over for the best pitches (anything beyond 6/over happens with few other short cameos, but a run a ball target is fair enough, by today's standards). In second innings of an ODI, the required strike rates are available and such 30-ball phases can be compared approximately with the target strike rates.

So in the short term, measuring quality of dot balls (being beaten or beating the bat) and number of dots to scoring shots is perhaps the best indicator of performance, due to the fact that dozens or hundreds of samples are available (by taking a ball by ball approach). It's a dot ball world for sure!

26.3 Breaking Averages

Seen those 'wagon wheels' on TV, indicating scoring areas for batsmen, with different colors for singles, twos, fours and sixes? Well, they miss out on a key issue– the 'chances' offered by a batsman. This is kind of unfair to bowlers, and for the batsman's own assessment, as batting is a Z-demand format, and the errors are catastrophic. This is not acceptable in an era of computers and communication, when we know that letting the team down is about the first major error (from a batsman's perspective).

The solution is simple, every time a batsman offers a *chance*– a catch which a fielder could catch or through the slips, or missed stumping, which from the batsman's effort, should have been the end of the innings (close lbw escapes, being out on a no-ball, inside edges can be shown on a wheel as 'lucky escapes' but those are not 'chances' since the fielding team could not have done anything to convert them).

The solution– please show multiple wagon wheels for each inning– since it was punctured after each chance. If a batsman gave 3 chances, in a score of 75 and another gave none in a score of 45, the viewers can get an idea which innings was qualitatively better—the 75 run inning may yet be better if the first chance came after 45, or if the largest 'break' was perhaps 60 odd, (to borrow a phrase from snooker).

Apart from wagon wheels, batting averages need to be presented in a better manner as well. **The first thing is that a batting average is not about runs scored as one might feel. It is about 'how many runs does a batsman make a major mistake'.** So giving a chance is no 'shrug the shoulders' kind of a matter, especially when players these days seem to get away with edges over the in-field or top edges flying for sixes as well.

For instance, in snooker, if a player made a score of 105, but had three mistakes in the frame (which were not cashed in by the opponent), that would be seen as an indifferent frame, no better. It could have three breaks of 25, 35, 55, which are fairly good breaks. **The total score in snooker or billiards is not a measure of performance (since your opponent could be playing poorly), but it is about the best or good breaks–** how many were scored in one visit until a mistake was made. So a snooker break of 85 in one visit would indicate quality. Unfortunately, in cricket, although such a notion exists (that was a chance-less innings), we do not present or measure it that way. Again, this is not acceptable in an era of computers and all the 3D charts.

So here are a few more aspects for presenting an innings for a batsman:

1. Different wagon wheel for each chance given as it was punctured. Sir Don Bradman said that his 254 at Lord's (1930) was his best knock since the ball always went where he wanted it to go, except for the ball which got him out. That would be one heck of a chance-less wagon wheel. Another example was of Brian Lara scoring 500 runs, (vs Durham) after being dropped when he had not reached twenty. This would involve two wheels, but would show how monumental the effort was, since the second wheel would be 480 runs big. In future if some big hitting bloke makes 500 after giving 7 chances, he cannot shrug it away, saying even Lara did not have a chance-less knock. But having a wagon full of wagon wheels is different from Lara's biggest break of 480 in that innings.

2. Each wheel can perhaps indicate lucky misses, which landed safe or a near lbw etc. This will give a closer indication of form, as many of the poorly played balls will be factored in.

3. Let-down average: The runs till first chance a batsman gave is the let-down score. Even if we do career or long term average this is a good indicator of what point a player let-down the team.

4. Breaking average: If you divide the runs in an innings, by the number of chances a batsman gave (including the one he got out), you will know how good the 'breaks are'. The breaking average is perhaps closer to a true average, because to be fair to the batsman, it gives him credit for the runs he made after every chance (it was a big error on his part, but to continue from then on is not his fault that he was let-off). **So next time we can hope we see the 'breaks' by a batsman not just the total runs scored.**

5. For Bowlers: likewise it just fair that we include chances as well as wickets, in relation to runs given. It was not the bowler's fault for a catch being dropped or stumping missed but that needs to be recorded more emphatically, than say a leg-bye!

It may all sound a bit tedious to try to present stats this way. However, when technology shows many other numbers not shown in the past, it is but right not to ignore the crucial aspects, which bowlers and batsman strive for. Fifty years ago they had simple score-sheets and they did pretty well with the tools they had. But it was difficult to record events on a dot ball (which is needed, to explain form— as it relates to being beaten and giving chances). However, today we have the tools to measure it better. Computing tools are like a microscope, and we can observe many details through graphs and numbers. We better not lose out the crucial ones.

27. New types of stats from agreeable concepts

In the previous chapter we discussed how known ideas need to be presented and emphasized in a proper manner. Now we need to take it a step further to be able to derive some new ways to analyze scores in context of some other agreeable concepts. The idea here is to see how we can use our understanding of the fact that **runs or wickets are relative measures, depending on pitch, opposition-quality, phase of a game, etc. However, runs or wickets are always shown as independent numbers.** This is perhaps acceptable in a particular game, since we will tend to interpret them in the context of that match anyway. But when we begin taking any average across samples, it is perhaps right to 'normalize' them to the pitch conditions and then see whether the performance of a batsman is below par or above par, compared to other players playing in other parts of the world or even in past eras. What follows is an attempt to make necessary compensation to runs or wickets based on 'par' pitch conditions, as they do in golf..

27.1 Normalized Scores

What is a normal score or score on a 'par' pitch condition in cricket? This is difficult to tell, as the same pitch behaves differently from match to match, and even within the same match.

But I can propose a way to find out what is a 'normal' score and then compare particular match scores to that normal.

Step1: Just before the match, compute 'cricket's average'. Take a history of all matches (for that format) played till the match being played. Total all the runs that were ever made and all the wickets that fell in the history of cricket, thus far. You can then arrive at "cricket's average'. In my estimation it will be somewhere close to 27 runs/wicket (closer to bowling averages, since usually only recognized bowlers bowl, but in batting even the tail has to bat). Run outs and extras will alter this estimate. Such an average this can be calculated very easily, since we know how many runs were scored and wickets fell in each test match, (there are just about thousand odd test matches). A refinement would be to consider 'history' as a 10-15 year period more akin to duration of player careers. Cricket's average perhaps changes over 7-10 year periods(?)

Step 2: Find cricket's average for that match (pitch). After the match, total all the runs and total all the wickets that fell in the entire match. Then you can get cricket's average for that match. There will often be some wickets which fall due to forced events such as declaration, but the fact that they fell that way was perhaps due to batsman having to keep them for later anyway. There will also be draws, but that is why we are taking 'actuals'– runs and wickets not innings. In the rare event, a match was terminated due to rain or for any reason, and only runs were scored and no wicket fell, you can consider a minimum of say 0.5 wicket to fall no matter what (just to avoid a divide by zero error). You will eventually **get an idea about the pitch– as to how many runs were scored per wicket** .

Step 3: Normalize all player scores: now compare the pitch average to cricket's average. You can now get a 'normalizing factor', for that game by cricket's **pitch average divided by historic average.** (How tough this pitch was in comparison to normally expected runs/wicket). Now divide each individual score to get the 'normalized' implication of an innings of a batsman and bowler.

For example, let say cricket's average (I do not know) is 27 runs/wicket. In a particular match where the team scores were around 170-190, the pitch average might be around 18 runs/wicket. You will get a normalization factor of 18/27= 0.66. This would imply that a batsman who scored 60 on this tricky pitch, it was worth like a 90 on a 'normal pitch'. Likewise a bowler who took 2 wickets for 40, it was like 2 wickets in 60 runs (since this pitch was perhaps bowler friendly).

This in my view will be a much better way to see career averages, not just in contemporary cricket but across eras. **Since we credit players based on what is expected in cricket during their era and then normalize each pitch result to a net runs/wicket factor, which is what batting and bowling averages are all about.** Similar ratios can be obtained for strike rates in ODI and tests as well.

27.2 Runs or Runs( )?

So runs are relative to opposition and phase of play, unlike other cue sports or *initiate and control disciplines*, where to a great extent a record-breaking or monumental accomplishment can be assessed as qualitative in itself, irrespective of opponent.

So just how relative are runs? We saw earlier in a tennis example, that when a player leads 5-3, with one 'break' and four 'held', the score of 5 games won, is clearly not achieved in homogenous manner. Likewise in cricket, to post runs, as just numbers is often misleading– especially in

ODIs and in moderate scoring test matches as well (since each batsman rarely plays all the bowlers).

And, how tough is it to determine the quality of effort from runs? Here is a little quiz, which will help us put things in perspective a bit. Say a **team 'A'** makes 300-350 runs consistently against South Africa. In similar conditions, a **team 'B'** makes 450-500 runs against Zimbabwe across many matches. From this one cannot conclude, which is the better batting team **A** or **B**– as making 350 against South Africa would be demanding indeed, but then 500 is a good score as well, although against a weaker bowling side.

To be fair, why not have a match between teams **A** and **B**, to find out once and for all, instead of trying to decide from involving other teams. Surely, a direct contest will decide who bats better. Now let's say **team A** consistently makes 100 odd runs more than **team B**. Now we know the answer, right? Wrong. It is just as inconclusive! Because team A batted against the bowling attack of team B, not their batting! And vice-versa, team B batted against the bowling of team A. What if the bowlers of team B, were only as good as Zimbabwe bowlers and the bowling of team A was as good as South Africa!?! **In fact, a direct contest between two teams, will never decide which team bats better, unless we know for sure that the bowling is surely equal.** Because of the asymmetric nature of skills in cricket, you can say that there are actually four teams involved in every game. This means that runs (and likewise wickets) have to be handled with care in deriving quality of effort, from the displayed scorecards.

So runs need to be displayed with some contextual indicator in brackets, perhaps, much like they do in maths functions. The problem is that 'runs are runs', when it comes to deciding a winner as the team total does not see runs in any context except plain numbers. True, but to ignore the context would be as silly as saying that holding serve and breaking serve, are just the same– as both give an increment of 1 game in a set.

27.3 Comparative Analysis

If you need to put some contextual aspect alongside runs, what should it be? Obviously, we cannot put information about all the bowlers a batsman faced, whether it was raining, or was it power-play 3, or the new ball was taken and which spell was going on. If we can, this would be good, as this is what differentiates batting prospects within an innings. It might seem as if we are needlessly complicating matters, but the problem is that details do get flashed around on account of a the hi-tech age we live in. So if details must be shown, the relevant ones are not the ones to be missed out. For instance, the minutes a batsman batted is of low relevance, as the balls played will indicate how long he played. Yet this goes into the displays, ignoring other potent facts.

1. It is quite surprising how many times ODI batting scores are shown without the strike rates. And once a match is finished, we even know how a batsman fared in terms of strike rate in context of the match. So only the relative strike rate (positive or negative % compared to opponent team's strike rate; and relative to your own team total) could be shown alongside runs (slight negative rate is acceptable if volume of runs is there, viewers can understand that). Relative rates are true for bowlers as well, since a bowler who gave away 5.5 runs/over in an ODI during a 350 run bonanzas from both sides, actually did fairly well.

2. We can display runs with a relevant contextual descriptor. In my view runs should always qualified as such, based on context of discussion since they are not absolute quantities. For instance, a simple way to make an improvement, is to qualify the runs, with the 'fall of over' at which a batsman comes in to bat and number of balls played as well.

So if alongside runs, we indicate the over-number the batsman came in and balls played, it will make a huge improvement. Instantly, we can then know that 'balls played' could be positive or negative, since it largely depends on phase. The over-number also indicates what kind of execution is possible and perhaps which spells the bowlers are in. So for instance in a test score card when a batsman has 30 runs (90 balls; 10th) it will make a lot of sense in test cricket as it indicates a constructive effort. Likewise 30 ODI runs (20 balls; 15th) will indicate power play and a good innings from a strike rate aspect.

3. One of the best ways to compare what is going on in a match or series, is to compare aggregates based on clear difference in phases. In most cases the toughest phases could be first 15 overs (in swinging conditions) and in some it could be overs 20-40 (on spinning tracks). In recent times, reverse-swing has made overs 35-50 kind of tricky. Whatever, it is, by observing when wickets fell most (in tests) and/or strike rates were good (in ODIs), we can say that a series typically had different phases which were crucial. (In ODIs, perhaps first batting and second batting have to be analyzed differently). **Then we can see which overs the batsman batted and do aggregates differently by recognized phases.**

If we compare between teams, it must be done in such a manner, that players are compared in corresponding manner of participation (in the corresponding overs, not in the batting order!). It makes little sense to discredit a player, when the player in the opposing team did not fare any different, in similar phases. If you do analyze competition, it cannot ignore the performance of competing rivals.

PART V: APPENDIX

Towards a formal assessment system

Can we express everything in terms of runs, wickets & strike rates?

Since runs, wickets and strike rates are what finally matter in cricket, it makes sense to try to evaluate all our expressions in context of these numbers. Players may contribute directly to the scores, or they may be involved indirectly—as we have seen throughout the book—by playing certain roles or altering the balance of resources by which scoring takes place. Whatever the method— one of passion and skill or by applying 'chess'— eventually we need to see them in context of how many runs or wickets, (and the rates) an activity was worth.

For instance, we all are aware of a batsman who 'plays out the new ball' or a bowler who was so demanding that 'he kept it tight at one end'. Sure it is useful but how much is it worth? Can we measure it in the scoring parameters which matter— as runs, wickets etc. If we cannot, even as an estimate, then it is perhaps difficult to credit such efforts. Any indirect activity must translate to a tangible state which can be measured in scoring parameters. Moreover, there will be even more subtle or emotional expressions, such as someone who 'played with grit and determination' or 'bowled his heart out'. These are fine, as the sport is after all about humans, creativity and passion. But every sport also has to be assessed in the competitive context— which in cricket, will be in terms of the scoring parameters, directly or indirectly.

As mentioned in the book, in a Test match, since about a minimum of 110 overs have to be played by a batting side to exhaust the span of 5 days, so each ball played must be of significance in batting. Then there are partnerships or breaking of partnerships. which are very significant as well. There are situations where wickets fall in a bunch or runs are made explosively. And then there is 'workman' like effort when a batsman comes in at a runs/wicket ratio, which is well below par for their team, and they help to score runs to make up this imbalance, and draw parity. These are just a few instances which most of us as followers of the game, are aware of. There will always be more intricacies amongst those who play it at a higher level.

So we can compile many known (usually agreed upon) situations of advantage or critical phases, where there is some credit given to batsmen and bowlers, as indirect 'runs and wickets' (beyond and in addition to, those which show up on the score sheets). But how do we value such indirect contributions? **The trick is to convert the English phrases in a manner by which we can express such efforts in terms of runs and wickets!** As of January 2007, I would say I have a pretty decent assessment system in place. There are some more issues which need to be handled. Stay tuned.

Can we really try to assess all activity in scoring parameters? Take the instance of **chess,** they have an assessment method to value every piece in terms of pawns. Kinghts & bishops are of equal value and worth about 3 pawns. Rooks are worth about 5 pawns and a queen is worth 9. You will find games or puzzles which do demonstrate that these values make sense for sure. But these are thumb-rules and their worth will vary in every different game and during different phases as well. For instance, knights are worth more than bishops early on, since they have the ability to jump around, when the board is quite densely occupied. But bishops are more effective later in a game, and then perhaps two bishops are worth more than two knights. These are subtle issues which are beyond the scope of enthusiasts like me but such valuations can be appreciated by all for sure.

Fortunately, cricket is not that complex to quantify as chess and you do not have to be like a GM assessing the value of a chess position. So we should be able to measure the impact of any contribution in cricket. (it will be in a another book though). However, there is an aspect of cricket, unlike chess, where the if-then scenarios are not very easy to assess. In chess, one can usually go back to an intermediate position, and try out other options to see 'what could have been'. This again is due to the exact nature of chess moves and piece behavior, whereas in cricket, what the next player might do—if some player was out or a another bowler was bowled instead—is hard to predict. Nonetheless, I guess giving credit to every effort made in terms of runs and wickets would be well worth it, even if it is just a thumb-rule to guide us in assessment.

Axiomatic approach for rule changes & variants

How does logic fit into a sport?

The rules and format for a given sport, usually will undergo refinements during its early development phase, and then change only when deemed necessary (as after the Bodyline series). Further, even though a sport is a man-made activity and we can define things the way we like, certain rules cannot really be changed, as it would make little sense to alter rules to an extent that there is no latitude for skills.

There will always be many sports-persons who are of the view that sports should be about quality of skill and all the academic complications should be kept aside. Fair enough, as we would like superb execution on field, be it in batting, bowling or in any other sport. But because a sport is an art and a competitive discipline, it is but natural that players will prevent you from doing what you are good at or are comfortable with. You will need skill as well as 'chess' (work with a few options which bring known results), to get to where you want to be—the winning post before your opponent gets there.

However, in what proportion should the 'skill' and 'applying chess' work out?

That is a question which can only be answered by the way the format has been defined. For instance, in cricket fielding restrictions are imposed due to the fact that a bowler initiate's play and he can bowl only one type of ball, for which there are only few natural replies.

In general, any format should be fair not just to both teams, but also to the variety of skills being tested. For instance, in English **billiards**, the best players are so efficient in garnering points within the small area on the top-table, that they can repeat shots with ease (only the top players can, not everyone, it still demands delicate skills). This perhaps does not adequately motivate players to try some other 'nice' patterns of play, simply because you score more points on the top table, and quickly too. The administrators did find a way to put some 'punctuation' in the process, by forcing players to go 'around the table' every hundred points. But this does not really solve the problem of inadequate sampling of the rich variety in English billiards (in the context of variety, billiards *can* be more colorful than snooker).

A good example of inducing some variety by format, is in tennis serves. Since the service alternates between right and left halves of the court, certain different angles are naturally tested. May be in future, with racquets offering power to beat the cross-court angles, they can perhaps try to force a serve down the line as well? (some such forcing of variety in service is perhaps needed in table tennis, where players have too many routine 'plays' from just one short serve).

In **chess** openings, have been so thoroughly studied that it is impossible to play the game if you are not ready to memorize many lines of play. This has led to Bobby Fischer formalizing his variant of Random Chess *(Ch 8, p82)*. Although, the format of the new variant is as brilliant as the genius himself, it is not easy to switch to, as it is sort of different. Although it keeps great chess ideas intact, due to symmetry and moves being the same, it is spontaneous as the starting points are random. But the classical format also has its great traditions, which give a reference point for everyone to compare, and then provide variety over known positions of strength and weaknesses.

So the question is— whether there is an axiomatic and abstract way to approach format related issues and how formats should be altered when certain skills dominate over others. How to change rules or invent variants which actually maintain tradition, in the light of players getting better in certain skills, either because of training and generations of knowledge, or because of innovations (and interference) in equipment due to technology.

> Surely, if we could express our sport in an abstract axiomatic manner, then we can actually 'arrive' at specific solutions, to change or add a rule, so that the original spirit, variety of skills and competitive rhythm is actually maintained, in an era of changing skills, training methods and equipment.

Regarding Twenty20 cricket

Many past legends have 'blessed' the twenty20 format, stating that the game 'evolves' and one has to accept change. Just as people from the test era, complained about one day 50 over format, and then gradually accepted it, so will we all accept twenty20. This may well be the case, but we need to be able to formally (as in abstract or symbolic ways), try to describe what the new variant is, and how far it deviates from the classical one. As Richie Benaud has said, that he would wish that twenty20, contributes something to test cricket, just as one-day cricket has done. This is an important point for sure, as it is similar to the discussion of adding or maintaining variety.

In an abstract manner, the Z-demand on batting in twenty20 is much reduced, as the price of the wicket is not quite that of an ODI. The X options- to do better than the bowler, is heading towards only big shots. So batting is getting closer to an X-demand discipline (since your better shots have to be good enough to score fours and sixes), with less emphasis on the price of a wicket, since a side being bowled out, is far less likely than an ODI. So the penalty for failure is much less, and we will perhaps see that, it is often apt to lose a wicket, to give the sequential format of batting, scope to 'develop'. Batting is getting reversed as an X-demand discipline.

Likewise, in bowling, we have already discussed that a bowler's strike rate is about 50-60 balls per wicket, in a test cricket context of beating the batsman in defence. In ODIs, with 10 overs a bowler and 60 balls each, the bowler can hope for a wicket or two, and more, if the batsman was squeezed into dots. In twenty20, with 24 balls per bowler, you cannot expect any magic. They are expected to bowl dots, and a dot in twenty20 is perhaps worth twice that of ODIs! Bowling is becoming Z-demand (where a failure– as byes or a boundary hurts a lot), with minor reward for the X-stuff (getting one heck of a ball to better the batsman will fetch a wicket, but a batsman's stay at the crease is anyway worth 2-3 overs. The next one in, is also perhaps going to do the same slog thing). So Chris Gayle, Jayasuria and Tendulkar perhaps have similar chance at bowling as compared to other world class bowlers. And they can bat a bit as well! Folks, we are headed for a team of perhaps 9 batsmen (some of whom, can dabble with the ball) and 2 'regular' bowlers (who can also swing their bats!?).

Mind-you **I am not complaining about a new variant, just that we should know what we are heading for, using a systematic approach.** Anyway, there can be other alterations to enforce the Z-demand of batting, and also encourage the X-side of bowling– by introducing some other scoring options, not present in conventional cricket. Try and guess what I am aiming at.

The point is that, we can arrive at different variants by playing around the basic principles of 'format'. We had seen how altering the symmetric nature, could lead to a two-phased ODI *(Ch 8, p81)*; or pairing of Twenty20s *(Ch 7, p77)* to give more space to all, and yet have two results; or introducing a draw in limited overs games *(Ch 18)*, to push the X-aspect of bowling, instead of getting away with dots.

Apart from adjustments, **we can have a whole new array of shorter variants, which are entirely new innovations—not just about reducing of overs**—and most importantly, every type of player will have a chance to play a meaningful role. Not in this book!

An Open Tournament for individuals

Here is an 'open' cricket tournament for individual players, that was 'arrived at in axiomatic fashion. Such a tournament would allow anyone to compete, just as in games like tennis or chess. But the idea is one of talent search and offer selection chances to individual players:

1. Cricket is a team sport, but being sequenced and one at a time, individuals get different amount of exposure at the crease.

2. Also, the natural pattern of performances, will have a failure or two in about 5 attempts. Batsmen on account of the Z-demand (can get out on the first error) and bowler on account of the X-demand (their best may be very good but somehow not getting a wicket), makes it difficult to judge a player from normal team tournaments.

Moreover, in my view many aspiring cricketers never make it to state level teams in the first place, as they perhaps were in a school which was not involved in cricket or not good enough to last many rounds at inter-school competition.

We can design a format of cricket, as an open tournament for individuals, to test their batting and bowling skills, and eventually get a 'winner' after many rounds, as in other individual sports. This would be a great way to find talent in a country, state or city.

A format for such an Open Tournament to test individual abilities:

1. Players fill in their entry as individuals- as a batsman or a bowler or all-rounder or wicket-keeper. We need to make groups of 11 players, say 5 bowlers (or four and one all rounder), 5 batsmen and a keeper.

2. The players then play amongst themselves, as they often do on the beach. Just that only the bowling candidates can bowl and only the batting candidates bat. Those who signed in as an all-rounder will do both, but in a lesser quota of overs, perhaps.

3. In one 'round', all 5 Bowlers can bowl two spells of 4 to 6 overs each, to make 50 overs of bowling. They will do so to the same batsman. What if he gets out? He bats again, and finishes his quota of 50 overs. The important feature is that each batsman, in turn plays the same 5 bowlers, and for the same number of overs (the non-striker is just a runner). Instead of getting 'out' we allow him to go on, but taking an average of how many times he got out in 50 overs. Further, the batsman's first 'break'—the runs when he was out the first time— can be given a heavier weight, since in real cricket he gets one chance (real cricket has zero weight to the other 'breaks'). Also his highest 'break' is noted for arbitration later on, if needed. As discussed in the book, a 'break' refers to runs scored till a chance is given, whether it was caught or not *(Ch 26.3, p262)*.

4. In this format, giving a chance and getting 'out' are the same things—since we are testing the skills, not luck. Just that it breaks that 'mini innings' and he plays on. The bowler also gets the credit of a 'wicket' when a batsman gave a chance, as it was none of his error (unless caught and bowled?). The fielder who drops it or should have reached it (umpire decides that), can be penalized a few 'points' (measure fielding efforts with a suitable point system). Also run outs have to be considered, but not as harsh, since the non-striker is as such not in your 'team'. We are trying to really test the core batting and bowling skills, even though fielding and running-between are important.

4. Each bowler can be given a new ball or an old ball, depending on his choice, being a pace bowler or spinner. Also, while bowling, if the bowler gets hit around, he must be asked to continue at least say 2-3 overs in a spell. He cannot just walk away. Bowling can then rotate or some creativity can be left to bowlers, within them. And obviously, field placing is done by the bowler.

This format will go on for perhaps 2-3 days since 50 overs are played by each batsman. Bowlers bowl their 10 overs, in each 50-over quota for different batsman.

Reduced over formats are possible. Another change could be that two batsmen at a time can be asked to play, so that bowlers do bowl to different batsmen. But each batsman must play the same number of balls–so each gets half the total overs (even if he takes a single, he retains strike for 'his' over). Also the overall distribution can be done so all bowlers and both batsmen play both sides of the pitch equally. In an over, therefore one of them will be the bastman and the other pays non-striker.

5. The top two bowlers (in bowling average) and top two batsmen (batting average) can proceed to the next 'stage' (if it is a knockout). For all-rounders, a run-wicket conversion will be needed by using runs/wicket ratio, of this pitch. We can also derive inspiration from what Sir Gary Sobers has been emphasizing in recent times about all-rounders– they should be good enough to find as a place in the team on just their batting or just their bowling, to be called all-rounders. Which means that they should break into the top 2-3 bowlers or top 2-3 batsmen, in such an individual tournament.

This format is fair to bowlers, as *chances* are credited as wickets. and fair to batsmen, as *chances* are punished as a wicket, but they still get to bat the same number of balls. If a batsman does not give a chance, and two such cases are there, then we can see the runs scored (and strike rate, if that was being tested as well).

So how did an axiomatic approach help arrive at such a format?

1. Firstly by recognizing that, to judge a batsman or bowlers, they have to play the same set of bowlers and bowl to the same set of batsmen on the same pitch. **Runs are not absolute!**

2. Secondly, understanding that the **Z-demand** and **sequenced format** (batsmen getting out on error, and not coming back) makes it difficult to implement that each bowler could bowl the same number of balls to a batsman, using conventional cricket rules. So we allow a batsman to play on, but take the 'breaking average' with more punishment on his first attempt (perhaps with twice or thrice the weight). This retains the zero error impact, as each time he gives a chance his average score in the 50 overs is reduced. So a batsman who scores 170 in 50 overs and gets out thrice, will not be as good as batsman who scores 110 and gets out once. We can also try to give some more weight to his highest *break*, so that *volume of runs* matters, just as much as not getting out.

3. By crediting a 'chance' as a wicket, you make the system fair to bowlers and the other batsmen who are competing (**form is about ratio of balls played to each time you get beaten**. But being beaten is still academic, so we should go by chances given). This way a fielder who is a bowler, cannot drop the catch intentionally, off the bowling of a rival bowler. The umpire can judge if the catch should have been taken or not. Catch attempts which a fielder touches, or it goes between the slips, or was high enough for a fielder to get under, and missed stumpings, are all chances, which credit the bowler as a wicket and penalizes the batsman as a break as well.

Put this system in place in India, it will give every junior a chance to compete on his merit, and only the best guys will come up tops, I can assure you. There can be a National Champion batsman or bowler, very soon.

My Background & Personal Acknowledgments

My humble sports background and acknowledgments

Computer Engineering by education; Content, Interface Design & Software Automation by profession, Travel Photography & Publishing by passion, are some of the things I am into. As far as my sports background goes, well, it is more of a background than anything else. I played serious table tennis at school, but was seeded from 4-8 in Mumbai, in my age group. The best I could do is win a team championship for my school once (Maneckji Cooper), and then once for my junior college (Mithibai College, XIth grade).

I did play some cricket and chess (once) for my school, but sporadically since my focus was table tennis. So I must thank all of my school friends who helped us when we were juniors. My school had excellent cricket players– Prakash Saraf and Dr. Kinjal Suratwala, were amongst the best in my time, and Rajat Patel, Mehrnosh Irani (Mangi), Anish Adalja, Irfan Pabaney were very good all-round sports persons. Bijoy Jain, was perhaps the highest achiever from my school (during my time)- he swam the English Channel, and was amongst the fastest Asians to do so. I have to thank Prakash Saraf, and Mr. Dubey our sports teacher, for giving me a chance to play table tennis for the school, at an early age, which eventually helped our school excel in table tennis when I was about to graduate. Needless to say my partner Marazban Thanewala (and junior, who beat me in the semi-finals of inter-school singles) is someone I can never forget. The others with whom I practiced table tennis at Jai-hind club, cannot be ignored– Sanjay Kava, Amit Gandhi, Ajay Arora, Jaykumar Nambiar, Sudarshan Arya, and our senior Ulhas Shirke (training juniors after work, after an hour of train travel– not easy in Mumbai). I also thank Hanumant Singh Jadeja uncle, for his chess tips to youngsters at the club.

I also am lucky that my parents encouraged me in just about every activity, while growing up, including their teaching me swimming and table tennis. My father, being a lawyer with keen interest in sports and photography, and my mother being a teacher of Indian classical music and creator of a synthetic system of Indian classical dance— would never tolerate insincerity or irregularity in my 'after-school' activities. Unfortunately, I often do not see such encouragement from parents, unless the results are apparent.

Finally, I have to mention– Goswami Shyam Manohar– 'full time guru of many part time students', for introducing me to the world of philosophy, both Western and Oriental, while I studied *Navya Nyaya* (the modern school of Indian Logic) out of interest in Artificial Intelligence during college days. I was first introduced to Bertrand Russell and many philosophers who were not easy to learn about before the web. I cannot ever comprehend writing such a book, had I not been involved in studying philosophy, even if it be for a brief period. This book is a combination of an abstract formal approach as well as about direct observations. Expressions which conform to experience, are the basis of all Indian schools, since millennia. As an Indian, I therefore hope that this book relates to the real world of cricket as well.

Jan-Ove Waldner & Tendulkar; and the rest…

So who have I admired as sports-persons?

I have admired many sports persons– and have learnt quite a bit from those I watched earlier during my school days—Sunny Gavaskar, the great Indian spinners, West Indian pace-men (till today), Viv Richards, Geoff Boycott; the great all rounders– Kapil Dev, Botham, Imran Khan, Hadlee– these were players most of us looked up to. Geet Sethi and Michael Fereira were great for every billiards enthusiast in India. Amongst snooker legends, Steve Davis and Stephen Hendry are perhaps the best to study (chess-wise and break building-wise). In table tennis, although Indians were never ranked alongside Chinese, and Swedes—I admired Kamlesh Mehta, Manjit Dua, Parthiv Vyas, and also a junior from Pune– Jayant Thatte (during my playing days).

However, in the last 12 years or so, I have been studying and at times, 'watching as if playing'– quite a few. Started off with Michael Jordan while in college in the US. Then I came back to India, watching cricket– Wasim Akram, Waqar, Alan Donald looked the most lethal. Kumble and McGrath have added to nuances to their art, which cannot be ignored, just as Shane Warne and Muralitharan have taken their art to another level.

What and whom did I learn a lot, to attempt such a book?

In the recent past, my understanding of sport has got better by trying to understand chess, browsing actual games (with commentary by experts) and several books–*My System* by Nimzowitsch, Capblanca's *Chess Fundamentals* are worth it for chess and other sports. Obviously as an Indian, Vishy Anand has to be given due credit for being a top player for over a decade. But I follow chess, game by game and am not good enough in my assessment to choose between GMs. Another sport which has made a huge impact is 9-ball pool—what a format! We need to thank Steve Davis, for bringing it to the snooker world.

But I have spent a lot of time studying table tennis videos–Jan-Ove Waldner in particular and his contest with the Chinese. As kids we could only imagine how Hungarians (Jonyer, Klampar) played. Today, thanks to the internet, DVDs are cheaper than mobile phone bills.

I can tell you that I find Tendulkar remarkably similar to Waldner–both giants of their eras, and just as versatile. But their secret of survival for over 16 odd years, is a story of mind over matter– how and when to use which skill. When to use momentum and when to provide it. When to allow and when to prevent. They do go into great mental depths instead of just relying on natural skills (someday I will show, with symbolic abstractions, that they are competitively similar).

Outside sport, Betrand Russell amongst modern philosophers is amazing– for his lucid manner of explaining the vaguest concepts. I have also derived a lot from my computer engineering education. The guys at Apple and Adobe, are not technocrats, they see their opportunities as a platform to make a difference in the world. I have been fortunate in many ways to get opportunities and have always tried to push the limits of what is possible, in any project I get into. However, it is time to relax a bit and get ready for fresh new ideas.…

After finding it out– write a book…

it's easier than playing out there!

Dot Chess– The Cricket in Between
Written & Published by Saumil Bhukhanwala
1st Edition, January 2007
ISBN 978-81-7525-824-2

www.saumilzx.com

www.ingramcontent.com/pod-product-compliance
Lightning Source LLC
LaVergne TN
LVHW091446170726
843492LV00001B/53